JK 1131 .J64
Johnson, Dennis W.
Congress online

W9-ART-850

DATE DUE

OCT 2 2 2007			

Demco, Inc. 38-293

CONGRESS ONLINE

CONGRESS ONLINE

Bridging the Gap
Between Citizens
and Their
Representatives

Dennis W. Johnson

SOUTH PLAINS COLLEGE LIBRARY

ROUTLEDGE
NEW YORK AND LONDON

Published in 2004 by
Routledge
29 West 35th Street
New York, NY 10001
www.routledge-ny.com

Published in Great Britain by
Routledge
11 New Fetter Lane
London EC4P 4EE
www.routledge.co.uk

Copyright © 2004 by Taylor and Francis Books, Inc.

Printed in the United States of America on acid-free paper.
Typestting: BookType

10 9 8 7 6 5 4 3 2 1

All rights reserved. No part of this book may be reprinted or utilized in any form or by any electronic, mechanical or other means, now known or hereafter invented, including photocopying and recording, or in any information storage or retrieval system, without permission in writing from the publisher.

Library of Congress Cataloging-in-Publication Data

Johnson, Dennis W.
  Congress online : bridging the gap between citizens and their representatives /
by Dennis W. Johnson.
       p.   cm.
  Includes bibliographical references and index.
  ISBN 0-415-94684-0 (cloth : alk. paper) — ISBN 0-415-94685-9 (pbk. : alk. paper)
  1. United States. Congress — Constituent communication. 2. United States.
Congress — Information resources management. 3. Legislators—United States—
Computer network resources. 4. Electronic mail messages — United States. I. Title.
  JK1131.J64 2004
  328.73'0731'02854678 — dc22

                                                                    2003022819

To Linda, with all my love.

CONTENTS

Part Three: Online Democracy and Communication

Acknowledgments

This book is one of the research products of the Congress Online Project, a collaboration between The George Washington University and the Congressional Management Foundation. For the past two years, I have had the privilege of serving as principal investigator for this project, which was funded by a generous grant from The Pew Charitable Trusts. Thanks to the foresight and vision of Rebecca Rimel, president, Michael Delli Carpini, Elaine Casey, Sean Treglia, and the board of trustees of The Pew Charitable Trusts, this project was developed and sustained. Through its two major annual reports, issue briefs, electronic newsletters, and technical assistance, the Congress Online Project has made an important impact on the way Members of Congress communicate with citizens in this emerging era of electronic communications.

Special thanks to my colleagues and partners at the Congressional Management Foundation: Richard Shapiro, executive director; Kathy Goldschmidt, project manager; Mike Callahan; Nicole Folk; and Brad Fitch. I benefited enormously from their insights and from the pleasure of our collaborative work on this project. From The George Washington University, I especially thank Christopher Arterton, dean, Graduate School of Political Management, for encouraging me to assume the role of principal investigator. My thanks also go to my colleagues: Carol Darr, director of the Institute for Politics, Democracy, and the Internet, and Michael Cornfield, research director; my talented research assistants, Lisa Butenhoff, Greg Talmage, and Ryan Waite; and to Rosita Thomas of Thomas Opinion Research.

Thanks to those individuals who read parts, or all, of this manuscript, who gave me sound advice, and helped make this a better book in the process: Chris Casey, Michael Cornfield, Charles Cushman, Carol Darr, Kathy Goldschmidt, Max Fose, Stephen Frantzich, Eric Petersen, Jeffrey Seifert, and Jonah Seiger.

This work would not have been possible without the assistance of Members of Congress who consented to be interviewed, their staff, and individuals in key technology and administrative roles. Many of the staffers were interviewed under the condition of anonymity.

Also of assistance for our overall project were technology experts in the private sector, especially John Aravosis, Graeme Browning, Janet Caldow, Max Fose, Kathy McShea, Chris Porter, Joiwind Ronen, John Sampson, and James Vaughn.

My special thanks to Rob Tempio, Angela Chnapko, Nicole Ellis, and Kathleen King at Routledge and to Eric Nelson.

Most important, my special thanks go to my wife, Linda, who, as usual, has sustained me throughout the long days of research and writing.

Dennis W. Johnson
Washington, D.C.

List of Tables

Introduction

Your votes and speeches may make you well known and give you a reputation, but it's the way you handle the mail that determines your re-election.

—Speaker of the House William B. Bankhead (1938)

In the early 1930s, life on Capitol Hill was slow-paced and unhurried. The House Office Building (now the Cannon Building) was the home of all the Representatives, each tucked away in one-room offices. In those days, congressional offices opened around 9:00 a.m. and closed at 4:00 or 4:30 in the afternoon. Visitors from back home were rare and sessions were relatively short, with Congress convening on March 4th and adjourning within four months, usually by July 4th. Air conditioning had just been installed in the House and Senate, but during the long, sultry days of late summer, official Washington resembled a languid ghost town.[1]

Members of Congress each had a clerk-hire budget of $5,000, allowing them to employ two secretaries. One estimate had it that more than half the offices hired just one secretary and paid the rest to a relative who never bothered to show up for work. Communications with folks back in the district were limited. Long distance telephone calls were prohibitively expensive; telegrams were rare and only for emergencies. Letters and penny post cards were the usual way citizens communicated with their lawmakers in Washington. The amount of mail varied from office to office, but typically, in a rural, western district, there would be no more than ten to fifteen letters a day, mostly from job-seekers or veterans looking for federal pensions.[2]

It was different, however, in the congressional office for the Fourteenth District of Texas. The Congressman was Richard Kleberg, a wealthy playboy who cared little about legislating and less about opening and answering constituent mail; but his energetic young secretary, Lyndon Johnson, minded very much. Johnson was a cultural and social naif when he arrived in Washington as a twenty-three-year-old aide, but he knew his politics. He knew that constituent mail was the life-connecting force with folks back home, especially those who lived some 2,000 miles away and could only afford to communicate through the mail. As the Depression gripped more people in economic desperation, they turned to Washington and to their Representatives for help. They wrote letters, many with plaintive hand-written requests for assistance or reassurance; more often than not, however, there was no help to give.

The Kleberg office saw its share of heart-tugging letters; no matter how desperate or futile a request might be, Johnson insisted that the two office clerks answer each letter the day it arrived. When things got quiet, young Johnson insisted that the Kleberg office send unsolicited letters of praise, congratulations, and condolences to Texas constituents. He carefully read every newspaper in the district and put a check mark beside the names of people who had celebrated anniversaries, retired from their jobs, lost loved ones, or won awards—each would receive the appropriate personalized letter signed by Congressman Kleberg. Every boy and girl graduating from high school in the Fourteenth District would receive a personal letter; forty to fifty slightly different boilerplate letters were prepared, so that the thousands of graduates would not receive the same letter. Johnson, the task-master of constituent mail, insisted that all letters be typed perfectly, and he would mark a big X through any letter that failed to meet his exacting standards.[3] These, after all, were letters all the way from Washington, sent from their Member of Congress on fancy embossed stationery, many to be framed and hung proudly on the living room or office wall.

The Kleberg-Johnson office was unusual in the amount of mail it generated. But during times of domestic turmoil or international crisis, nearly every congressional office had been briefly deluged with mail. For example, on September 13, 1939, just two weeks after Germany invaded Poland, President Franklin D. Roosevelt called for a special session of Congress to consider revising the Neutrality Act of 1937. Roosevelt's announcement activated strong and vocal isolationist voices both in Congress and throughout the nation. Republican Senator William E. Borah of Idaho, a leading isolationist in Congress, warned that war was imminent if Roosevelt meddled with the neutrality law. Aviation hero Charles A. Lindbergh and popular radio priest Father Charles E. Coughlin went on the air to lambaste Roosevelt's plans. Coughlin's radio audience was huge: about thirty million listeners—one out of every three radios in America was tuned to him—and the public was listening intently. In just days Congress was overwhelmed with more than a million letters, post cards, and telegrams denouncing Roosevelt's actions.[4] Congress had never seen anything like this: an unprecedented outpouring, whipped up by attacks over the radio, with mountains of bulging mail bags choking the offices and hallways in the House and Senate.

Perhaps two or three times a decade, Congress has been similarly overwhelmed with letters, telegrams, and telephone messages from angry or alarmed citizens. In recent decades, it happened during Watergate and Richard Nixon's impeachment hearings, the Iran-Contra investigation, the savings and loan crisis, and the House banking scandal. After each episode, however, the communication pattern would return to its normal flow.

Then came the online communications revolution coupled with the scandals and impeachment trial of Bill Clinton. Undoubtedly, the first time that many citizens ever went to the Internet to retrieve a federal government document was when the Starr Report on President Clinton was released in September 1998. Anticipating heavy demand for this report by the special prosecutor, Congress made it available on seven government websites and offered it to the websites of major media outlets as well. All were swamped: CNN Interactive had twice its website's daily average of visitors, America Online had a 30 percent surge, and the Associated Press website had a twenty-fold increase in traffic. Altogether, it was estimated that twenty million people, or 12 percent of adult Americans, used the Internet to view the Starr Report.[5] Before any in Congress could fully absorb the controversial report and its salacious findings, it was downloaded by millions from computers throughout the United States and the world.

At nearly the same time, the husband-wife team of Joan Blades and Wes Boyd created a website address for $89 and an activist organization out of thin air. Their organization, MoveOn.org, rallied citizens who were fed up with the attempt to impeach President Clinton, and sent over two million e-mails to Congress. MoveOn.org called this a "flash campaign": citizens who heretofore had little in common, upset by events in Washington and rallied by a website, generated an unprecedented number of messages through this new weapon of online communication. This inventive e-mail campaign certainly drew attention on Capitol Hill and throughout the emerging electronic advocacy community, but in the end it did not prevent the impeachment of President Clinton.

At the peak of the impeachment proceedings, in January 1999, House offices were receiving 1,000 e-mails a week and some Senate offices were receiving up to 10,000. Yet once the impeachment hearings and trial had ended, instead of returning to a normal flow of communications, e-mail continued to increase in volume. In December 2000, just after the contested presidential election, the House of Representatives alone received seven million messages; the short but bitter confirmation fight over John Ashcroft for Attorney General fueled another round of e-mails and anti-Ashcroft websites[6] and following the September 11, 2001, terrorist attacks and anthrax contamination, Congressional e-mail shot up once more.

By the end of 2001, a million e-mail messages to Congress *a day* had become routine, and these were on top of the hundreds of thousands of letters, post cards, telephone calls, faxes, and telegrams received daily. What happened to all that e-mail and how could Congress possibly manage this enormous flow of communication? Further, where did all of this e-mail come from? This book addresses those questions and focuses on Congress, its use of online communications, and how Congress can better communicate with the American people.

Who Uses E-mail and the Internet?

In the most comprehensive study to date, the Department of Commerce found that Internet use in the United States had grown substantially in the late 1990s and early 2000s, growing at a rate of two million new users per month.[7] The study found that 54 percent of the nation is online, with 143 million Americans using the Internet (an increase of twenty-six million in thirteen months), and 177 million people (or 66 percent of the population) using computers.

Children and teenagers use computers and the Internet more than any other age group. A remarkable 90 percent of children between the ages of five and seventeen (48 million) use computers, and 75 percent of fourteen- to seventeen-year-olds and 65 percent of ten- to thirteen-year-olds use the Internet. Not surprisingly, households with children under the age of eighteen are more likely to use the Internet than households with no children.[8]

The U.S. Commerce Department study found that 45 percent of the population uses e-mail and 39 percent of individuals make online purchases or seek service information. Sixty-five million employed adults use a computer on their job and twenty-four million of those individuals also work on their computers at home.

Internet use by the lowest income households (less than $15,000 a year in earnings) increased at an annual growth rate of 25 percent; nevertheless, the lowest income levels saw only one out of four individuals with Internet access. By contrast, 80 percent of the highest income levels (more than $75,000 per household) use the Internet.

These and many other studies confirmed what we observe in daily life: that e-mail and the Internet are becoming part of the core communications for many Americans. In the average day, about 60 million Americans go online.[9] Somewhat surprising, however, is how quickly electronic government services are catching on with the public, even outpacing some commercial Internet activities. Instead of standing in line, citizens are increasingly going online for government information, forms, and assistance. One survey of adults who use the Internet found that in 2000, 55 percent of those surveyed had visited a government website, with 50 percent of those visiting a state or local government site, while 33 percent had visited a federal site.[10]

Another study in April 2002 found that sixty-eight million American adults had used government agency websites, a considerable increase from the forty million who had used government sites a year earlier. Further, those who sought information on government agency websites were happy with what they found, with 80 percent indicating they were able to find what they wanted on those websites.[11]

The top fifteen federal and state government websites each have had more than a million visitors a month according to a February 2001 survey. But even the most visited federal site, the Internal Revenue Service, had only 6.7 million visits in February (its busy tax season), compared to sixty-nine million visits to the AOL Time Warner Network, sixty million visits to Microsoft sites, and fifty-seven million visits in February 2001 to Yahoo!. The AOL Time Warner site ranked first, while the IRS site was forty-fourth overall in traffic.[12] Yet by taking all federal government websites as a whole, the U.S. government ranked, in another study, as the fifth largest web property with over thirty-nine million unique visitors in February 2002.[13]

The Internet, e-mail, and websites have become integrated into the lives and routines of millions of users. In another report, the Pew Internet and American Life Project interviewed 1,500 people in March 2000 and then re-interviewed them one year later to determine how their attitudes and use of the Internet had changed over that period of time. The researchers found that as people became more familiar with the Internet and e-mail, online communications became more serious tools woven into their daily lives. E-mail had gone "from the remarkable to the reliable" and the Internet became more of a communication tool used in everyday work.[14]

Until 1999, even computer and e-mail-savvy citizens preferred postal mail as the best way to communicate with Congress. However, there were some indications of a shift in attitudes. By late 1999, Juno Online Services found that 58 percent of users of Juno services would rather use e-mail, while just 25 percent said they preferred the postal mail; just 11 percent said they would use the telephone, and only 2 percent said they would use a fax to try to contact their legislators.[15]

How Congress Communicates with the Public

The focus of this book is not primarily on Congress as an institution, but rather on its constituent parts. Congress does have a central telephone exchange and postal address, but it routes communications to the appropriate subunit, whether it be a committee, administrative office, or individual legislator. The same holds true for electronic communication. The House of Representatives and the Senate created their own Internet sites in the mid-1990s. Those sites are useful, though still somewhat underdeveloped portals whose main purpose is to point visitors to other congressional sites.

First, the most important and most frequently visited websites are those of the individual lawmakers, the 435 Members of the House, 100 Senators, and the delegates from the District of Columbia, Puerto Rico, U.S. Virgin Islands, America Samoa, and Guam. It has often been observed that Congress is a collection of 540 separate small businesses, each with a unique constituency, political problems and opportunities, policy agendas, and re-election challenges.[16] In many instances, the legislators and their personal office staffs have little interaction with lawmakers from their own state delegation, and certainly little connection with the office three doors down, representing another state. The manner, frequency, and effectiveness of traditional or online communication is up to the individual lawmaker, subject only to limitations of funds and congressional regulations. While the Senate and House both maintain a central office to assist with computer, online communications, and other technology issues, there is no central authority telling individual legislators what they must do. A first-time visitor to twenty separate House websites, for example, will find twenty different designs, and most likely, several very well-constructed sites and some that barely serve as communication tools.

Some offices are at the leading edge of online communications; others are barely aware of the possibilities and opportunities missed. Much depends on the attitude of the Members of the Senate or House, filtered down to their senior communications staff. Some legislators are very Internet-savvy, pushing their staffs to devise inventive and labor-saving ways of communicating with constituents. Other legislators cannot even access their own website without the gentle help of staffers showing them how to click the mouse on the appropriate web page.

The second component of Congress consists of the standing committees and a few select committees. The communications traffic between the committees and the public is usually far less than what is found with the personal offices, but there is wide variation, depending upon the issue jurisdiction of the Committees and their constituencies. Committees like the House and Senate Committees on Appropriations, the Senate Finance Committee, or the House Judiciary Committee will have external professional audiences, seeking specialized technical information. The House and Senate Committees on Veterans Affairs, or the House Agriculture Committee, reach a significant non-technical audience, whose interests must be addressed with readily understood and communicated information.[17] The Senate Foreign Relations Committee will have a much different audience from the House Rules Committee. Likewise, the audience for the Senate Committee on Rules and Administration will be far more focused than the audience for the House Committee on Energy and Commerce, with its far-flung areas of jurisdiction.

The third component consists of the Leadership offices, such as the Speaker of the House or the House Majority Whip. Not all leadership offices have websites and those that do are usually more focused on internal congressional communication than with constituents or the press.

Different Audiences

Just as there are several distinct components of Congress, there are also different audiences. The most diffuse and largest audience is the public at large. There are some legislators who have developed a national following and communicate to a broad audience, far beyond their own districts. But by and large, legislators are fairly parochial and pragmatic when it comes to their own constituents. Members of Congress typically will respond to communications from citizens who live only in their districts, or perhaps live in their state; Senators often confine themselves to communications within their state as well. There are very strong pragmatic reasons: the crush of communications dictates that priorities must be set and boundaries drawn; and those who receive attention first are those citizens who live (and vote) in their districts. Many also consider it political bad form for lawmakers to encroach on their colleagues in other congressional districts. This geographic and political focus is especially true with online communications. Special filters that search for ZIP codes or key words (such as the name of a state or its abbreviations), are used to automatically sort congressional e-mail. Citizens who decide to blast e-mail to every Member of Congress will find their electronic missives go only to their own legislator, with the rest bounced back with an auto-response, or more likely, simply evaporating into cyberspace.

A second smaller audience consists of individuals actively involved in advocacy. For this segment of the public, online communications have become very important, not only for sending communications to Members of Congress, but also as organizing tools, keeping like-minded citizens informed, or rallying them to action. Grassroots activism, which has grown more sophisticated and prolific in recent decades, hit its stride with online communications, opening up a whole new, potent way to communicate with elected officials. However, there are limits to the effectiveness of grassroots activism, and advocacy campaigns based on mass e-mailings are by no means assured of success.

A third audience is the specialized audience of lobbyists, professional activists, government officials, other legislators, and a variety of others for whom legislation, policy making, and agenda setting is their principal occupation. This is a small audience indeed, but a very critical one. For them, e-mail and the Internet are invaluable, but certainly not the only or most important means of communicating with Congress.

Finally, the press constitutes a fourth important audience. Increasingly, journalists turn to electronically-posted news releases, reports, real-time audio- and video-streamed hearings, and press conferences to assist them in understanding and writing about Congress.

Members of Congress often spend much of their time working to get re-elected to another term. For many, re-election is an overriding concern, and day-to-day communication with the voting public is a high priority. But while much of their concern is re-election, there is a legal divide between campaigning and legislating. No taxpayer money can be used directly to help Members of Congress get re-elected, and congressional staffers are prohibited from working, during their regular hours, on their boss's re-election campaign or in giving money to the campaign. Legislators cannot solicit campaign funds from their offices, and they are prohibited from linking their official websites to those of their political party, their own campaign websites, or to other partisan sites.

Forms of Communication

Communication between audiences and Congress takes many forms, and although e-mail and the Internet are the latest and most talked about, they certainly are not the only, nor the most important, forms of communication.

Face-to-face meetings may be the most important of all communications between constituents and Members of Congress. They come in a wide variety of forms: the town meeting in a high school auditorium, meetings of senior citizens, firefighters, religious leaders, Boy Scouts, or a whole assortment of groups in cities and towns throughout the district or state; meetings scheduled with groups or individuals in the district offices of Members; high school, civic or labor groups coming to Washington to meet with the legislator. Members now spend more time back in their districts and give increased priority to district office staffing and constituency problem solving. Members know that constituent service, problem solving, and keeping in touch with those who elected them to office are paramount to their career.[18]

As the young Lyndon Johnson knew, mail has been the key communication tool for Members and their constituents. For decades, it was the most common form of communication, but now has been far surpassed by e-mail. Postal mail has a ring of authenticity to it that some legislators cannot ignore. In talking to many congressional staffers, we found that their bosses far preferred sending responses to letters and e-mails using letterhead stationery, with the gold embossed seal of the House or Senate, and the legislator's signature. Further, there are legislators who feel that e-mail simply does not have the same weight as postal mail: that somehow it is far simpler to send an e-mail than a regular letter and that the sender has not invested the same amount of time and energy by sending an e-mail.[19]

But postal mail service ground to a halt after deadly anthrax spores were found in Senator Thomas Daschle's mail on October 15, 2001; mail service was hobbled months afterward. Despite the efficiencies of e-mail, and the fact that those who send e-mail prefer receiving responses back quickly and through e-mail, letters remain a preferred form of communication for many lawmakers.

Post cards and telegrams also deliver messages to Capitol Hill and are often generated by organized massive appeals from grassroots organizations. It takes only a handful of such post cards and telegrams (or letters) before the lowliest legislative correspondent or intern in a Senator's office knows that another mass grassroots campaign is underway. Some offices have a policy of never answering this kind of mail, others will answer only from their own constituents, and the only contact these post cards have with a Member is a tally sheet at the end of the week, where the legislative correspondent shows the Member how many of the post cards or telegrams from constituents were in favor of a position, and how many opposed.

The telephone has always been an important means of communication from constituents to Member offices, but two things have occurred to complicate things. One is the rise, especially in the early 1990s, of radio talk show programs, with commentators bringing up highly controversial issues, ranting about them with their audience, egging on listeners to call particular legislators, giving the phone number out over the air, and jamming up all incoming telephone lines in the Washington congressional office. The result might be an 8:15 a.m. drive-time harangue, especially on the dominant conservative talk radio programs, followed by a day full of telephone calls blocking out everyone else. However, jamming telephone lines is often no more than guerilla theater, radio talk show pranks and high-jinks, rather than legitimate attempts to persuade legislators.

A more sophisticated form of telephone communication, but with perhaps the same unintended consequences, relies on patch-through technology. An organization, worried about an upcoming vote in the Senate and working on a very tight deadline, would hire a telemarketing firm, which then makes calls to the organization's membership. The person who receives the phone call is told the dire consequences if the Senator votes a certain way, and becomes so upset that he wants to write his Senator. Better yet, says the telemarketer, why don't we patch you through right now (while you are still upset) directly to the Senator's office in Washington. Throughout the day, into the evening, and all the next day, the telephone lines for the Senator's office are jammed with calls from irate members of this organization, all orchestrated by a slick and expensive telemarketing campaign. Such campaigns, however, are very risky— they tend to irritate the Senator and the staff more than enlighten them.

Facsimile machines began appearing in the early and mid-1980s in

Congressional offices, and became another new tool for communication, especially from organized grassroots efforts. "Blast faxing" became a common term, as telemarketing, direct mail, and communications firms sent appeals to legislators on behalf of their clients. The telemarketing firm would use lower telephone charges after midnight, a congressional office might open up the next morning to discover that the fax machine had run all night, used up all the fax paper, and still had several hundreds of copies waiting to be printed.

At first, the facsimile machine offered new and interesting technology. It certainly was a quick way to send information, avoiding the delays and backups of the House or Senate mailrooms. Faxes became a great mechanism for congressional district offices to send morning newspaper clippings from towns and cities back home immediately to the Washington office. But faxes soon lost the luster of newness and became nothing more than another form of communication, no more or less important than a telephone call or a regular letter.

Added to this mix are electronic mail and the Internet. Congressional acceptance of e-mail and websites as communication tools has been relatively slow, unorganized, and halting. There was no sudden mandate that each of the House and Senate offices adopt standard e-mail software and online technology, nor were there any requirements for a common website design or web content. Unlike a business enterprise that receives an enormous amount of communication from the public, and has vast customer service offices, with standardized protocols, equipment, and procedures, Congress chugged along fitfully adapting to new communications technology. Some offices quickly adapted, seeing the great advantages of online communications; others barely noticed and only reluctantly participated. Given the organizational nature of Congress, the nature of political life, the 540 separate offices, and individual personalities, this is to be expected.

Electronic communication, for a growing number of citizens, is the more convenient and preferred form of contact with elected officials. It can be timely and efficient in targeting the right offices; but electronic mail can also be blasted ineffectively to every office on the Hill, and it can suffer from the perception that it is often not carefully constructed and deliberative communication, but simply a message patched together or orchestrated by an organized electronic grassroots effort. Unlike telephones or television sets, computers, e-mail, and websites are not universal appliances and tools. For many, electronic communication is now a moot issue. Some 40 percent of American citizens do not use or have access to e-mail and websites. This percentage will undoubtedly diminish in the future, but the digital divide must be recognized and considered an important factor in any complex of communications.

About this Book

This book is divided into three parts. The first, Wired Citizen, Wired Government, concerns the growing phenomenon of citizen involvement in electronic communication. Chapter 1, New Tools for the Active Citizenry, discusses how citizen activism and grassroots communication have been transformed. Both spontaneous and organized grassroots efforts have found electronic mail and websites to be powerful resources for gathering and disseminating information, quickly sending messages to elected officials, and creating new interactive communities. Many of the messages sent by wired citizens went to Members of Congress. Chapter 2, The Rise of Electronic Advocacy, looks further at the new phenomenon of electronic advocacy. It has become a tool of newly-created, ad-hoc groups, but even more so for established organizations that have found e-mail and websites to be important additions to their arsenal of communications. This chapter discusses the attractions of e-mail and websites as advocacy tools and the new electronic advocacy business. Chapter 3, The Promise of Electronic Government, discusses how state, local, and federal government agencies have entered the new age of electronic communication. Many agencies have recognized the growing efficiencies of putting information online and allowing bills, taxes, and fines to be paid electronically. Many have realized significant reductions in staff time, printing, postage, and other costs. More and more citizens are now being connected with government agencies through e-mail and agency websites. Congress as an institution and through its individual Members and committees can learn from the experiences of government agencies as they have attempted to better communicate with and inform citizens.

The second part of the book, Congress Responds, looks at how Congress has adjusted to the new reality of electronic communication. Congress was fairly slow to react both as an institution and through individual Members, but by the end of the 1990s, all Members, committees, and the Congress itself had established at least rudimentary websites and were receiving e-mail from constituents and others. Chapter 4, Old Communications and New, discusses the early days of congressional electronic communication, from the mid-1990s push toward a CyberCongress; how Members and the institution itself accommodated to electronic communication; the technology adjustments and upgrades needed; and the criticism of those internal efforts. Chapter 5, The E-mail Overload, looks at e-mail and Congress. Congress has been inundated with e-mail, particularly since the Clinton impeachment trial, and especially after September 11, 2001. This chapter looks at how e-mail is handled in individual offices, how it is viewed in importance and seriousness in comparison with other forms of communication, and how e-mail correspondence, properly handled, can add to the efficiency and management of congressional offices. Chapter 6, Congressional Websites, looks at the 610 websites now hosted by Members, committees, leadership offices, and the institution of Congress itself. There has been a marked improvement in congressional websites, with now one half of all such sites earning a favorable rating; unfortunately, the other 300 or so websites still are in need of improvement. This chapter outlines a best practices model and notes the premier websites and outstanding features in others. It also discusses persistent problems, features which are not on congressional websites, and the need for a Congressional portal site.

The third part of this book is entitled Online Democracy and Communication. Chapter 7, Challenges and Opportunities, looks at a number of challenges and opportunities facing Congress and electronic communication. It examines what state legislatures are doing and it looks at a pilot project on digitizing congressional mail, access to committee hearings, and communication after September 11. The final chapter, Congress and the Deliberative Process, discusses some of the ideas and possibilities of a virtual Congress, one that would permit congressional business to be conducted remotely. The chapter ends with a discussion of congressional communication, democracy, and communicating across the digital divide.

This book explores the electronic communications revolution and the ability of Congress as an institution, and its individual Members and offices, to meet the challenges of twenty-first century communications. It is one product of a two-year research and assistance program, called the Congress Online Project, a collaboration between the Congressional Management Foundation and The George Washington University, sponsored by The Pew Charitable Trusts. The fundamental mission of the Congress Online Project has been to determine if there are better ways for Congress to communicate with the American people using online communications.

Our findings lead us to this simple conclusion: indeed there are.

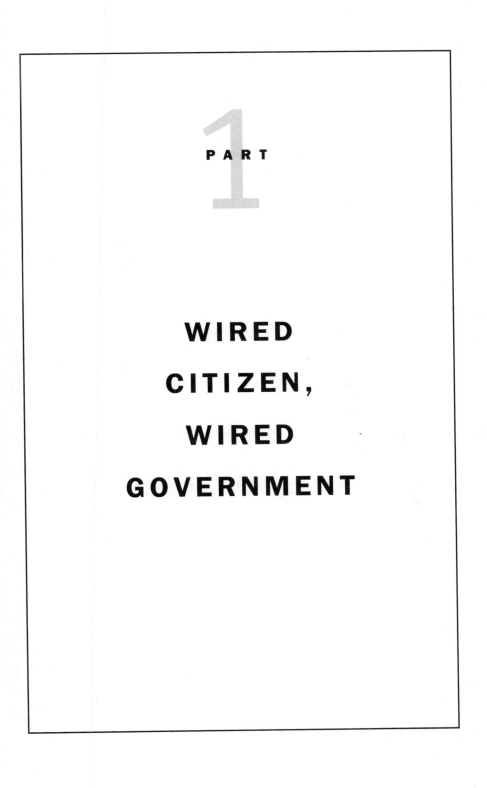

PART 1

WIRED CITIZEN, WIRED GOVERNMENT

New Tools for the Active Citizenry

Publicity is justly commended as a remedy for social and industrial diseases. Sunlight is said to be the best of disinfectants; electric light the most efficient of policemen.
—Louis D. Brandeis (1913)

Electronic Filing + Internet Disclosure = Digital Sunlight
—Digital Sunlight, a project of the California Voter Foundation

Citizen activism and grassroots political power are being transformed by online communications. Through e-mail and websites, individual citizens and grassroots organizations have found new ways to retrieve information, organize quickly and inexpensively, and create interactive communities. Through the Internet, citizens in just minutes can find out how their Senators voted, where the candidates for governor stand on particular issues, who is on the ballot for the upcoming election, or which of their neighbors gave money to candidates for office. Citizens can determine what harmful chemicals are found in the soil in their communities and compare those levels to national averages, download otherwise hard-to-find government documents, and find the names, addresses, and pictures of sex-offenders living in their neighborhoods. During local elections, citizens can join discussions about public policy alternatives, view online debates between candidates, contribute money, or sign up to volunteer. Through websites and e-mail, citizens can be rallied to write to their Member of Congress, to sign an electronic petition, or participate in an online poll. Activists can form their own Internet-based cyber-communities around issues of concern to them, and citizens may be able to vote using online technology at a polling place and perhaps even at their homes. Some even foresee citizens participating in nationwide cyber-referenda, voting online on major policy issues. Others think that it is not far-fetched to consider alternatives to our traditional representative form of government with citizens having a greater role in direct participatory democracy through online priority-setting and decision-making.

Much of the discussion about electronic citizenry is wishful thinking, hyperbole, or pure fantasy. But the power, reach, and potential of online communications cannot be ignored, especially by elected officials. Like nearly all governmental institutions, Congress has come late to online communications. Many Members and staffers enthusiastically embrace new techniques and technologies of communication; others are content to follow or to ignore them. As elected officials, Members of Congress (and for that matter any elected body) must keep attuned to the needs, wishes, and sentiments of their constituents. Many of these constituents are comfortably and actively moving into electronic citizenship and electronic activism. For this new breed of citizen, transparency, accountability, and immediacy are valued principles. For their own careers, elected officials need to know that the rules are changing, and activist citizens are demanding more from them.

Most citizens are not activists; the majority, in fact, barely do more than vote in presidential elections. There is a whole shelf full of social science literature on why citizens do not participate in politics, do not think or care about public policy issues, and do not pay much attention to elections and government. The revolution in online communications will not make activists out of the politically comatose. But for those who are interested, vote, want to participate, and want to make a difference, online activism gives them many tools. It lifts them to new levels of strength and, ultimately, to power. It also creates a new breed of participant—the five-minute activist, who is recruited through e-mail by an employer, union, or friend, family member, organization to fire off a (usually) pre-written e-mail letter of protest to Congress or other elected officials.

Information at the Click of a Mouse

One of the biggest hurdles that citizens and activist organizations traditionally have faced is the lack of information regarding elected officials, candidates and their activities, and the means to quickly and efficiently disseminate that information to their allies. What is the city council's agenda at its next meeting? How much money did the mayor receive in her bid for re-election and where did that money come from? What does this candidate for Congress really stand for? How did my Senators vote on that important appropriations bill? What trips did that Member of Congress take, who paid for them, and what were the reasons for going?

In the past, citizens were often frustrated because this information, while technically open to the public, was not readily available and required considerable digging to obtain. For professional campaign researchers it used to be arduous and time-consuming to find information in the pre-online days. It often meant sifting through paper, microfiche, or microfilm documents, found only at city hall, the statehouse, or in Washington. Sometimes materials were not indexed, were incomplete, or just not available. When the documents were found, it required time, money, and often considerable doggedness to sift through them. At times, the public papers were carefully guarded, the researcher had to sign in and explain why they were needed, and then the files were grudgingly opened up, under the condition that they could not be taken from the room and could not be photocopied.

Those were the days of microfilmed or paper files, before documents were maintained and stored electronically. Many documents, especially older records, are still only available in those formats. But now electronic filing and storage are becoming standard procedures for most government agencies and public documents are far more readily accessible. As seen in chapter three, governments at all levels now post a wide variety of public documents on their websites, and with the assistance of enterprising non-profit and for-profit organizations and the electronic media, citizens have extraordinary access to information about public officials, campaigns, votes recorded, and policies enacted. Certainly not all public information is available; some is held from the public for security or confidentiality reasons while other material is not made public because lawmakers simply do not want the information scrutinized. Yet increasingly, openness and transparency are becoming the norm: if the material is public, it is becoming readily accessible to anyone willing to seek it out. In general, more information is available from federal sources than from state sources, and more comes from state resources than from local government. Public interest and watchdog websites have been created, rich with content and public disclosure information, and there is now a small industry in publications that help citizens find material on websites.[1]

What do citizens want to know about Congress? In focus groups, we found that their responses went directly to the heart of representative democracy. Above all, people want to know how their legislators voted on key issues that affected their lives.[2] Finding the answer in the pre-online days was not easy. Then information on key roll call votes was available to the general public, but was not easily accessible. It would be located in a good library that subscribed to specialized publications like *Congressional Quarterly Weekly* and it was sometimes available in local newspapers when a major issue was voted on. But citizens would look in vain to find key congressional votes on local television news, the source of news information for most people. Dominated by happy talk, heavy doses of local crime stories, weather, and sports, there is rarely any discussion of congressional decision-making or accountability.

Don't look to Congress and the websites of individual legislators for this information. Many lawmakers boast of their achievements through laudatory and self-serving press releases, but few will list the key votes they have taken, why they voted a certain way, or list important votes that might soon be scheduled and ask constituents to comment on them. Third-party presidential candidate and congressional critic Ralph Nader complained that Members of Congress play "hide and seek" with their legislative records, noting that no Senators and only two Members had placed their voting records in an easily searchable format.[3]

Now this information is readily available on the Internet, free of charge, and in a format that is both easy to access and understand. Ironically, it is not being offered by Congress but by private non-profit and for-profit organizations. Many special interest groups post their own congressional scorecards on their websites and visitors can see how their Member of Congress voted. Such legislative scorecards are fine for framing the issues and responses that are important to each interest group, but they do not give a complete picture of how Members of Congress voted. Other websites give information about Congress, but two stand out in giving easy access to citizens wanting to know how legislators voted on key issues: Project Vote Smart's website and Capitol Advantage's Congress.org.[4]

Project Vote Smart

Starting in 1992 with a team of volunteers and student interns in Corvallis, Oregon, Project Vote Smart has been a resource center for citizens who wanted to know more about how candidates for office had voted and what they stood for. Project Vote Smart compiled information on candidate voting records, policy positions, financial backers, and ratings from seventy national interest group scorecards. By election day in 1992, Project Vote Smart had answered 209,000 telephone calls on its 800-number requesting information on policy positions, voting records, and financial supporters of candidates for Congress and the presidency. With its budget of $40,000, Project Vote Smart was able to send out 300,000 "voter self-defense manuals" containing much of this information and 50,000 teacher/student study guides. On Election Day 1992 alone, volunteers handled 34,000 telephone calls. Then came the online revolution.

Project Vote Smart now runs on an annual budget of $2 million, with funds coming from individual contributors and the Markle, Ford, Hearst, and Carnegie foundations, but it refuses all donations from corporations, political action committees, unions, or any other special interests. This is done, according to founder Richard Kimball, to "ensure that citizens, both conservative and liberal alike, have at least one remaining source to which they can turn in absolute confidence for untainted independent information about those seeking the power to make the rules we must all live our lives by."[5] During the 2000 election cycle, Project Vote Smart received over a million inquiries a day from citizens eager to learn how their candidates had voted in the past, what they stood for, and other information about them.[6]

Project Vote Smart provides a database of major roll call votes for Members of Congress. The information goes back to 1987, so that the complete key voting record of nearly every incumbent is now available. The roll call vote analysis is divided into fifty-five legislative categories, is easy to read, and unencumbered by technical jargon. Here is an example of how it works: go to the Voting Data section; click on a state on the map of the United States (Colorado is chosen at random); then go to Elected Officials and click on House of Representatives, then choose (again randomly) Rep. Mark E. Udall, a Democrat representing the Second District. The viewer can read a short biographical statement, learn about his campaign finances, and the issue positions Udall has taken through Vote Smart's National Political Awareness Test (NPAT). Project Vote Smart also provides a listing of about 100 interest group scorecards, arranged by category. For example, the National Association of Social Workers gave Udall an 89 percent approval rating for his votes in 1999, while the Americans for Tax Reform gave him an 18 percent approval rating for his votes in 2000.

How did Rep. Udall vote? Click on the first of the 55 categories, Agriculture, and the viewer finds that he voted against passage of H.R. 2646, the Farm Bill which passed the House of Representatives in October 2001. The official language of the bill is long, technical, and hard to understand; Vote Smart simplifies the description but gives it in sufficient detail. The viewer can then find out how every other member of the Colorado delegation voted, how each of the other members of Congress throughout the country voted, and how the two parties lined up. In similar fashion, thousands of other votes can be checked from the key votes database.

This kind of detail is given for every member of Congress, providing a wealth of accessible information. Unfortunately, this database is limited to congressional votes; votes from state legislatures remain unavailable in one convenient website for interested voters.

Congress.org

Congress.org, the free citizen-oriented site operated by Capitol Advantage, is one of the best websites for citizens to see how members of Congress voted, learn about policy issues, contact their legislators, and become involved in civic activity. What started in 1986 as a small company that created congressional directories tailored to the interests of client organizations, Capitol Advantage has grown under founder and president Robert Hansan into the major electronic resource for information about Congress, the federal government, and, increasingly, state and local governments. Over 1,000 clients, ranging widely over the political and ideological spectrum, have their websites designed and powered by Capitol Advantage, and tailored to their interests, membership, and policy goals. In addition, some of the highest-volume government-related websites, like America Online's MyGovernment, are powered by Capitol Advantage's software.

Congress.org is particularly easy to use for searching key roll call votes in Congress. It provides detailed, but relatively jargon-free descriptions of key legislation; for each bill, it lists sponsors and cosponsors and provides a legislative history. In its key votes section, citizens can look up categories of votes and see how their representatives in Congress voted. Another very useful feature, called MegaVote, lets viewers receive e-mail updates weekly showing how their legislators voted.

Another Congress.org service, Write Elected Officials, makes it easy to contact federal, state, and local officials: enter a ZIP code (55052 in Minnesota, as an example), then hit "Go": up pops a federal page, with information on President George W. Bush, along with his e-mail address, Senators Norm Coleman and Mark Dayton, and Representative John Kline with links to e-mail addresses, information, and key votes for each. By clicking on "information," for Rep. Kline, the reader will have a thumbnail sketch of the Member, contact information, recent election results, committee assignments and links to committee sites, and Federal Election Commission data on political action committee contributions. The viewer could also click on state officials and find the e-mail and information link to Governor Tim Pawlenty. The viewer is asked to provide a full nine-digit ZIP code because 55052 crosses into two state legislative districts. If the ZIP code isn't known, then simply supplying an address will match with the state and local officials. Searching by ZIP codes gets the viewer focused on the local governments of Rice and Waseca Counties, Minnesota, with names of officials, e-mail addresses, mailing address, and telephone numbers. Congress.org provides a virtual electronic mailbox for the e-mail, telephone and fax numbers, and mailing addresses for nearly all elected and many appointed officials throughout the country. In addition to the e-mail addresses of elected officials, the viewer can also click on to the e-mail addresses of local media, and send a letter to the editor, for example, to newspapers or television outlets in the surrounding area.

Other Helpful Sites

Another helpful website is sponsored by the Center for Congress at Indiana University, under the direction of Lee Hamilton, the seventeen-term former congressman from Indiana. The website's central purpose is to explain Congress to the average citizen. Through its website and other sources, the Center looks into public perceptions of Congress, the role of Congress, and its impact on the lives of ordinary people. The website has a section outlining the main criticisms of Congress, needed reforms, and how citizens can make the system work for them. The Center for Congress presents balanced, reasoned, easy-to-understand information about how Congress works. For too many citizens, Congress is a remote, frustrating place, not easily understood, and seemingly not interested in their day-to-day concerns.[7] This is an excellent site which tries to help the average citizen better understand how Congress works.

Taking a different approach is YourCongress.com. Salted with humor and irreverence, YourCongress.com, is a website founded by former Hill staffer Christopher Porter. Inspired by the financial services advice group Motley

Fool, which infused whimsy into the sometimes grey world of stocks and bonds, YourCongress.com focuses on an audience that may not have paid much attention to Congress. It provides a free e-mail service, called Your-Congress.Watch, which will send viewers complete statements or speeches of the Member or Senator of their choosing within 24 hours. YourCongress.com also has two e-mail tools, QuickBitch and QuickThank, so that within five seconds viewers can communicate directly with their legislators. For a fee, YourCongress.com provides a legislative and issue tracking service and a grass-roots advocacy package.[8]

While roll call votes serve as a good entree into the working of the House and the Senate, they give only one picture of the many activities and decisions made there. Through key votes, viewers see only the end product of the often complicated and tangled process of lawmaking. Other important votes, like those taken in committees or subcommittees, are not available on any of these websites, and some significant actions, such as the recent congressional pay raises, are taken without resorting to any roll call votes.

C-SPAN (Cable-Satellite Public Affairs Network) is the private, non-profit public service of the cable television industry, which provides gavel-to-gavel coverage of floor proceedings of the House of Representatives and the Senate. It has grown significantly in both the depth and scope of its coverage since it began telecasting House floor action in March 1979. Now with a staff of 260, C-SPAN provides round-the-clock programming to 77 million households, with three television networks (C-SPAN, C-SPAN2, and C-SPAN3), C-SPAN Radio, Washington Journal, BookTV, and other features.[9]

Through its website, C-SPAN offers some valuable features for those interested in keeping up with Congress, through its seamless combination of televised programming and audio and video streaming activities over the Internet. Users of its website can browse through ten issue categories to find which corresponding programs were televised (and audio and video archived by C-SPAN). For example, click on the category of "White House/Executive," and during the month of May 2003 were listed seven public affairs speeches, debates, or meetings, including State Department and White House briefings, the testimony of Secretary Thomas Ridge before the Homeland Security Committee, a joint news conference of President Bush and Philippine President Gloria Macapagal-Arroyo, and an address by former President Bill Clinton at the University of Arkansas.

The U.S. Senate, in an arrangement with C-SPAN, wired twenty-six hearing rooms in the Dirksen, Hart, and Russell office buildings to provide on the C-SPAN website audio-stream versions of the 8–12 hearings held each day when the Senate is in session. However, no such arrangement has been made with the House of Representatives. For over a year, a private company, HearingRoom.com, provided audio and transcription service in most House committees, but its services were available only to subscribers and it ceased operations in January 2002.[10] However, the House is in the middle of a major project of wiring all committee hearing rooms and many of the House standing and select committees now audio- and video-stream their hearings. The House Committee on Government Reform went several steps further in early 2003 when it began to electronically database its hearings with searchable text applications using the Internet. By using a combination of advanced database, voice recognition, and transcription software, the recorded hearings could be databased, then searched for the desired text or video clips.[11]

The C-SPAN website has extensive links to executive branch websites, campaign finance databases, a wide variety of policy organizations, and even to the Hague trials of Slobodan Milosevic. Further, there are extensive links to the websites of legislatures throughout the world, with audio and video links to 27 legislatures, including the Canadian Parliament, the British House of Commons, the Israeli Knesset, the Japanese House of Councillors, and the Slovenian National Assembly.

Also providing extensive coverage of national politics, elections, and international affairs are the online versions of the *Washington Post*, the *New York Times*, along with solid online coverage from CNN and ABC News.[12]

Much of the information about government and the legislative process is free on the Internet, but a considerable amount of inside information comes in the form of expensive products, only open for subscription use. *Congressional Quarterly's* GovStaff.com, for example, is an exceptional interactive website that has put in one database the 100,000 federal government contacts, from the executive branch, district courts, to congressional staffers. Organizations and interest groups can download these names for mail, telemarketing, fax, or e-mail campaigns. This knowledge base, however, comes at a price: an annual subscription of $1,500.[13]

Where Candidates and Elected Officials Stand

In October 1999, the Federal Election Commission (FEC) ruled that non-partisan organizations could host debates for political candidates over their Internet sites. Democracy Network (DNet), a non-profit organization, had been hosting non-partisan debates since 1996, inviting candidates to post their opinions and issue stands on selected topics. It was not clear, however, if these electronic "debates" should be considered as corporate contributions, since they provided a platform for candidates and their issues. The FEC ruled that such debates were not contributions, and granted both non-profit and for-profit organizations latitude in hosting online debates.[14]

The League of Women Voters assumed control of Democracy Network (DNet) in 2001 and took it nationwide, covering 26,000 national and local candidates in the 2000 and 2001 election cycles, everything from local, congressional, gubernatorial, and presidential elections. It also covered more than 280 ballot measures in 2001, providing summaries of the policy issues and presenting arguments for and against each. For 2001, which was an off-year election cycle with the principal races in New Jersey and Virginia, DNet had a pre-election spike in viewership of 3 million hits in the two weeks before the November elections, culminating in a million hits before noon on election day itself.[15]

DNet presents unedited issue statements that are provided by the candidates themselves, giving links to their websites and their campaign calendars; it also gives campaign finance information on the candidates, along with non-partisan background information on the issues they address. DNet works like an electronic town hall, allowing candidates (not just frontrunners) to debate one another over the Internet, permitting citizens to e-mail candidates directly with questions or comments, to volunteer their services, or to make campaign donations. All information about candidates is based on ZIP codes and the viewer need only type in that information to see which offices are holding elections, who the candidates are, where they stand on issues, which ballot measures are being decided, and where to vote.

The Markle Foundation created an online election project, named Web White & Blue 2000, which offered political information and interactivity for the 2000 presidential election. From June 28, when it went online, until election day, November 8, 2000, Web White & Blue 2000 received over 7.5 million page views and between October 1 and November 8, one of its key features, the Rolling Cyber Debate received 738,000 page views. Rolling Cyber Debate, consisted of daily exchanges between candidates on topics provided by the campaigns themselves and citizens.

An evaluation by the Markle Foundation determined that viewers expressed greater confidence in the quality of political information after seeing it on this Internet site, and that 70 percent of the viewers were able to find the information they needed about candidates and the issues through Web White & Blue 2000.[16]

Candidates for public office, especially incumbents, are bombarded with policy-oriented questionnaires from interest groups. A candidate for the House or Senate might be asked to fill out policy and vote preference questionnaires from 30–50 organizations. An instinctive tactic, especially of campaigns run by professional consultants, is to ignore as many questionnaires as possible, and make as few specific issue positions known to the public, especially on highly controversial issues. Candidates want to run on their own message and want to define the contest in their terms; they don't want to get pinned down or have their message diluted by issues and controversies that aren't helpful to their campaign strategies.

Project Vote Smart, however, tries to pin down candidates. It asks them to fill out a detailed policy questionnaire, then displays the answers on its website. During the 2000 election cycle 12,510 candidates for federal and state office were asked to fill out the National Political Awareness Test, a detailed questionnaire crafted by the Project Vote Smart research staff, national leaders, political scientists, and political journalists. Altogether, 4,802 candidates in 2000 completed the questionnaire. For those candidates who did not participate, mostly state legislative candidates, Project Vote Smart argued that something was learned: "Even when they do not respond, the public learns something valuable about candidates who refuse to provide the public with answers to fair-minded, balanced questions relevant to the jobs the candidates are applying for in the campaign process."[17]

The questions asked were fair, well-constructed, and written so that candidates could check off a yes or no box, but also expand on their answer. "I have not seen a questionnaire that does as good a job of pinning candidates down," said Peggy Lampl, former director of the League of Women Voters.[18] The NPAT left no room for equivocation and asked some very detailed, but important, public policy questions. Presidential candidates in 2000 were asked specific questions about gun issues, abortion policy, campaign financing, budgets and spending priorities, taxes, crime and sentencing, and many other key policy areas. Similar questions were asked of congressional candidates and detailed questions were tailored to state legislative candidates.[19]

The NPAT survey caused controversy in the 1994 Texas gubernatorial race, when Republican candidate George W. Bush's campaign sent a mailout to thousands of Texans, with Bush's picture on it, with a quote from Democratic Governor Ann Richards saying that she "believes no changes are necessary" in the welfare system, with this notation: "If you want an independent confirmation of Governor Richards' status quo views on welfare, call the non-partisan Project Vote Smart at 1-800-622-7627." Richard Kimball said that the Project Vote Smart hotline was deluged with telephone calls from irate citizens "assuming we are party to this unauthorized and misleading use of" its name and reputation. Kimball asked for a public apology, but none was forthcoming from the Bush campaign.[20]

The questionnaire is almost too good: By asking detailed questions on all facets of public policy, it scares off many candidates for office. (A sample of the NPAT questions is given in Appendix F.) A number of prominent candidates did not fill out the NPAT form, including Bill Clinton, Steve Forbes, and Patrick Buchanan in the 1996 presidential race, while Al Gore, Bill Bradley (a former Project Vote Smart board member), and George W. Bush refused to fill out the form during the 2000 contest.[21] The percentage of completed questionnaires by candidates at the local and congressional level has gone down during the past several cycles. The reason, Project Vote Smart surmised, was that Republican and Democratic political parties and leaders at all levels were urging their candidates not to fill out the forms.[22]

The Federal Election Campaign Act amendments of 1974 require candidates for federal office to report to the FEC all campaign contributions above $200 and since 1996 much of the FEC data has been online. At the state level, election laws and reporting requirements vary widely. Charles Lewis, founder and executive director of the Center for Public Integrity, complained in 1998 that citizens in nearly two-thirds of the states had to visit election board offices in person to examine campaign contributions, and that records in dozens of states existed only on paper.[23] Thanks to projects sponsored by the Center for Public Integrity and others to convert paper files to online files, much of the mystery of state contributions has been taken away.

One of the most important research centers is the National Institute on Money in State Politics, and its website, Follow the Money.[24] Through its research, citizens can see who are the biggest donors and the largest recipients of funds on a state-by-state basis. Viewers can see, for example, where the $1.88 million from Enron and its chief executive officer went to state-level candidates and state parties and the funds received from hundreds of candidates in thirty-two states from Enron during the 2000 election cycle. A joint investigation by the National Institute on Money in State Politics, the Center for Public Integrity, and the Center for Responsive Politics, called "State Secrets" looked at the $600 million in soft money, largely unnoticed, that was given to state parties during the 2000 election cycle. This information was invaluable not only to citizens and activist groups, but to journalists who now through online-assisted research can focus more sharply on the connections between money, power, and elections at the state level.

Occasionally newspapers will assist in unraveling the mysteries of state campaign finances. In Virginia, a state then notorious for its paper-only campaign finance records, the 1997 gubernatorial campaign contributions records were made available to the public thanks to the pooled resources of five newspapers, a state university, and other sources to create the Virginia Public Access Project website. Approximately 40,000 records were computerized, making public the names of top donors to each of the gubernatorial candidates and the corporations that gave money to nearly all candidates.[25]

The oldest independent website that analyzes federal election contributions is Political Money Line, set up by two former FEC staffers, Tony Raymond and Kent Cooper.[26] It has an extensive database of contributions, including political action committee dollars given to Members of Congress, by committee assignment, soft money contributions, lobbying database and registration information, ranking of Leadership PACs by funds received, along with a variety of FEC reports. Viewers can see individual donors by name or ZIP code, find who is registered as a Foreign Agent, or look at the listing of 187 records of illegal contributions made by corporations or individuals, plus prison terms and executive resignations as a result of those transgressions.[27] Much of the data is available only through subscription, but there also is a public website dedicated to the topic of political money.

The Center for Responsive Politics website, Open Secrets, is especially helpful in looking at political action committees grouped by industry, with clear, easily understood charts and graphs to explain money given by top contributors and money received by top recipients.[28] Open Secrets also has topical features such as reports on Pro-Israel and Pro-Arab money, contributions from Enron and Arthur Andersen LLC, and analysis of the gambling industry's lobbying and campaign contributions. Open Secrets also maintains FEC Watch, posting FEC rulemakings and policy statements, court decisions on election law, enforcement actions, and advisory opinions and advisory opinion requests.[29]

The Internet is providing activists groups, citizens, and the media the twenty-first century equivalent of Justice Brandeis' sunlight and electric light. Government entities, at all levels, public interest groups, and for-profit companies have made available an extraordinary range of information that was heretofore unobtainable. Some federal, state, and local agencies have been far more forthcoming in making public information usable online; others have clung to the old ways of microfiche, paper, and inaccessibility. The U.S. Congress is struggling with its responses to the online revolution. As will be seen in chapter six, the public now has far greater access than ever before to reports, votes, committee activities, and legislative actions. Much of what is available, however, comes after the fact—after votes have been taken, reports filed, and decisions made. Increasingly, however, Congress is providing information on a real-time basis, letting the online public know while it all happens. Yet, Congress as an institution and through its constituent parts could do so much more to provide the public with public information.

Connecting with Other Citizens

Through the Internet, citizens are finding potent ways of sharing and organizing valuable information, providing listservs and bulletin boards, using instant and text messaging, and coordinating e-mail with telephone, fax, and postal campaigns.[30]

Candidate debates over the Internet and political discussion groups can be an integral part of that connectedness. The first political debates conducted over the Internet were in the fall of 1994, when a group of good government activists created Minnesota E-Democracy. This was a tool to capitalize on both the emerging technologies of the Internet and electronic communications, but also to promote good government and good citizenship. It presented an alternative to traditional candidate debate: members of the established media asked questions of the candidates, and they in turn responded, but with no interaction with the public, no follow-up questions, and no chance for lesser known candidates to have an equal voice. Minnesota E-Democracy created two forums, MN-Debate, a source for candidates, who could post their answers, and later rebuttals, to debate issues, and MN-Politics, open to the public as a citizen discussion forum. Perhaps because of their novelty, these sites attracted national attention, even having Vice President Al Gore appearing online during a debate to endorse one of the Senate candidates.[31]

Others followed the Minnesota example in the 1996 elections, with the most successful being the Democracy Network (DNet), begun in Los Angeles, and then taken nationwide by the League of Women Voters in subsequent elections. The intentions were good and honorable: broadening the base by having non-partisan civic organizations sponsor the projects; leveling the playing field by letting every candidate participate in the debates; being available twenty-four hours a day; and being interactive, so that citizens could enter in their responses or criticisms. It was also thought that such electronic debates would add much-needed discussions of substantive issues that affected the citizenry, rather than the hype and gloss of television commercials, or the utter lack of discussion of issues by television stations. During the 2002 election cycle, DNet covered more than 25,000 candidates and 630 ballot issues, and had over fifteen million hits during the five days before the November elections.[32]

The further hope was that young voters—notorious as the least likely to participate in politics at any level—might find electronic debates and e-mail discussion something of interest to them. Perhaps the candidates themselves were still a generation removed, but maybe through their medium—electronic communication—some of that barrier could be removed.

Still, the audience for the first experiments in Minnesota was quite small, despite the publicity generated by because of its novelty. Few then had computers, there were no public access terminals in public libraries, and it frankly attracted from among its own—the small, already active crowd of Minnesota good election-types and techno-activists.

Minnesota E-Democracy branched out to sponsor a political issues forum for the city of Minneapolis. The site, Minneapolis-Issues, had been characterized as a "24-hour letters to the editor without an editor," said Craig Miller, a landlord who often posted information about local housing issues.[33] During September 2001, there were over 600 participants.[34] Steven Clift, chairman of Minnesota E-Democracy, noted that when an interactive site reached somewhere between 500–1,000 participants, rules of participation had to be enforced. This was a particular challenge given the feistiness of comments, the inherent sparks of contested elections, and the anti-incumbency mood of many of those who participated.[35]

After the September 2001 primary for the mayoral race in Minneapolis, the "chat" became so heated and contentious that the list manager and founder of Minneapolis-Issues David Brauer nearly quit. He had to eject three people for violating prohibitions against insults, threats, inflamed speech, and one-on-one disputes; 20–25 others dropped out because of the online shouting. Brauer, whose other job is managing editor of a downtown community paper, *Skyway News*, spent up to 15 hours a week managing the list. This was a labor of love: He created it out of his frustration over lack of sufficient coverage by the Minneapolis *Star Tribune* and the weekly *City Pages*.[36]

Electronic advocacy can be a timely tool at the local level, where community watchdogs keep an eye on city hall, city council, and other public officials. In the San Francisco Bay area, for example, several self-appointed watchdog and political gadflies use the efficiency and speed of e-mail to bring information to citizens and calls for action. Jeannette Sherwin's website is a feisty newsletter that targets Oakland mayor Jerry Brown and members of the city council. She and others use online forums, such as Yahoo! groups, to communicate, sending via e-mail their opinions, documents, and calls to action.

In 1999 Sonoma County citizens interested in grassroots social change, the Town Hall Coalition, hosted a series of public town hall forums on a variety of environmental, health, and development issues. The Coalition has been fighting for an initiative to limit rural sprawl; it is a major local source for environmental news and has spawned other anti-growth organizations in neighboring counties. The Town Hall Coalition's website has been the vehicle for bringing them together and sharing information. Another site, maintained by Alice Barnes, self-appointed San Bruno watchdog, followed the progress of BART (Bay Area Rapid Transit).[37]

Like these examples from the San Francisco area, community watchdog websites have several advantages over the old-fashioned way of communicating with like-minded citizens. Through their websites, citizens can gather information, link with allies, alert fellow citizens to upcoming events, raise money, send electronic petitions—all of this done very efficiently, quickly, and cheaply through the Internet. It is almost impossible to alert 500 citizens about an emergency meeting occurring in 36 hours by mail, very difficult by telephone, but simple and painless to do by posting on an Internet site, better yet, sending an e-mail through a listserv. Five hundred angry e-mails to city council may have some impact, but 500 angry citizens jammed into city council chambers will certainly have a bigger impact. More and more, we find those 500 angry citizens assembled because they have been alerted by e-mail or by an activist website.

There are also some dangers in having wide-open community-based websites where citizens are free to rant and rave against elected officials, corporations, and other citizens. From 1998–2000, hundreds of lawsuits have emerged in which webmasters have been subpoenaed to identify online critics who have posted online forums, bulletin boards, or listservs, where private individuals, corporations, and public officials have allegedly been defamed or falsely accused. Rebecca Fairley Raney has reported[38] on a website called Eye on Emerson, which posted information on the community of Emerson, New Jersey. Part of the website was devoted to a policy forum, where residents could discuss local issues and use anonymous nicknames like "Frustrated Voter" or "Seeing Red" to blast away at what they perceived as municipal indifference or incompetence. In the summer of 2001, four local officials struck back, suing for defamation of character and issued subpoenas to find out who their anonymous critics were. While the online publishers were not held responsible for the comments posted by third parties, they could face significant legal fees, and in the case of the webmaster for Eye on Emerson, the costs were thousands of dollars in legal fees.

Raney noted that most of the subpoenas against anonymous critics come from corporations, who have a strong interest in protecting their stock prices, reputations, and their ability to recruit employees. Civil libertarians and especially groups like the American Civil Liberties Union, the Electronic Frontier Foundation, and Public Citizen are worried that such subpoenas will chill online free speech. America Online has been subjected to hundreds of subpoenas in recent years, and has adopted a stringent policy: When AOL receives a civil subpoena, it immediately notifies the persons involved and gives them two weeks to respond. In many cases, AOL contests the subpoenas. The Eye on Emerson episode made it clear that posting materials on a community watchdog website can come at a price.

Many policy-oriented websites contained petitions, which viewers could read, sign electronically, and forward to elected officials. Capitol Advantage went several steps further by posting the electronic petitions of its 1,000 paying clients on its citizen-oriented website, Congress.org. There were forty-nine public policy issues areas listed on the Congress.org website, and for each policy issue, clients can post links to their own websites and issues. Several Capitol Advantage clients have five or more policy issues listed on the Congress.org website. For the clients, it is free publicity, a way to generate public interest it their causes, and a way to send messages to members of Congress or to state or local elected officials. For example, under the Agriculture/Food section, there were thirteen separate organizations with links to their issue message, coupled with a link to Members of Congress, including the advocacy organization 20/20 Vision ("Tell Kraft to Hold the Genetic Engineering"), Vote Hemp, Inc. ("DEA's New Rules on Hemp"), National Farmers Union ("Stop 'Fast Track' Dead in its Tracks"), and Western Pennsylvania Conservancy ("Preserve a Way of Life by Supporting Senator Harkin's Farm Bill"), and others.

Other entrepreneurial websites included E-The People, which dubbed itself as "America's Interactive Town Hall," and had gathered a total of 231,338 electronic signatures on 5,585 petitions through early May 2002.[39] Its "people's poll" for May 6, 2002 asked whether visitors favored opening up the

Arctic National Wildlife Refuge for oil drilling. Its most popular national petitions in 2002 were one to support the Second Amendment to the Constitution and one concerning innocent men wrongly convicted of murder. The visitor could then send any one of the petitions to a government official. Type in "Senator Hollings" and up popped the addresses of eight staffers in Senator Ernest F. Hollings South Carolina district offices. E-The People would let the viewer send the petition to three recipients at one time.

Political consultant Dick Morris's website, Vote.com, claimed that by mid–2003 over 52 million votes had been cast in his online questionnaires. Vote.com features a new question concerning politics or policy almost daily, such as this question for June 3, 2003: Should the U.S. pick Iraq's interim leaders? Earlier questions included: Should D.C. residents be exempt from federal taxes until they get voting representation on Capitol Hill? Should commercial airline pilots be armed? Should the House and Senate pass resolutions supporting Israel and rebuking Arafat? Should the Senate confirm Judge Charles W. Pickering, Sr., to the Appellate Court?

Vote.com promised: "We *always* e-mail your vote to key decision-makers." Morris prominently displayed a quote from President George W. Bush, "I believe that when you e-mail a congressman or a senator, it makes a difference." President Bush might think so, but that was hardly an opinion shared on Capitol Hill. From dozens of interviews conducted with House staff, petitions such as those generated from E-The People or Vote.com receive the lowest attention, or no attention whatsoever, from busy staff members trying to cope with the daily avalanche of electronic and regular mail. Individual e-mails from constituents, thoughtfully written, and unconnected to a mass electronic mailings or petitions would receive staff attention and time; most everything else was viewed as nothing more than electronic junk mail.

Ad hoc Advocacy

Internet entrepreneurs Joan Blades and Wes Boyd, the creators of MoveOn.org, invited friends, then other like-minded citizens, to urge Congress to censure, not impeach, President Bill Clinton and then move on with other pressing business. Thus began an historic e-mail campaign, springing up from nowhere. Blade and Boyd, best known as the inventors of the flying toaster screen saver, were frustrated that they, their friends, and many thousands more were not being listened to by Congress and were wasting their time and subverting the country's priorities by pursuing Clinton.

A new term—"flash campaign"—was added to our political lexicon with the MoveOn Internet and e-mail campaign.[40] It is a campaign that develops almost overnight, sparked by a controversy, with citizens deluging public officials through organized e-mail messages. The MoveOn campaign was remarkable for its ability to reach so many people, who until this point, had no political or partisan connection with one another. The "flash campaign" using e-mail quickly mobilized, generating over 250,000 telephone calls and 2 million e-mails to Congress regarding the impeachment proceedings against President Clinton.

Some anedoctal evidence suggests that their e-mail campaign changed some minds, or stiffened backbones. For example, Representative Carolyn B. Maloney (Democrat-New York) received 3,121 e-mails from MoveOn, more than any other House member, and these e-mails reportedly strengthened Maloney's decision to stick with the Democratic leadership and vote for a limited inquiry. Representative Bart Stupak (Democrat-Michigan) received 205 MoveOn.org e-mails over a thirty-six-hour period, convincing him to vote for a limited inquiry as well.[41]

MoveOn.org brought with it three innovations: First was website support for a word-of-mouth campaign (or as MoveOn calls it, "word of mouse"). The original website was very plain, with no graphics, no links to other sites, concentrating on the simple act of signing a petition and sending it to others. Second was the use of its website as a "command and control" center for volunteer operations. Despite some daunting tasks of communicating two-way with volunteers in the field, MoveOn.org found the best way was to use the website itself to communicate with and to monitor field volunteers, using detailed worksheets, step-by-step instructions on how to talk to Members of Congress and staff about a subject. The third innovation was the use of the website as an effective bundler of campaign donations. One minute after the House vote to impeach, an e-mail was sent out to all petitioners, and by the next day, $5 million was pledged for the 2000 elections. Eventually $13 million and 800,000 volunteer hours were pledged, though substantially less money was actually donated. MoveOn.org bundled money and developed a complete online solution to the processing, transmission, and reporting of donations, meeting FEC requirements.[42] By mid-October 2000, MoveOn.org had raised about $1.85 million for Democratic candidates. The funds came from over 43,000 individuals and donations averaged approximately $42 per person.

Following the student massacre at Columbine High School in Littleton, Colorado, Joan Blades and Wes Boyd started an online gun control drive section on their website. In just weeks, they had gathered more than 70,000 signatures for a "Gun Safety First" campaign, which promoted federal child safety standards for gun manufacturers, and tougher background checks for purchasers at gun shows. As the Senate debated a bill to reduce crime among juveniles in May 1999, printouts of the petition signatures gathered during the month since Columbine by MoveOn.org were delivered by hand truck to the offices of Senate majority leader Trent Lott and minority leader Tom Daschle. MoveOn.org said that more than 100,000 individual e-mail messages had been sent through its site to senators throughout the nation.[43]

By 2001, MoveOn.org had a roster of 300,000 online activists, whom they called "five-minute activists," busy people who wanted to be effective citizens, and now could have their voice heard through organized online communications. Its website, in the aftermath of the September 11th terrorist strikes, featured electronic petitions advocating a dramatic increase in the U.S. public health infrastructure; another called for the U.S. committing to protect innocent civilians and ending the cycle of violence. The petition statements were vague, general, and soft: one implored the "President and Congress to act to ensure reasonable energy prices," while another asked to "Preserve the estate tax on the very rich, and defend our country's proud legacy of charitable giving."

MoveOn.org also has something akin to a policy chat room, asking through its "Issue Forum" what are the great goals that the nation should pursue. In the 2000 election cycle, the top issues were campaign finance reform and protection of the environment.[44] As of late October 2001, some 297 individuals posted their "great ideas," allowing MoveOn.org participants to voice their agreement or disagreement, and to rank the issue from one star (not important) to five stars (very important). In March 2001, MoveOn.org joined forces with the nonprofit advocacy site Generation Net, with Peter Schurman, who founded Generation Net in April 2000, becoming a full-time, salaried executive director.[45] By mid-2003, MoveOn.org had signed up roughly 1.2 million activists.

In late February 2003, MoveOn.org worked with a coalition of over thirty anti-war organizations that called itself the Win Without War Committee to coordinate what it called a Virtual March on Washington, a first-of-its-kind campaign aimed at flooding Senate offices and the White House with e-mails, telephone calls, and fax messages.[46] The Win Without War website touted that on February 26th, every Senate office and the White House would receive a telephone call every minute from constituents, together with a flood of faxes and e-mails. The collective message from the Virtual March participants: Don't attack Iraq. "Every Senate switchboard will be lit up throughout the day with our message—a powerful reminder of the breadth and depth of opposition to a war in Iraq," the website noted. An estimated million individuals called or faxed their Senators and another 500,000 had pledged to send e-mail messages.[47] The website asked for volunteers to commit to making three calls to their Senators and to the White House at a time they would select from the hours listed on the website. Further, participants were asked to include a brief comment on the website indicating what they would communicate to their Senators' offices or to the White House; these comments would then be displayed online and on the Win Without War "anti-war" room.

Other organizations have successfully sprung up and used the Internet for advocacy purposes. John Aravosis, president of Wired Strategies Internet Consulting, together with four friends created an advocacy website, StopDrLaura.com, designed to stop Paramount Television from giving the controversial conservative talk show hostess her own television show. Dr. Laura Schlessinger reportedly had declared that gays and lesbians were "biological errors," and that comment prompted the creation of the anti-Schlessinger website. It was created as a simple six-page site, paid for with an $18,000 budget raised mostly by selling over the Internet t-shirts that proclaimed, "You are a biological error." During the year-long period that the site was active, it gathered fifty million hits and three million visitors, resulting in pressure that forced 170 advertisers in the United States and Canada to drop Dr. Laura and Paramount to cancel the planned television show. Aravosis noted that one of the reasons the site was so successful was that its audience, many of whom were gays or lesbians, took the affront personally, and then acted upon it. "She's outrageous. She's beyond the pale of 'I'm a Christian, I don't like gay people,'" Aravosis said of Dr. Laura.[48]

Using the Internet and e-mail for rallying like-minded individuals and for sending petitions to Congress is now commonplace, and part of the arsenal of citizen activists and citizen organizations. Into the swirl of true grassroots activism, however, is a mixture of manufactured responses, uncontrolled viral campaigns, and out and out prevarication.

Mark Twain supposedly quipped that a lie can travel halfway around the world while the truth is putting on its shoes. The Internet can be something like that as well. Sometime in early 1999, a report filtered through the Internet and through e-mail that Congress was about to enact legislation to tax the use of e-mail and computer systems. "Please read the following carefully if you intend to stay online and continue using e-mail," warned the original message. "Under proposed legislation the U.S. Postal Service will be attempting to bilk e-mail users out of 'alternate postage fees.' Bill 602-P will permit the Federal Govt. to charge a 5 cent surcharge on every e-mail delivered by billing Internet Service Providers at source." One writer on a computer discussion group warned: "One congressman, Tony Schnell, has even suggested a twenty to forty dollar per month surcharge on all Internet service. Don't sit by and watch freedoms erode away! Just say 'No!' to Bill 602-P." Readers were urged to flood Congress with e-mails in protest.

To anyone who would check, this whole issue was a hoax. There never has been a "Congressman Tony Schnell" and neither House nor Senate bills are ever numbered as "Bill 602-P." A Canadian version of the e-mail message had been bouncing around cyberspace earlier, and the message was later tailored to an American audience. Thousands of e-mails arrived in Congress, even after this was exposed as a hoax. Yet, the phony Bill 602-P would not die: It became part of the New York Senate campaign debate between Hillary Rodham Clinton and Representative Rick Lazio, with both candidates opposing the non-existent legislation. Further, Representative Fred Upton (Republican-Michigan) proposed and the House ultimately passed in 2000 legislation prohibiting such an Internet tax from being enacted. The Internet hoax altered political reality. To this day, some Members of Congress have felt it necessary to post on their official websites a notice that the Internet tax is a hoax and that there is no such thing as Bill 602-P.[49] There are e-mails, created years ago, warning of such dangerous taxes, still bouncing around cyberspace.

The reach of e-mail and Internet campaigns is worldwide: Jody Williams, with others, launched a major international campaign to ban land mines; international protest movements have focused on World Trade Organization meetings; rallies at the U.S. Capitol grounds have been orchestrated by both supporters of Israel and supporters of Palestinians; protest movements in East Timor and rallies against the American war in Iraq—all of these and more have been launched or coordinated through e-mail and the Internet. Cell phone text-messaging helped rally protestors and bring down Philippine president Joseph Estrada; and "smart mobs," with no identifiable leaders and no central officer, have emerged throughout the world.[50]

Activists can go to one convenient site to find out when the next protest will be, whether it is Milan, Ho Chi Minh City, or Washington, D.C. Evan Henshaw-Plath created Protest.Net to offer the schedules of worldwide protests. From June 1998 when the site was created until late March 2002, there had been 23,605 events posted, with 4,768 upcoming events from around the world posted in March 2002. The website doesn't necessarily endorse the protest causes and will not remove a protest event or prohibit one from being on the website "unless it's really offensive, like the KKK," Henshaw-Plath said.[51]

Direct Electronic Democracy

Will direct democracy be the next frontier for electronic citizen activism? Will there be a time when citizens, at their computers, mark electronic ballots that have binding effect on states or the U.S. Congress? Twenty-four states and the District of Columbia now permit some form of initiative, referendum, or recall, offering citizens the constitutional right to make decisions in place of or in concert with their legislative bodies. Today, ballot issues form a curious mixture of grassroots civic-mindedness, individual entrepreneurship, big bucks corporate and labor backing, combined with professional political consultants.[52]

Electronic citizen activism attempts to cut out the intermediaries of politics: bypass the established media, and let all candidates have their fair shot through cyber-debates; subvert the costly route of purchasing expensive television commercials for campaign ads, and go directly to the people through a campaign website; look at original documents and raw data rather than relying on the gloss of a television commentator; or speak directly to office holders, cut out their aides and intermediaries. Direct democracy has already laid the path to dis-intermediation, the elimination of middlemen. Here, the so-called middle men are elected officials, and the solution is to go directly to the people through online communications.

To extend that argument, why not go directly to the people through online voting for ballot initiatives, and to extend it further, consider the possibilities of a national initiative system, where citizens throughout the country could directly tell their representatives in Congress what is important to them, what priorities should be set, and, indeed what outcomes should be realized. These ideas, mostly pie-in-the-sky, but seriously floated by some, could fundamentally change our representative system of government, and not for the better.

The direct democracy movement, especially in its biggest laboratory, California, is fraught with problems. As critics David Broder and Peter Schrag[53] have shown, direct democracy, California style, subverts democratic institutions, is skewed to help those with deep pockets; and once in the hands of political consultants, virtually any issue can be manipulated and polished to present simplistic and misleading choices to relatively uninformed citizens. Critics who see the flaws of direct democracy should be doubly concerned over online direct democracy.

The central problem with online direct democracy, however, is the simple but profound fact that millions of people have no access or familiarity with e-mail and computers. Despite the glowing, robust figures of increased e-mail and computer use, even among the poor, roughly 40 percent of Americans do not use electronic mail and one-third of Americans do not have access to or use computers. There indeed is a digital divide between those who are computer-savvy and those who are not. A voting system, such as online direct democracy, which leaves out, or short-changes in any way, any citizen is flawed and cannot stand. Those voting systems that combine online direct democracy with traditional methods of voting also must come under close scrutiny, to assure that the simple act of voting is available to all who wish to exercise it.

Constitutional problems abound: for any national initiative—online or traditional—to have legal or binding authority, a constitutional amendment would have to be enacted permitting it. Even if that extraordinary hurdle could be surmounted, what kind of ballot initiatives could be enacted and how would they be implemented into binding law? A nationwide endorsement of gun control, a ban on all abortions, a pay reduction for all federal workers, a national holiday honoring Ronald Reagan and Bill Clinton? Who could create a ballot initiative; who would account for its validity?

What would most likely be missing in electronic direct democratic action is the deliberative nature of legislative politics—the give and take, the compromise, the multiple proposals and amendments boiled down to workable language, the nuances of language, the regional and interest-based concessions. As unappetizing, irrational, and ignoble as representative deliberation is at times, it is far better than nationwide direct democracy.

These and other problems do not stop those who think that electronic direct democracy can work. Tracy Westen, chief executive officer of the Center for Government Studies, argued that certain checks and balances could be put into place so that citizens can weave a new course between the "'impulsiveness of the mob' and the 'elitism of unresponsive representatives.'"[54] Westen has called for an electronic "cooling off period," a time during which signatures on an electronically circulated ballot measure would be valid only if the voter signs the proposed measure twice, separated by at least a week. Citizens would be required to review the pros and cons of the measure and consult a list of proponents and opponents. These would appear on pages before a signer could reach the electronic signature page. Westen would also insist on citizens answering an online questionnaire, "requiring the signer to 'educate' himself or herself about the issues first." Further, according to Westen's scheme, electronic ballot measures would need a higher acceptance (say, 60 percent) of the electorate to become effective, or must be approved twice in two successive elections, or they would "sunset" automatically in ten years.

Under our current system of direct democracy, no citizen is required to sign a measure twice or show any degree of knowledge about the measure, and no ballot issues, except for some constitutional amendments, require super-majorities. But for Westen's deliberative online future, citizens and measures would need to do more.

According to Westen, the democratic process in the future will consist of interactive, electronic dialogues between elected representatives and participating citizens. "Voters might initiate, circulate and vote on electronic ballot initiatives addressing the 'hot ticket' issues of the day. Legislators and legislative bodies will respond with modifications, corrections, and follow-up actions."

An organization called the Democracy Symposium wants to go a step, or three, further. It proposes a National Initiative for Democracy, which it dubs as "the first constitutional amendment and federal statute ever to be enacted directly by the People of the United States of America." Developed by former U.S. Senator Mike Gravel (Democrat-Alaska, 1969–1981) and others, the National Initiative would include a Democracy Amendment to the U.S. Constitution, which asserts "the People's sovereign authority and legislative power to create and alter governments, constitutions, and laws, independent of existing governments." Coupled with this is the Democracy Act, which would establish legislative procedures through which the people can, in an orderly and deliberative manner, enact laws using ballot initiatives. The Democracy Act would create an Electoral Trust, to administer the procedures on behalf of the people.

According to the rationale on the Democracy Symposium, the National Initiative "resolves a problem faced by the Framers when they drafted the Constitution in 1787. At the time, the Framers had no alternative but to design a representative structure for our government since the technology of the day did not allow for the assembly, in person or otherwise, of the American people. Of course, that is no longer the case. Recent advances in communi-cation technology now permit the people to exercise *First Principles,* which were last used to ratify the Constitution but now have, through lack of use, become long forgotten."[55]

As individual states and the federal government grapple with the challenges and opportunities and pitfalls of online voting, so too are citizen advocates thinking about online voting for ballot initiatives in states that already permit such democratic measures. In the next several years, we may have to confront the hard questions and practicalities of online ballot initiatives in states and localities. National initiatives and other forms of nationwide ballot initiatives might seem remote, wacky, or impossible to operationalize. They should, first and foremost, be considered a direct assault on our representative form of government. Yet, thanks to the emerging robustness of electronic communications, the temptation is to dream and speculate about a new land of true online democratic vigor. What would Aristotle, that great critic of mass democratic rule, make of all of this? What would Congress?

The Rise of Electronic Advocacy

There's about to be a prairie fire out there in grassroots. There's a whole new industry taking shape here that is selling online lobbying, activism, and communications strategies to clients.
—Michael McCurry, Grassroots Enterprise, Inc.

E-mail is uniquely effective as a means of organizing, educating, and engaging a constituency to show up at rallies or call a talk show, but it is uniquely ineffective at projecting the voice of that constituency into a legislator's office.
—Jonah Seiger, co-founder, Mindshare Internet Campaigns

Not many grassroots movements begin outside of Washington, D.C.
—David Rehr, president, National Beer Wholesalers Association

Lobbying often conjures up the image of well-dressed, high-paid Washington insiders, working for law firms, trade associations, interest groups, or consulting firms who are more or less permanent fixtures in Congress and have extraordinary influence over the setting and crafting of public policy. These are the inhabitants of "Gucci Gulch," spreading around political action committee money, taking lawmakers on golfing and hunting junkets, whispering advice in their ears, handing their aides ready-made amendments, favors, and exceptions to be inserted into pending legislation.[1] This personal, high-priced lobbying is integral to influencing and shaping federal law and policy, but it is by no means the only way that lawmakers are pressured or courted.

Organized grassroots lobbying emerged in the 1970s and 1980s as a new, potent tool to contact and persuade lawmakers and other elected officials. It was based on the political fact that elected officials can be swayed by well-timed, persuasive arguments from groups of like-minded voters. The simple, but formidable, tasks of any grassroots effort are to identify and contact likely constituent groups, gearing them into action, so that they contact their lawmakers with the right message at the right time. The constituent groups might be a company's employees, shareholders, customers, and suppliers; they might be an industry's coalition of companies. The constituency may have to be assembled, such as a coalition of consumer groups, environmental activists, farmers or ranchers, anti-gun activists, or others, depending on the issue. Grassroots might concentrate on leading elected local officials, respected figures in the local community, or other well-known individuals whom the industry calls "grasstops" activists. Grassroots persuasion may mean having a coalition of political operatives throughout the country who show up at local city council or town hall meetings to push for a particular policy. It could mean inundating Members of Congress with telephone calls, petitions, or packing the audience at a local town meeting when the legislator comes home to visit the district. Grassroots activism might involve a concerted letter-writing campaign, staging media events, with protests, signs and displays, or other artful gimmicks.

E-mail has become an essential tool for any group that wants to have its voice heard in Congress. Over the past several years, thousands of organizations and interest groups have overhauled their grassroots lobbying efforts to include online communications, using e-mail and advocacy websites. For many well-funded organizations with sophisticated communications tools already at their disposal, e-mail and websites have become welcome additions to their advocacy arsenals. For many groups, especially those with low budgets but big ambitions, online communication has become vital in getting their message across.

Where Do All the E-mails Come From?

In the 1970s and 1980s, organized interests began adding another dimension to their lobbying activities, grassroots advocacy.[2] Citizen activism and organized protest in the 1960s had demonstrated what could be accomplished at the grassroots level, and with congressional reforms and fragmentation of power coming in the 1970s, the opportunities for new voices became clear. Organizations and interests simply could not rely on Washington lobbyists or law firms to pursue their interests; they needed other means of communication and pressure. First labor unions, then membership-based interest groups and corporations began focusing on their members, employees, or customers to communicate with elected officials. With electronic advocacy emerging in the 1990s, the possibilities of grassroots activism have grown dramatically. With e-mail and Internet sites, it is so much cheaper, faster, and more efficient to keep a grassroots constituency informed, motivated, and ready for action, should the time come. Online advocacy is also an important way for creating new constituencies of like-minded individuals or groups who are drawn to a particular issue. Certainly there are some spontaneous movements welling up from citizens, but most grassroots activities that deal with issues in Washington come from organizations based in Washington and are orchestrated through their lobbying and policy departments, setting the message, establishing the time frame for the communications, and coordinating with other lobbying efforts on Capitol Hill. Congress is inundated with e-mails and other forms of communication to a large measure because of these coordinated grassroots operations.

As an instrument for policy advocacy, grassroots e-mail first appeared during the early days of the Clinton administration. In 1993, the Clinton administration backed the "Clipper Chip," a key escrow encryption system, a method for individuals to scramble their electronic communications. The original system called for a two-part decoding key—two large numbers—that would be held by separate government agencies. Once a court order was approved to wiretap telephone conversations, then law enforcement officers could get copies of the two keys, put them together and unlock the encryption. Critics worried that it would be too easy to eavesdrop on telephone conversations or computer or fax traffic. While e-mail usage was still in its earliest stages and years before the majority of members of Congress had e-mail installed in their offices, some 47,000 e-mail messages in one month were sent to leaders in Washington from the Computer Professionals for Social Responsibility. This, according to Jonah Seiger, co-founder of Mindshare Internet Campaigns, was the "first example of the Net community working to change something of this magnitude."[3]

Later, Internet service providers banded together in what has been described as a "virtual Boston Tea Party," protesting the 1996 Communications Decency

Act measures that were found in that year's Telecommunications Act. For forty-eight hours in February 1996, thousands of Internet service providers, including Netscape and Yahoo!, participated in the "Black Page Protest," transforming their normal web pages to stark black backgrounds and white lettering. The legislation passed, despite this and other protests, but the black pages stunt gained considerable media attention, and demonstrated how a grassroots protest could be abetted by the Internet.[4]

During the mid-1990s, e-mail and websites started to become common communication tools in business, education, and everyday life. It took advocacy groups, businesses, trade associations, and labor unions a few more years before they were able to begin tapping into the potential of online advocacy. Even by 2002, electronic advocacy was still in its infancy. By then, according to Michael Cornfield, an expert on online advocacy, groups were finally "awakening to the potential of the Internet."[5]

By 2000, a new specialty industry had been born, experts in electronic advocacy communication, who were assisting a wide range of clients in the creation of advocacy-centered websites, helping them create databases of members and potential supporters, and assisting them in orchestrating and coordinating e-mail campaigns together with their other advocacy resources.

In 2000, for example, the Washington, D.C.-based online consulting firm of e-Advocates, headed by Pam Fielding, helped the American Society of Anesthesiologists (ASA) in its fight against a proposed Medicare rule that would have allowed nurse anesthetists to administer anesthesia without requiring a doctor's supervision. The Department of Health and Human Services through its website provided a link so that visitors could make comments to the Centers for Medicare and Medicaid Services (CMS) which was doing the actual drafting of the rule. Until this point, the ASA had never considered online advocacy as a means of communicating to members and to officials in Washington. With the assistance of e-Advocates, the ASA, an organization made up of 36,000 medical doctors in the speciality of anesthesiology, launched an advocacy website, AnesthesiaSafety.net. Its slogan was "Keep Surgery Safe for Seniors" (to say nothing of keeping anesthesia firmly in the hands of medical doctors). During a two-year period of time, more than 200,000 e-mail messages were generated from this site, and the ASA developed a database of 70,000 online advocates, persons who had signed up at the website and took some action, such as writing letters to Members of Congress.[6]

The advocacy campaign did not rely solely on e-mail, but broadened its communication by using the old reliable methods of letters, faxes, and telephone calls to federal policymakers. In November 2001, the Centers for Medicare and Medicaid Services released its final report ensuring, as ASA had strongly advocated, that physicians would continue to supervise patients' anesthesia care in Medicare- and Medicaid-approved hospitals and ambulatory surgical centers. This, however, did not end the policy fight because the new CMS rules gave state governors the latitude to opt out of physician-supervised anesthesia requirements. The ASA then turned its attention to individual states, and focused its already developed online grassroots efforts to potential threats found at the state level.[7]

The Attraction of E-mail as an Advocacy Tool

For the ASA and hundreds of other organizations that were attempting to communicate with Congress, e-mail, coupled with an advocacy website, became an extraordinarily effective tool. It is not hard to understand why e-mail has become the communications tool of choice.

E-mail is inexpensive; it costs virtually nothing to send an e-mail message to Washington or anywhere in the world. Upfront costs can be expensive, however, especially in creating the database of members, allies, and friends who should be alerted to take action. In comparison, postal mail costs 37 cents for first class, in addition to the cost of printing and stationery; faxes cost approximately 25 cents for each minute of telephone time used; letters delivered via special services like Federal Express cost from $12–14; patch-through telephone calls cost approximately $1.00 plus long distance charges; a Western Union telegram costs $6.00, while it costs between 13 to 34 cents for First Class letters to be hand-delivered to the House Postal Office.[8] Sending 1,000 messages from an organization's membership to Congress would still cost nothing when sent by e-mail, but would soar to $12,000 (depending on any discounts) for a service like Federal Express, or $1,000 for telephone patch-through calls. This is probably the key reason that many organizations are turning to electronic mail advocacy—the sheer cost advantage of e-mail.

Further, e-mail is immediate, most of the time. When circuits are not clogged, e-mail can get through without delay; but there have been instances of delays of several hours, even days, when the circuits in Congress—especially in the Senate—were so overloaded that e-mail could not be processed. Only patch-through telephone calls have the same immediacy as e-mail, provided, of course, that the congressional lines are not saturated with incoming telephone calls. All postal mail to Congress, since the anthrax episode in October 2001, has been sent to one of two facilities, in Ohio or in New Jersey, to be irradiated; this caused delays in their delivery of at least four to six days.

Likewise, specially delivered mail, such as through Federal Express, also have been delayed by four or five days because these packets also have to be irradiated. Telegrams promise delivery the next business day. While e-mail shines for its cost efficiency and immediateness of delivery, it is by no means the killer application, that perfect vehicle for getting a message across to Congress.

The Perfect Communication Tool

What is the perfect tool for communicating with Congress? Simply put, there is no perfect tool: It all depends on who is delivering the message, its timing and context, and its reception. For the Member of Congress who still has to be convinced about a certain piece of pending legislation, the perfect communication could be a last minute phone call from a highly paid, influential lobbyist with a key nugget of information, or it could be the arm twisting that she was subject to in the political party caucus earlier in the week. The lawmaker might have been convinced by the spontaneous outbursts of anger erupting in senior citizen homes when she visited the district two weeks ago. Or the perfect communication may have been the advice from her political mentors back home, the mayor and city council members that helped her get elected to Congress in the first place. It might have been the 500 telephone calls that jammed her district offices, or something her spouse said five minutes before they retired the night before. She may have been convinced by the last-minute telephone call from the White House, or the sincerity and tenacity of the forty blue collar workers who took a day off work without pay, and rode in a hot bus 400 miles to Washington to deliver their message in person. It could have been the results from a recently completed poll of her constituents, or the 1,200 letters and postcards urging her to vote a certain way. It could have been the 3,000 e-mails the office received in the span of just one week.

Those who run successful advocacy campaigns know that one vehicle is usually not enough to draw media attention, convey their message, and convince lawmakers. Amid all the clutter and noise of modern communications, it can be very difficult for an organization or group of citizens to break through, be heard, be remembered, and have an impact on an issue.

This is what one large, powerful, and well-funded interest group did to get its point across. AARP (formerly the American Association of Retired Persons) relied on a wide variety of sophisticated communications tools, including a state-of-the-art grassroots program that capitalized on its vast membership (35 million), many of whom are politically active senior citizens. E-mail was just one of the many tools that AARP utilized. The Public Affairs Council, a corporate-based educational organization in Washington, D.C., gave its top prize for Grassroots Innovation to AARP, which delivered a clear, clever, and memorable message to Washington: on the 36th anniversary of the Medicare program, the one thing that was missing was a prescription drug benefit. AARP held rallies on the Capitol lawn, in many of the state capitals, and at the Truman Presidential Library in Independence, Missouri, where President Lyndon Johnson signed the Medicare legislation and presented President Truman with the first Medicare card. At the heart of the AARP campaign was a birthday cake, honoring the 36th birthday of Medicare. Not just one cake, but cakes arriving at all 535 offices of House and Senate Members, and at their district offices. Usually nothing gets the attention of congressional aides faster than free food, especially sweets, and these cakes were particularly memorable. Each of the birthday cakes had a slice missing—symbolizing what AARP considered the missing piece in Medicare, the prescription drug benefit.

The cake-with-missing-slice campaign caught a lot of attention, garnered considerable press, and was an effective way of showing AARP's policy concerns. The efforts didn't stop with the cake with a missing slice. AARP followed up with public meetings nationwide that they called "kitchen-table discussions" and events featuring senior citizens holding hot-air balloons to symbolize the rising cost of prescription drugs. Then AARP targeted specific audiences online by using a new integrated database developed by Democracy Data & Communications (DDC).[9]

AARP understood that one method of communication was not enough and that a coordinated effort was vital. It understood the value of keeping its members and allies informed through electronic communication. AARP's website featured a series of e-mail newsletters to which members could subscribe, including the AARP Advocate Newsletter, which gave subscribers information on timely legislation and public policy issues and assistance in writing to their members of Congress and other elected officials.[10]

Websites as Advocacy Tools

One of the key strengths of online advocacy is the ability to give citizens and activists at the grassroots level valuable, timely information. One of the best examples is the set of issue-based websites established by the Environmental Defense Fund (EDF). The original EDF website evolved over the years from essentially a brochure site, containing basic information, to a sophisticated range of websites tailored to the interest of specific audiences. The sites include Scorecard.org,[11] a detailed accounting of environmental problems, such as lead hazards, superfund sites and land contamination, animal waste from factory farms, toxic releases from industrial facilities and many more. All of this information is accessible by ZIP code.

Selecting a ZIP code at random, 48016, yielded this information about Oakland County, Michigan, a heavily populated, industrial county west of Detroit. Air quality in Oakland was among the dirtiest 10 percent of all U.S. counties; and 1,194,156 people in the county faced cancer risks that were more than 100 times the goal set by the Clean Air Act. In a section called, Who is Polluting Your Community?, the top twenty polluters in Oakland County were identified, starting with the GMC GMTG Pontiac East Assembly plant in Oakland, which was releasing annually 1,709,363 pounds of contaminants, followed by Fiber Mark of Rochester, releasing 1,460,962 pounds of contaminants. The top twenty polluting materials were identified along with the amount of contaminant released. Oakland County ranked 78th of the 177 Michigan counties in the amount of animal waste released, with 2,400 tons in 1999. The names and status of the three Superfund sites in the county were given, and there was a detailed study of pollution and environmental justice. Much more was available on Scorecard, sortable by ZIP code or custom-fit to the interests of the viewer.

Also impressive was the Environmental Defense Action Network, claiming to have 750,000 e-mail activists interested in environmental policy. Action Network linked twenty-four environmental organizations, like Alaska Action Network, Environmental Advocates of New York, Texas Action Network, and Ohio SOAP Network. Each network, in turn, had links to its own state environmental organizations. Ohio SOAP (Sustainable Ohio Action Partnership) Network, for example, linked to the Buckeye Forest Council, the Ohio Chapter of Sierra Club, the Ohio B.A.S.S. Chapter Federation, and six other environmental/conservationist organizations.[12]

Environmental Defense also maintained Hog Watch, a central source for information and action on industrial hog farming in North Carolina. The site gave a virtual tour of a hog factory, first-hand accounts from North Carolina citizens of what it was like living downwind from a hog factory, detailed maps showing the location of hog sites, and for those who needed to know, a second-by-second update on the amount of hog waste deposited in North Carolina, with a whirling ticker called Hog Watch's Poop Counter.[13]

Along with its excellent websites, the Environmental Defense Fund staff wisely used other forms of communication to build and manage its relationship with activists, journalists, policy specialists, decision makers, and consumers: direct mail campaigns, publications, paid advertisements, public service ads, banner ads on websites.[14]

For decades, Congress and the states wrestled with the question of whether to have and, then, where to place a high level nuclear storage facility to receive the nuclear waste from America's commercial nuclear power plants. In recent years, the focus has been on the Yucca Mountain nuclear waste site, in a desolate section of Nevada. Earlier, the politics and debate centered on the location of the site, but lately the Environmental Working Group and the EWG Action Fund, in Washington, D.C., among others, tried to focus public attention on the dangers of transporting nuclear waste to the Nevada site, rather than the site itself. By the summer of 2002, the House of Representatives had voted overwhelmingly to support President Bush's decision to seek a license from the Nuclear Regulatory Commission to build the Yucca Mountain storage site.

Now the spotlight shifted to the Senate, and opponents of the site were focusing on a new tactic: the potential dangers of transporting nuclear waste by rail and over highways. Altogether, it was proposed that some 70,000 metric tons of radioactive waste stored in 131 above-ground nuclear power plants and facilities in thirty-nine states would be shipped to Nevada over the next twenty-five years. More than 123 million people live in the 703 counties through which the Energy Department planned to use highway transportation, and 106 million people live in counties along railroad routes. Data from the U.S. Public Interest Research Group showed that trucks or trains carrying nuclear cargo would go through Chicago every fifteen hours, every ten hours in Des Moines and Omaha, and every seven hours in Salt Lake City.[15]

Through its website, mapscience.com, the Environmental Working Group and the EWG Action Fund presented a powerful combination of information about nuclear waste storage and transportation issues, the dangers of nuclear waste, terrorist threats, and past safety records of nuclear waste shipments, plus a call to action for citizens to contact their federal legislators. The site is ZIP code-driven. A random selection of ZIP codes brought up Merrillville, Indiana, a bedroom community immediately south of Gary, in the northwest corner of the state. A map appeared, showing a nuclear transportation route, via the railroad just one-tenth of a mile away, and three major Interstate and federal highway transportation routes less than four miles away. The map also showed the location of hospitals and schools that are near the transportation corridors. The website also revealed that 86,577 Indiana citizens lived within one mile of a nuclear transportation route, and that there were twenty-four hospitals and 419 schools in the state within one mile of such a route. The site gave statistics on the number of train wrecks and fatal tractor-trailer wrecks in Indiana over a recent period of time, and showed that over the life of the Yucca Mountain project, forty years, that there would be 32,913 shipments by truck and 9,819 shipments by train of nuclear waste material through the state.

The website asked me to take immediate action, and conveniently gave the names of the Indiana senators, with their local offices and Washington office telephone numbers. The site also provided an e-mail form, with suggested language (and Indiana data already imbedded in the language): "Dear Senator: Please oppose plans to ship deadly nuclear waste through towns like mine for the next 40 years. The vote on the Yucca Mountain nuclear waste dump is not just about Nevada. It's also about my community and our state. I live within 0.1 miles of a nuclear waste route. . . . Thousands of people would have to live near a nuclear highway or railroad in Indiana under this dangerous proposal. We should not be asked to send children to the 419 schools that are along nuclear waste routes in Indiana. . . ." Citizens can choose other tailored paragraphs expressing their concern about terrorism or accidents, or about the dangers of transporting nuclear waste through a big city. They are encouraged to write their friends, with these ready-made phrases: "I live near a nuclear waste transportation route. Do you?" "I just found out that I live 0.1 miles from a proposed route to ship dangerous radioactive waste if the Senate approves the nuclear waste dump at Yucca Mountain in Nevada."

On July 9, 2002, the Senate approved funding of the Yucca Mountain site. Certainly many forces were at work in trying to persuade Congress; this nuclear hazards transportation website was one of them. It was one of many voices, but certainly no competition for the $72 million that the nuclear energy industry and the U.S. Chamber of Commerce had spent since 1994 lobbying for the project. The information about transportation problems and possible horrors certainly were known to the Senators. John Ensign, the junior Senator from Nevada, carried an inch-thick folder to the offices of forty of his Republican colleagues, with detailed maps of rail and highway routes to be used for transporting the waste through their states. But in the end, Ensign and the Environmental Working Group were unsuccessful. Senator Robert Bennet (Republican-Utah) bluntly expressed the sentiment of those who wanted Yucca Mountain—not their communities—to receive the hazardous material: "Given the choice before us, I would rather have the waste go through Utah than to Utah."[16]

One of the important features of online communication is the ability to recruit supporters who may otherwise never have heard of an issue or did not know how to get involved. This is what Microsoft was able to do, starting with a small database of unsolicited letters of support sent to chairman Bill Gates. Microsoft for years was slow in setting up a lobbying presence in Washington or in state capitols, and only during the latter part of the 1990s did the company aggressively turn to political donations and other traditional forms of lobbying of lawmakers. But its most impressive action was to launch a web-based grassroots program that, according to business reporter Jeffrey H. Birnbaum, was "the envy of the influence-peddling world."[17] The program was called Freedom to Innovate Network (FIN), which began with the names and addresses of persons who had written Gates, then mushroomed into 250,000 names and e-mails of individuals supportive of Microsoft and willing to approach their lawmakers on behalf of Microsoft policy initiatives. FIN was created in response to what Microsoft calls the "overwhelming amount of correspondence we received from around the U.S. and overseas regarding the trial with the Department of Justice and other policy issues." During the last two months of 2001, Microsoft had its FIN members send e-mails to 30 lawmakers who were key to the passage of fast-track trade authority and three months later FIN urged its members to send e-mails and letters against Digital Rights Management (DRM) standards that were soon to be debated in a House committee session.[18]

Another example of seeking out new recruits came from the Heritage Forest Campaign, which targeted e-mail subscribers to Juno, one of the largest e-mail and Internet access providers during the 1990s. Juno's business was built on providing free e-mail access to individuals, who, in turn, provided Juno with demographic and lifestyle information. That information was then used to help Juno target its advertising, and it helped the Juno Advocacy Network create a custom-made audience gathered around particular interests.[19] The Heritage Forest Campaign, which was hosted by the National Audubon Society, created an Internet branch, called OurForests.org, designed to gain citizen support and have them contact federal forestry officials in support of tougher regulations for road building and logging in national forests.[20]

Heritage Forests Campaign first targeted 500,000 Juno users who had listed hiking and camping as their leisure interests; this list proved to be flush with individuals sympathetic to the anti-logging message. Next, they added 2.5 million other subscribers of Juno. When the targeted e-mail users logged onto their e-mail service, up popped an ad for the Heritage Forest Campaign.

Altogether, more than 150,000 new activists were recruited, and over 320,000 e-mail messages were sent to federal government officials.

OurForests.org, the online campaign, was created and run by TechRocks (formerly the Rockefeller Technology Project & Desktop Assistance), a Philadelphia-based national organization which helps progressive non-profits use new technologies in political advocacy. TechRocks used a variety of tools for its grassroots outreach campaign. Among other things, TechRocks designed an "electronic postcard" on the OurForests.org website, which visitors could send directly to the U.S. Forest Service and elected officials; it arranged for twelve of the top websites and Internet advertising networks to donate banner advertising; and it linked to or had placed banner advertising on the websites of coalition partners. In addition, the web address was included in all of the traditional organizing materials, like petitions, print and television advertising, direct mail, and flyers.

Altogether, over 1.6 million official public comments were received by the Forest Service in 1999 and 2000, the vast majority of them in support of forest preservation, together with hundreds of thousands of e-mails, post-cards, faxes, and telephone calls to the White House and Congress. On January 5, 2001, just days before he left office, President Bill Clinton announced the largest federal land conservation action since the Carter Administration, setting aside 58.5 million acres of forests in thirty-nine states.[21] Did the hundreds of thousands of citizen comments prod the Clinton Administration to take this action? Like most complex policy decisions, there could have been many reasons for Clinton's action: fulfill a long-standing policy agenda item of conservationists, agree with powerful constituencies in the Democratic Party, complete one of the President's own policy goals, or seek a tangible conservation accomplishment to burnish his Administration's domestic policy record. No one can pinpoint the answer, but certainly hundreds of thousands of communications at the right time in the policy cycle certainly could not hurt.

One of the benefits of such an online advocacy campaign is the opportunity to create a database of names, addresses, and e-mails of potential activists, who have helped out once and can be called upon to help again. Such databases, listservs, and membership lists become vital to online campaigns, because of the unique ability of e-mail and Internet communications to multiply. The phenomenon is known as "viral marketing": a message is passed from one group to another, or from one individual to another. A message sent to a relatively few can be multiplied many fold and sent to thousands of e-mail locations. One simple example of this came immediately after the terrorist attacks of September 11, 2001.

On the morning after the September 11th terrorist attacks, an Afghan-American, living in San Francisco, Tamin Ansary, sent an e-mail to about twenty friends, passionately arguing against a U.S. bombing retaliation against Afghanistan, a "bombing back to the Stone Age," as some Americans had suggested. "Trouble is," Ansary wrote, "that's been done. The Soviets took care of it already. Make the Afghans suffer? They're already suffering. Level their houses? Done. Turn their schools into piles of rubble? Done."

The e-mail, sent to a small circle of friends, took on a life of its own. Ansary's telephone never stopped ringing, his e-mail box was filled with thousands of messages; two websites with fairly substantial readerships, Tompaine.com and Salon.com, posted his letter. His letter was cited on a special edition of the television show "The West Wing"; he was on "Oprah" and had been interviewed by Charlie Rose; and by early October, Ansary, a textbook and children's book writer, secured a book contract for his memoirs about growing up in Afghanistan. Ansary's e-mail was copied and pasted, perhaps hundreds of thousands or millions of people had his e-mail land in their computers.[22]

Successful online campaigns rely on this viral marketing feature, and will provide convenient e-mail forms for visitors to tell a friend, thank an elected official, or to visit like-minded websites.

Advocates are forever seeking like-minded individuals, hoping to inform them of issues and generate a comment or response to elected officials. They look particularly at individuals who hold strong beliefs, but would not necessarily invest the time and energy to become actively involved in an issue. Online communications makes it easy for arm chair activists to become involved. They are often dubbed "five-minute activists," or in the case of one ideologically-based website, "sixty-second activists."

Longtime Republican and conservative political consultant, Richard A. Viguerie, heads Richard Viguerie's ConservativeHQ.com, a website dedicated to generating support for conservative causes. Part of that site is the "Sixty-Second Activist Club." Conservatives who join will receive each day a brief e-mail outlining an issue of interest to them, asking them to either "defeat a liberal proposal or pass a conservative bill." The Activist Club promises to make support and activism quick and easy: sixty seconds or less to read the brief e-mail, with information right at the member's fingertips on who to contact, how to reach them, what information they should convey. The

Activist Club boasts of having sent over a million faxes, 260,000 petition signatures, 16,000 mailgrams and FedExs, and 350,000 e-mails to Congress, the President, and other elected officials.[23]

One of the problems of mounting an online advocacy campaign is making sure that membership and allies are comfortable using computers, e-mail, and the Internet for communications. One such effort has come out of the labor movement. Organized labor, long used to old-fashioned shoe leather and handbills rather than high-technology, has made a concerted effort to bring computers and online technology to working men and women. The A.F.L.-C.I.O. in 1999 developed its own Internet service provider, workingfamilies.com, to help bring its 13 million members online. The purpose of all this was to bring online access and computers at discounted prices to union members, with the hopes that union workers and their families could respond quickly and forcefully when legislation or policy affected them. Part of the strategy was to help bridge the digital divide, so that workers with lower incomes could have access to online communications. Ironically, union households own and use computers at a higher rate than the general public, with 57 percent of union members owning a computer and 81 percent of them going online, compared to 54 percent of the general public owning computers and 70 percent of those households online.[24]

Certain websites are interested not only in advocating changes of law, but also in the enforcement and implementation of pre-existing law and regulation. One such campaign tries to assure that federal protections are enforced against gender discrimination in sports at federally-funded educational institutions. The Women's Sports Foundation teamed up with actress Geena Davis to create an advocacy website for women and girls and the issues surrounding Title IX of the Education Amendments of 1972, which prohibit sex discrimination at educational institutions. The site is named after Ms. Davis, an avid amateur archer. The award-winning website, Geena Takes Aim,[25] was particularly good at explaining what Title IX is, who is covered, and what myths and misconceptions surround it. The website provided over twenty issue briefs on a variety of Title IX matters, and viewers were encouraged to fill out an online report card, a detailed survey that checks for inequities in sports facilities, funding, and opportunities at schools.[26] Geena Takes Aim also encouraged students to take action, by writing the President, members of Congress, and other elected officials to support women and girls in sports. Visitors were urged to sign up for a service that provides an issue action alert, learn more about gender equity legislative issues, and receive an e-mail weekly of their representative's roll call votes. Like many other advocacy organizations, Geena Takes Aim was powered by Capitol Advantage's CapWiz service, which provided the vote and issues databases, which were then linked to the viewer's ZIP code.

Electronic Advocacy Business

Since 2000, many organized interests have quickly adopted online communication advocacy tools. One company, Capitol Advantage, has been at the center of the online revolution. As seen in the preceding chapter and from several examples above, Capitol Advantage hosted a public website called Capitol.org, where many of the services it provided to paying clients were available free to the general public. Capitol Advantage, through its CapWiz software packages, provided architecture and database information for approximately 1,000 clients, ranging from the U.S. Chamber of Commerce, Disabled American Veterans, Medical Society of Virginia, to Intel. CapWiz is also an integral part of American Online's AOL Government Guide, Yahoo!, *Slate* magazine on MSN, and *USA Today* and *The New York Times*.

Just from Capitol Advantage clients alone, a total of 7.5 million messages were sent in 2001 to Congress, the federal agencies and the White House, and state and local officials. During 2002, there was an increase of 54 percent in e-mail use over the year before.[27] For its clients, Capitol Advantage offers a wealth of services and information. It provides educational tools, such information on both federal and state elected officials (photos, bios, mailing address, key staffers, links to their web sites, sponsored legislation, and committee assignments, endorsements, political action committee contributions) and federal legislation (tracking of bills and votes for current and several past sessions, voting scorecards, committee and floor schedules of Congress). It further provided contact information for all members of Congress, hundreds of cabinet officials, foreign embassies in the United States, and independent agencies, as well as thousands of state and local government elected officials, and over 9,600 media contacts. Capitol Advantage's services also made it easy for its clients to target individuals and organizations for policy alerts and messages, and to post alerts on popular Internet sites like AOL, MSN, Yahoo!, and national and regional media sites.[28]

Very little of this ever occurs spontaneously. Grassroots mobilization is manufactured, planned, and orchestrated. What is "real" about grassroots is the sentiment that is channeled and organized: citizens, groups, employees and others genuinely irritated or stirred up, willing to have their voices heard. A grassroots effort falls flat on its face without that potential (then actualized) constituency. To make it legitimate and credible, the constituents who are now mad, activated, and "wired" cannot be misled or misinformed, and their support must be genuine. When wired citizens are misinformed, or ill-informed, critics rightly charge that the whole grassroots effort is nothing more than "astroturf," phony representation, and it usually can be detected within minutes of the first telephone calls hitting Capitol Hill offices.

Many large companies, trade associations, and coalitions first turned to phone bank specialty firms, such as Bonner and Associates and Direct Impact, a division of the giant public relations firm, Burson-Marsteller. Other grassroots specialists included Dewey Square Group which has a network of grassroots operatives throughout the country, and Dittus Communications with a sizeable grassroots practice. Along with these and other grassroots specialists were relatively new firms that concentrate on electronic advocacy.

One of the earliest organizations to realize the potential of online advocacy was Issue Dynamics, Inc., a Washington, D.C.-based firm that began its Internet advocacy services in 1993. Among its clients were Verizon, Blue Cross Blue Shield, American Express, and the Human Rights Campaign. Another Washington-based firm is Grassroots Enterprise, headed by former Clinton press secretary Mike McCurry, with forty-five employees and a roster of clients such as Campaign for Tobacco Free Kids, the Greater Washington Board of Trade, and TechNet, a coalition of 300 technology CEOs and senior executives. Starting out as Grassroots.com in 1999, the business has transformed itself from one based on developing online political communities, political news and perspectives, and online candidate campaigns to one focused on the grassroots mobilization and crisis management. Mindshare Internet Campaigns and e-Advocates are also pioneer firms that specialize in electronic advocacy, along with firms such as Democracy Data & Communications (DDC) which create and manage databases.[29]

Electronic advocacy firms have pointed to several attractive features in their products beyond the cost-efficiencies and speed of online communications. Grassroots Enterprises, for example, touted one of its software products, Grassroots Multiplier. Through this software program, clients could grow their own bases of support, manage their issues, and mobilize their organization's support base.[30] Mike McCurry described the ultimate object of electronic grassroots advocacy: "The real Holy Grail is [finding a way] to seamlessly communicate via e-mail with the audience you're trying to reach and get the end user to pick up the phone or send e-mails to Congress."[31]

Using grassroots software, client membership or organization data can be highly segmented so that messages and issue alerts can be tailored to specific audiences. Using advocacy software, a client can track the past response rate of its members, and determine immediately how many of them have responded and to whom they have sent e-mail messages. By using advocacy software, clients have a much greater understanding of how well their message was being delivered.

Electronic Grassroots and Future Advocacy

Is electronic grassroots the next Big Thing, the killer application that will revolutionize how Congress interacts with citizens, interest groups, and the world? Those in the business of marketing electronic grassroots campaigns certainly think and hope so and they promote the many benefits of advocating online. Larry Purpuro, a former deputy chief of staff of the Republican National Committee who headed up its e.GOP project and now heads his own firm, RightClick Strategies, made the case for e-mail advocacy: "E-mail can displace about 10 lobbyists if it's done effectively in terms of your coverage. If a lobbyist's challenge is to deliver information immediately, efficiently and dramatically, absent a one-to-one meeting, e-mail is it."[32]

But many prefer the tried-and-true methods of traditional lobbying, coupled with electronic grassroots advocacy, and view the latter as simply another weapon in their arsenal of persuasive tools. Often the best advocacy efforts combine both the old and the new, with the director of government affairs or the senior lobbyist in Washington quarterbacking the persuasion effort.

Law firms, trade associations, lobbying firms, boutique influence shops are populated with Washington insiders—former Members of Congress, former staffers, persons who know Washington, who know how to work their particular niche of the policy and influence market, whether it be defense, agriculture, energy or a myriad of other issues and causes. Many law and lobbying firms have former Democratic and Republican staffers or Members working for them, hedging their bets by appealing to both sides of the political aisle. So too are lobbying firms choosing to either ally closely with or buy into a firm doing non-traditional, electronic advocacy.[33]

The electronic revolution in grassroots advocacy has been a driving force leading to the enormous increase in e-mail traffic to Congress. Interest groups, using specially designed, easy-to-use software, have been able to target their membership, and coalitions of friends and allies, to bombard Congress with e-mails and traditional forms of communication. The electronic advocacy revolution has made it possible for marginally-funded organizations to spend relatively little money to reach their own members, like-minded citizens, and then to reach Members of Congress, the White House, and the agencies of the Executive branch. A new class of activists has emerged: individuals who perhaps otherwise would not become involved, would not write to Congress, and who would not take time off work to protest an issue. The online activist is asked to do something relatively simple: read the e-mail, and if you believe in what we say, click on the name of your legislator, and write an e-mail, or click onto our website, choose paragraphs and phrases that best fit your sentiments, and then send the message to Congress.

E-mail has become so easy to use and it has increased so dramatically as it flows into Washington. The question is, does Congress listen and respond? Or do e-mails just stack up in an electronic in-box, answered automatically by correspondence software, and only seen by the lawmaker on a chart at the end of the week with tallies for or against an issue? Does e-mail reach the intended lawmaker's office system, or does it disappear into cyberspace? Has e-mail become such a universal commodity that the more it is used, and the more it is organized and orchestrated, the less important it becomes and the smaller its overall impact?

Electronic communication between citizens and Members of Congress is still a work in progress. As chapter five will illustrate, some Congressional offices now effectively use readily available e-mail software to manage the flow of electronic mail; others, often following the lead of the Member, rank e-mail as a rather low priority, both in the way it is handled internally and the qualitative importance assigned to it. Some Members insist that e-mail is not as important as "real" mail; many refuse to reply to e-mail with an electronic reply, even though most individuals who send e-mail to Congress prefer such electronic responses.

3

The Promise of Electronic Government

*Done right, digital government promises to transform Industrial Age
big government into Knowledge Age smart government.*
—Robert D. Atkinson, Progressive Policy Institute

*Electronic government can fundamentally recast the connection
between people and their government. It can make government far
more responsive to the will of the people and greatly improve transactions between them. It can also help all of us to take a much more
active part in the democratic process.*
—The Council for Excellence in Government

The Transformation of Government

uring the Industrial Age, governments at all levels suffered from
a poor public image. Fair or not, government was often seen as
unresponsive, uncaring, doing its best to irritate or frustrate
citizens and businesses alike as they sought assistance, information, or simply the right form to fill out. Citizens seeking government
assistance would be forced to come downtown to dingy reception areas and
offices with garish fluorescent lighting, stained carpets, uncomfortable chairs,
pea-green paint chipping from waiting room walls, only to be confronted by
long delays and surly civil servants.

Service was not customer-oriented with long lines and limited hours, with offices open from 9 A.M.–5 P.M. on weekdays only, more at the convenience of civil servants than their customers. It seemed that in the most customer-intensive agencies, like the Division of Motor Vehicles or Office of Taxation, service was at its worst, often approaching Kafka-esque dysfunctionalities. Outmoded, unreliable mainframe computers, relying on generations-old software, frequently broke down, compounding the frustration and delay.

Citizens frequently did not know which agency to turn to or what services were provided, and too often agencies did not go out of their way to help. Citizens might stand in long lines at one counter, only to be told once approaching the window that the form they needed was at a different agency, two floors (or two buildings) away and another long line. Of course, an exasperating second trip and time away from work would be required to complete the transaction.

In Industrial Age government, the dominant operating culture was "agency-centric" rather than "customer-centric." The businesses large and small in the competitive private sector learned long ago that in order to survive, they had to pay attention to their customers. However, that elemental business credo, "the customer is always right" rarely took root in the Industrial Age public sector. The focus was on the agency, not the customer; citizens frequently were viewed as nuisances rather than customers who paid the taxes and salaries of the public servants. Businesses trying to obtain permits, meet regulatory requirements, and simply to work with government agencies were in for the same unresponsive treatment.

Government could also be mystifyingly complicated. It was difficult for both informed citizens and those with limited knowledge to figure out just where to turn to receive assistance or find answers. It might be as simple as finding out if car insurance papers must accompany an application for a new driver's license, or as complex as finding out which agencies, among the federal, state, and local, can provide assistance to a low-income single mother. Industrial Age government too often made it difficult for citizens to obtain information, make comparisons, or find out the right person to talk to.

The problems were compounded because agencies, in public administration parlance, engaged in "stove-piping," running their own departments independently of others, not sharing information or resources, jealously guarding their own data and knowledge bases. Stove-piping abounds throughout government. For example, Congressman Robert Goodlatte (Republican-Virginia), co-chair of the 180-member Congressional Internet Caucus, saw problems of stove-piping firsthand as head of a subcommittee of the House

Agriculture Committee. In the U.S. Department of Agriculture, there are 28 different agencies, each with separate authorities, segmented plans, and priorities. "People in some buildings can't e-mail people in others," lamented Goodlatte.[1]

The September 11th terrorists attacks highlighted the problem of stovepiping, particularly with its impact on national security. A principal reason that the White House moved swiftly to establish a new office of Homeland Security was to put a halt to turf wars, get agencies to cooperate, and share information and resources. Homeland Security was fighting an uphill battle, going against an ingrained security culture, where agencies did not trust one another and did not share information and intelligence. Homeland Security's task was made even more difficult with the need to have state and local law enforcement agencies drawn in.[2]

Citizen participation, particularly at the local level, was often hampered by a basic lack of communication and information: when public meetings were held, a published agenda, minutes of meetings, transcripts of witness statements, and follow-through information. Citizens were often left in the dark, even in jurisdictions that prided themselves in their accessibility to public hearings and open door democracy.[3]

Beginning in the mid-1990s, sometimes in halting steps, governments began improving their communications technologies and their accessibility to citizens and businesses. One of the first steps was the implementation of automated telephone answering services. What seemed like an efficient way of handling customer calls is familiar to us all: An automated voice would say "select 1 if you have a question concerning taxes," "select 2 if you want to order a city form," and so forth. Laid out in a logical format, however, these telephone trees often extended to limits beyond customer patience. For example, before the government of the District of Columbia installed a mayor's hotline, with inquiries answered by an actual person who was knowledgeable (even friendly) about city services, it used an automated telephone answering system. In a simple experiment the author tried to find the answer to a relatively easy question about automobile title transfer. The telephone call to the central District of Columbia number started with "press 1 if you want this message in English, press 2 if you want it in Spanish." Fair enough, but it then took six distinct layers of "press 1s and press 6s" in order to get to the question. Users of such systems have to be lucky enough not to press the wrong number and determined enough to listen through the ladder of options that it took to get to that sixth level.[4]

This automatic routing does have built-in efficiencies for the government receiving the calls, but the inconvenience and impersonal nature of the transaction leaves many customers cold, if not exasperated, wishing there was a real, live, friendly, and helpful voice at the other end, who at most would pass inquiries off to just one other agency staffer.

A dramatic improvement in the way citizens are treated and problems solved was the telephone call center. One of the best is found in the city of Chicago. In 1999 through Mayor Richard M. Daley's IT initiative, Chicago launched the 311 call center, a citizen hotline non-emergency service, modeled on the 911 system. It has become a successful communications system, widely praised and has attracted much attention throughout the United States and abroad. The key features are customer service, order tracking, resource management, and accountability.[5]

The old system in Chicago suffered from many Industrial Age stove-piping maladies: lack of accountability, absence of coordination, and data not being shared. Under the old system, the mayor's office did not know which agencies were doing a good job in response and follow-up and which were not.

The 311 system handles three million calls per year, a ten-fold increase in just three years since it was created. It is manned twenty-four hours a day, seven days a week by rotating teams of thirty civilian operators and police officers, who learn key phrases in twenty-five languages. Chicago citizens call about everyday annoyances and problems. Most calls concern abandoned vehicles, streetlights, location of wards, garbage, graffiti, stray animals, tree trimming, and open hydrants. Chicago street maintenance must be doing something right, because complaints about potholes ranked only twentieth in citizen concerns. Roughly 30,000 calls a day have nothing to do with Chicago or its services, and when possible, they are routed to the right government agency.

One of the most important accomplishments of the 311 system is permitting the mayor's office, citizens, and alderman to monitor bureaucratic performance. They can track the status of service requests as they travel through the 311 process to any of the forty-two city departments, and see, for example, how long it takes for an abandoned automobile to be removed or garbage carts to be delivered.

A telephone call center, manned by trained workers, can bring communications technology to every citizen, with little concern for digital divide issues. On the user's end, it is sheer simplicity: anyone who can use a telephone and can dial 311 has access to city service. No computer skills are required and no knowledge of the Internet is necessary. Yet behind this system is a sophisticated telecommunications network, which puts no burden on the caller.

In July 2000, the Federal Communications Commission designated 511 as a traveler's telephone information number and permitted states or groups of states to create their own 511 information systems. Eight states, led by the Iowa Department of Transportation, have pooled their resources and expertise to develop a 511 voice-enabled telephone service for travelers. They use Voice XML (Extensible Markup Language) standards and technologies to create a voice-enabled traveler service. Once connected, a traveler could seek information by speaking keywords rather than responding to a series of number choices. A voice-enabled traveler service was created in Utah in December 2001, and in 1999, Iowa along with four other states formed a partnership to develop Condition Acquisition and Reporting System (CARS), a reporting system that gave access to information on road conditions, work zones, and incident management information collected from the Internet.[6]

In addition to telephone technology, governments, large and small, have increasingly turned to online solutions. To a large degree, they have been swept up by the same lofty expectations, hyperbole and enthusiasm found in the dot.com and Internet revolution. Much has been written about the wonders and promise of electronic government, but the sobering reality is that the challenges are daunting, bureaucratic sluggishness (and rivalry) is deeply-imbedded, and resources are invariably pinched. The public sector has been wrestling with the challenges and opportunities of the so-called information superhighway and the re-invention of government. Managers and administrators have had to re-think how government operates, how it communicates, and how it can better serve the public through advanced technologies. Through electronic government initiatives, the public sector has focused on three layers of communication: government-to-government, government-to-business, and government-to-citizens.[7] Our concern is primarily with the third layer—government communication with citizens.

State and Local Governments Go to the Web

Since the mid 1990s, there has been an impressive transformation of communications at the state and local government level. Websites at the state and local government level now are almost universal. By 2001, a total of 84 percent of all municipalities had developed websites, and for those jurisdictions which did not have a web presence, 70 percent were planning to create one within a year.[8]

Typically the first versions of these websites were nothing more than electronic brochures. They gave information on key services, telephone numbers and sometimes e-mail addresses of officials and staff, and posted information on upcoming events. A more advanced version was the interactive website, which permitted relatively simple transactions: forms could be downloaded or simple questions answered through a frequently-asked-questions format. The next stage of website development was the transactional stage, providing more complex levels of assistance, such as permitting payment of taxes, fees or fines, allowing businesses to submit bids and proposals. The final, most sophisticated, level was the transformational stage, achieved by just a few jurisdictions, which sought to change how government operates, broke down organizational barriers, and emphasized citizens and their needs.[9] One of the goals of a transformational web presence was to provide, simply put, a government "without walls, doors or clocks."[10]

Many websites for local governments and small to medium-sized cities, however, are little more than simple electronic brochures. Civic Resources Group, a Santa Monica, California research organization, analyzed the websites of all cities in the United States with populations of 100,000 or more, using seventy different variables. Researchers found that for most websites, information was static and the sites had limited interactivity. For example, just 11 percent of the cities provided interactive features for public participation in the planning process, public hearings or online meetings.[11] Clearly, for many governmental units, the hope of moving from electronic bulletin boards to the transformational web configuration is still a work in progress.

What makes a good state and local government website? Costis Toregas, president of Public Technology, Inc., has argued that electronic government should improve the delivery of service to citizens, assist in the creation of economic activity, and safeguard democracy. Further, e-government must be oriented toward citizens, who do not care what level of government or agency provides the needed service. Moreover, electronic government demands that its services be available to all citizens, not just those who can afford to pay for or find the electronic infrastructure. Toregas warned that merely automating current systems was an inadequate way of meeting the potential of electronic government.[12]

A number of organizations have established best practices criteria and periodically rate websites to determine which ones are doing the best job in promoting electronic government. For example, the Center for Digital Government[13] and *Government Technology* magazine promote an annual rating of state and local government websites and have developed criteria to determine which sites measure up as "Best of the Web." These best practices include:

- Innovation and use of web-based online technology to deliver government services. What innovations are there in the areas of government-to-citizen communications, government-to-business and/or government-to-government services?

- Efficiency or time saved. What amount of time is saved in agency operations and by citizens; how able is the government to handle a complete transaction for services or business online; and what amount of information is available online?

- Economy or money saved. How did the government save money by using web-based services and how much was saved? Were there innovative ways of funding these e-government projects; and were public/private partnerships involved?

- Ease of use and improved citizen access. Were customers satisfied using the website; was it easy to navigate and clean in appearance; is handicapped accessibility a key component of the site; and could citizens participate in online government or interact with government and affect policy?[14]

Promise of Websites

Citizens and governments alike have seen the advantages in shifting to online technology. Through their government website information is available twenty-four hours a day, seven days a week; there are no long lines, no overworked civil servants to confront, and no busy signals. Instead of driving on congested city streets, fighting for a parking place, and standing in line for a form, transactions can all be done with a click. If a government provides nothing else online, nonetheless, it has gone a long way toward enhancing its reputation with the public for efficiency and service. For citizens and businesses, there can be savings from reductions in travel time and in time associated with person-to-person business with government officials, or in reduction of costs in complying with government rules and regulations.

Using the Internet, governments can also reduce the cost of providing services. The Virginia Department of Motor Vehicles, for example, estimated that the cost per transaction over the Internet is half the cost of over-the-counter transactions.[15] Arizona, the first state to have vehicle registration renewals online, found that electronic renewals cost $1.60 versus $7.00 for the paper process.[16] Instead of printing massive copies of reports or other official government information, a small number can be printed, with the reports then posted on the government website, for everyone to view. For example, Fairfax County, Virginia, in 1999 published 240,000 copies of its "Citizens' Handbook," at a cost of $500,000; with this publication now available on its Internet site in a readable and downloadable format, available to all, the county in 2001 printed just 25,000 copies, at a cost of $20,000—a savings of $480,000 in printing costs. Further savings came in reduced copying and mailing expenses.

Fairfax County officials assume that a minimum of five minutes in staff time resulting from a telephone call or a counter visit could be avoided by gaining information from the web—to say nothing of the convenience and customer satisfaction. With one million website visitors a month, and an average staff cost of $16.25 per hour, the estimated savings is over $16 million a year.[17]

A successful government website must include services that citizens want to have online. Some jurisdictions have used market surveys, questionnaires, and focus groups to determine what citizens wanted out of electronic government and their government's website. Several studies have been conducted to determine what should go on government agency websites. One poll, commissioned by the Council on Excellence on Government, found that citizens were eager to have certain public services online.[18] Above all, they wanted to be able to renew a driver's license online, find health information online, have change of address forms disseminated automatically and electronically to all government agencies, review online voting records of candidates, and respond to jury summons online. Citizens wanted just what the Commonwealth of Virginia's website promised: "Get *on*line, not *in* line."

Congress could learn lessons from Fairfax County and other jurisdictions that use questionnaires and conduct focus groups to determine what people want on government websites. As will be seen in chapter six, it is the rare congressional office that asks constituents what they want to see on their lawmaker's website.[19]

Examples of Best Websites

A number of universities, technology magazines, and research organizations have begun rating state, municipal, and local government websites to determine which provide the best service, are easiest to use, are accessible to those with physical disabilities, which offer timely materials, and are applying innovative solutions to communication and service deliverability issues.

For example, from the research conducted by the Center for Digital Democracy in 2000 and 2001, the Council of State Governments in 2001, and Digital Cities in 2001, these have been judged the best state executive, state legislative, local government, and state judicial branch websites.

BEST OF STATE AND LOCAL GOVERNMENT WEBSITES, 2000–2002

State Government Sites	My California (portal); NC@YourService (portal); Pennsylvania; Maine; Virginia; Washington; Georgia; Virginia DMV; New Jersey Home Page; Georgia Secretary of State; Illinois Criminal Justice Information Authority; eMaryland Marketplace; Virginia VATAX Online.
State Legislatures	Minnesota; Alaska; Louisiana
Local Government	New York City; Montgomery County, Maryland; Conyers, Georgia; Miami-Dade County, Florida; Chicago; City of Seattle; San Jose (California) Permits Online; Honolulu; Colorado Springs; Houston; Plano, Texas; Des Moines, Iowa; Salt Lake City, Utah; Roanoke, Virginia; Boulder, Colorado, Costa Mesa, California; and Bellevue, Washington.
Judicial Branch	North Dakota Supreme Court; Arkansas Judiciary; Utah State Courts.

There has been a steady improvement in design and features of the websites. Cathilea Robinett, executive director of the Center for Digital Government, observed that the 2001 entries were the strongest in the history of its awards. "The sites, in general, are very good. Everybody is getting better."[20] For the Center for Digital Democracy awards in 2001, the My California portal beat out 168 other entries in the state government category while New York City bested more than 200 entries in the municipalities category.

The award-winning California portal site permits visitors to personalize the home page, hence the name My California.[21] Viewers fit into one of several "communities": California resident, business person, media/press, state employee, student, or tourist, and website information tailored to each community becomes readily available. The website also has gained a certification from the Accessibility Center of Excellence, meeting the highest measures of the World Wide Web Consortium (W3C) Web Content Accessibility standards. Beginning in July 2001, My California added a new wireless feature, allowing Californians to receive up-to-date information about energy costs, traffic delays, and the latest news from the Governor's office through pagers, cell phones, or hand-held personal digital assistants (PDAs). The Center for Digital Government noted that this was the only state government portal to have an array of wireless capabilities.

In 2001, the best sites were portal-style, where the homepage served as a master site, directing viewers to a wide array of information. The Commonwealth of Virginia, which launched the first personalized state webpage, My Virginia,[22] routed viewers to the correct community portal (such as My Richmond) once they had entered their ZIP code or tax jurisdiction number. The portal also had the unique feature of giving users "Live Help" as an option at the bottom of its homepage. The state of Maine website had a helpful electronic service called "Remind Me," which notified citizens by e-mails when it was time to renew driver's licenses, vehicle registration, and register to vote. The Maine website offered nearly 40 electronic transactions and allowed citizens to renew 131 types of professional licenses online.[23]

The New York City website, with more than 30,000 pages of content and more than 100 transactional services, had 52 million page views in fiscal 2001, doubling its 1999 rate. The New York City site offered online traffic hearings and a one-stop e-payment center. The small suburban town of Conyers, Georgia, recognized that 65 percent of its citizens commuted to nearby Atlanta each workday and were often unable to conduct business in person in their home community. To meet its citizens' needs, Conyers emphasized practical services like online tax and traffic fine payments, and access to police accident and incident reports.[24]

Case Study: Fairfax County, Virginia

Fairfax County, Virginia, the large, affluent county in the Washington, D.C. metropolitan region, has 970,000 residents, making it larger in population than seven states, a median family income of $84,000 in 1997, and a total of 399 square miles in land area. The county has 350 parks, and the sixth largest library system of its kind in the United States. It is also the home of many high-tech industries, the second largest concentration of commercial shopping on the East Coast, and a large and growing immigrant population. Fairfax County also has an award-winning website and commitment to provide services online from the elected county Board of Supervisors.[25]

When the Fairfax County government website debuted in 1996, it contained some 600 pages of information about county government and services and received an average of 8,000 visit a month; by 2001, the website had 20,000 document pages and more than a million visitors each month.[26] This high volume of public inquiries and the growing amount of information on the website prompted county officials to redesign the website so that it provided easier access. The redesigned website was more customer-friendly and intuitive, moving an essentially agency-oriented website to a customer-oriented one. More than fifty county agencies provide information to the Fairfax website, and it is managed by 120 staff from different agencies who work on web development.[27]

The new design further meets the mandates of the Americans with Disabilities Act (ADA) and section 508 of the Rehabilitation Act of 1973. By using the website, Fairfax County residents can pay county taxes using credit cards; access information about county job vacancies; download Request for Proposals (RFPs); look at recent real estate sales through the GIS parcel maps; visit the county library system to see if their books had been checked out or reserved and access the online card catalogue; look through an historical newspaper database containing about 1.5 million articles; and report lost pets, among other things.

In preparation for redesigning its website, Fairfax County conducted citizen and business surveys and focus groups.[28] County officials learned from the focus groups that citizens were not always aware what tasks each county department or agency handled. The next phase of redesign involved moving Fairfax County to a content management system that would allow staff to use information across platforms. A concentration on content management had the potential for greatly increasing the ability of the county agencies and department to quickly publish and update their information. Furthermore, there would be greater access to information because it would be available over handheld devices and cell phones.[29]

Fairfax County operates three technology platforms for its e-government activities: information kiosks, interactive voice response (telephone call center), and the county's website.[30] It has twenty-four kiosks located in twenty-one county libraries, public buildings, shopping malls and other locations. Created in 1996, the multimedia kiosk program by May 2001 had registered four million inquiries for information; the newly-designed kiosk enclosures also met ADA standards. Fairfax County shares information with other government and private entities, such as the Washington, D.C. Council of Governments, the Virginia Department of Motor Vehicles, the local private

Inova Health Systems, the Virginia Railway Express, and several other local governments.

Technology certainly isn't perfect. At a demonstration at the Fairfax County Government Center of the kiosk, I asked for one page to be printed out and twelve pages came spilling forth. Voice instructions on how to use the kiosk came from a sound dome, but the sound was too soft to be heard over the ambient sounds of the building's lobby. The kiosk information was in English only, yet Fairfax County public schools have students whose parents speak some 150 languages.

Customer-Centric Sites

State and local governments are trying to refocus their efforts from being agency-focused to customer-focused. It is a simple idea, but one that requires basic rethinking of programs and new approaches to communicating with the public. Much of the problem stems from the simple fact that citizens often have no idea what governments can provide or where to turn when they need assistance. The state of Texas is trying to break through the often formidable knowledge barrier between citizens and state assistance. In October 2001, the Department of Human Services launched STARS (State of Texas Assistance and Referral System) to help citizens determine their eligibility for more than fifty types of state assistance programs. The bilingual web-based system is part of a larger program called TIERS (Texas Integrated Eligibility Redesign System) to provide a comprehensive system to determine eligibility for the full range of public assistance services in the state; and provides full caseload-management support. State officials have found that STARS has provided faster, more efficient access to information; it has improved customer service, giving the Department of Human Services 12,000 case workers throughout the state's 500 local offices better information, and it affords better citizen access by being available through schools, libraries, hospitals, and county human services agencies.[31]

Another example of a customer-centric website is Oklahoma's redesigned website, Your Oklahoma, which was unveiled in October 2001.[32] It presents viewers with simple, easy to understand categories: Business, Working, Living, Recreation and Travel, Education, Health and Public Safety, Government, Facts and History. Under the somewhat vague Living section, the viewer can click on "Automobiles and Transportation," along with eight other subcategories, and find state government information about bicycling, drivers' licenses, fuel efficiency, maps, road conditions, planes, trains, buses, vehicle insurance, vehicle lemon laws, vehicle titles, registration, and license plates.

Opportunities and Issues with Government Websites and E-mail

While many state and big city websites are doing a better job at providing information, interactivity, and accessibility, others still have far to go. Civic Resources Group in its 2001 study, determined that while many U.S. cities are moving toward information online yet they are "are ill-prepared to deal with the organizational challenges and complexities of e-government operations."[33] Civic Resources Group summarized the tasks ahead for local government as "daunting, even for the most well resourced and tech-savvy municipalities."

Civic Resources Group found that while 64 percent of cities surveyed provided e-mail addresses of elected officials, only 5 percent included user-friendly response forms to encourage and facilitate interaction. Further, 21 percent of cities did not provide online access for meeting agendas and 33 percent did not provide online minutes of public meetings. Just 5 percent of cities use online video and 3 percent use web-based audio for meetings of elected officials. Only 8 percent of city websites analyzed include a privacy statement and only 5 percent were accessible to the disabled.[34]

In a study of mayors and city council members of the National League of Cities, the Pew Internet and American Life Project in 2002 found that local officials had embraced the Internet and most used e-mail to communicate with their constituents.[35] In contrast to Members of Congress, the local officials surveyed were not overwhelmed with e-mail from constituents, and found that e-mail lags behind the more traditional forms of communication, such as telephone calls, letters, and in-person meetings.

One particular concern has been protection of citizen records and information from electronic abuse. According to the Internet Alliance, just eight states had passed laws regarding government use of private information. Specially aggressive in giving law enforcement access to databases during 2001 were Colorado, Delaware, Illinois, New Jersey, Ohio, and Georgia. States that had passed privacy laws include Arizona, Arkansas, Massachusetts, Montana, Nevada, New York, Texas, and Utah. Only fifteen states have passed financial privacy laws since enactment of 1999 federal legislation.[36]

One of the marvels of useful government websites is that they can provide information otherwise very difficult to obtain, often in full reports, or in a useful database format. This includes public documents and public information which may be sensitive, present security issues, or embarrass individuals or organizations. An ongoing debate, however, will concern where to draw the boundaries between material that should and should not be posted on official websites.[37]

Prompted by a 1996 federal statute, known as Megan's Law,[38] all states and the federal government are now required to register individuals who have been convicted of sex crimes against children. As part of the law, certain information must be made available to the public and many states have placed this information on their websites. In compliance, the City of Chicago maintains a listing, updated daily, of 4,451 registered sex offenders, giving name, sex, race, date of birth, picture, and street address (but not the exact address) of the offender, and whether the victim was under eighteen years of age. At the same time, the website maintained by the Illinois State Police lists all sex offenders in the state (including Chicago), and includes full address information. The Minnesota Department of Corrections maintains a file on sex offenders out of compliance with registration, complete with pictures, personal information, and where they last resided.[39] Private organizations, especially the Klaas Foundation for Children, also maintain extensive links to state, city, and county websites that maintain sex offender information.[40] Megan's law and similar legislation had been challenged in federal courts in Connecticut, New Jersey, and Alaska as being too harsh or in violation of the due process clause of the Fourteenth Amendment. In a ruling by the U.S. Court of Appeals, Second Circuit, a Connecticut statute was found to be "too blunt" and "fails to accommodate the constitutional rights of persons . . . who are branded as likely to be currently dangerous offenders irrespective of whether or not they are." The U.S. Supreme Court, however, unanimously upheld the statute in a March 2003 ruling.[41]

· Already public documents, such as marriage and divorce records, bankruptcies, liens, civil lawsuits, and professional licenses are available on the web, but usually to companies that run credit, employment, or criminal checks, not to the general public. There are some safeguards for the person being investigated: the federal Fair Credit Reporting Act, for example, requires anyone running a criminal check for employment or credit screening to obtain the applicant's permission in writing and to notify that person if he or she were denied a job or a loan because of that information.

Now, however, criminal records are being sold directly to the public. In May 2002, a small company in Tennessee, RapSheets.com began selling national criminal background checks to the public for $20 or $30 each, using a database of 50 million criminal records in thirty states. Peter Schutt, the president of RapSheets.com, stated that he wanted not just corporations but citizens to be able to find criminal records: "If your daughter was going out on a date with someone for the first time, there is no reason you can't check the guy out." RapSheets.com requires customers to check an online box pledging to honor the Fair Credit Reporting Act, but there is no way for the nine employees of the company to check on customers. The biggest employment screening company, ChoicePoint Inc., announced that it would soon start selling criminal record searches to the public.[42]

Another problem that governments must face is the accuracy and timeliness of sensitive, but publicly available information on their websites. For example, a Virginia-sponsored website contained profiles of 31,000 physicians who practice in the state. Included was information about disciplinary actions taken against doctors in Virginia, other states, or by federal agencies or hospitals. In September 2001, the *Washington Post* identified five physicians in Virginia who had misrepresented or omitted crucial facts about disciplinary actions taken against them in their online profiles. According to the *Post* investigation, it could take up to five months or more for the Virginia Board of Medicine to adjudicate the cases of these five and an additional five physicians. One physician's medical license was suspended in Pennsylvania for three years and had been convicted of a misdemeanor charge of having unlawful sexual conduct with a patient; another had been forced to surrender his license in North Carolina; one doctor was on indefinite probation but the state had concluded that he posed a "danger to the health and safety of his patients." None of this and other information had been available for consumers to see, since the information is furnished by the doctors themselves and the information is not independently verified.[43]

Likewise, a report by the staff of the House Committee on Government Reform found that a website, Nursing Home Compare, which is an official site of the U.S. Department of Health and Human Services, had excluded more than 25,000 violations reported by state investigators. The website was launched in 1998 to allow consumers to search for safety records and violations of virtually every nursing home in the United States, and was having some 100,000 hits per month.[44]

In the wake of the September 11, 2001 terrorist attacks, a number of states and the federal government have been rethinking what they put on their official websites. Fearing possible terrorist attacks, the Utah Department of Environmental Quality, for example, no longer identifies on its website where toxic substances were stored throughout the state. This information came from the 1986 Toxic Release Inventory, which was designed to alert citizens of potential toxic hazards in industrial plants, chemical suppliers, mining operations, and other operations that might use dangerous substances. Similarly, officials in New Jersey have deleted from the state's official website databases with information on the state's reservoir system and hazardous chemical storage sites, while New York City consulted with the FBI about what information was appropriate to have online.[45]

Federal and state sites are being re-evaluated throughout the country. Federal agencies have been removing from their websites data such as security plans of hazardous chemical sites, information about weapons of mass destruction, or aviation accident reports. The National Imagery and Mapping Agency no longer sells its detailed digital maps on the Internet. The Energy Department suppressed 9,000 documents from its Information Bridge Web service, the Department of Defense scrubbed information about the location of personnel, and the Environmental Protection Agency, which receives more than 100 million hits a month on the Web, removed sensitive materials from its Envirofacts database.[46]

E-Democracy at the Local Level

Some local governments provide information about meetings to be held, agendas, and access to local officials through e-mail. The city of St. Paul, Minnesota, for example, provided a service so that citizens could automatically receive e-mail of city council minutes and agendas.[47] In Wisconsin, local governments were found to be doing a good job of providing basic service information. Two-thirds of the 225 local government websites were used primarily to publish information such as agendas and minutes of government meetings, department directories, and descriptions of services available online. Yet only twenty-five of those websites allowed online payments for government services, and only two cities established services so that parking tickets could be paid online with a credit card.[48]

There are 87,504 government units in the United States—school boards, city councils, county commissions, state legislatures, and other bodies. J. H. Snider of the New America Foundation has estimated that these government units hold more than one million meetings, which must, by law, be open to the public.[49] However, only a small number of citizens attend such meetings. The combination of poor attendance by the public and poor records by the public entity, makes for, in Snider's view, a "private meeting."

Snider has argued for all public meetings at the local level to be truly in the public record, meaning that they should all be videotaped and citizens provided with verbatim transcripts, provided by a speaker-dependent voice recognition system, using web technology. Further, citizens should receive agendas and minutes via e-mail, agendas should be linked to appropriate documents such as proposed budget items, and there should be a public comments forum. Snider also believes that citizens should be able to view and participate in all meetings anonymously and remotely.[50]

The greatest opportunity for democratic participation is at this local level. Snider's vision of openness and citizen online participation may never be fully realized, but electronic government at the county school board, city council, or other level, if through nothing more than e-mail notification of meetings, agendas, minutes, and audio- and video-broadcasting on their websites, would go a long way toward making local government more accessible.

These electronic tools would make it easier for activists and ordinary citizens to have better knowledge of local government activities. It would make it far easier for activists to find information, communicate with their allies, and organize opposition or support of local government activities. Ordinary citizens, who are only marginally interested in civic issues, and may be galvanized only when issues directly affect them, nevertheless could find online local government to be quite useful. Electronic notification, access, and information make it all the more easy for like-minded citizens to organize and to assemble before local elected officials. It may do little, however, for the majority of citizens who simply do not follow politics. No matter the immediacy of online information or ease of access, there has to be a basic level of civic interest to animate those with no interest in politics.

The Federal Government on the Web

One of the earlier steps in online communication was legislation passed in 1996 to give easier and quicker access to federal government documents. That year, Congress passed and President Clinton signed into law the Electronic Freedom of Information Act (EFOIA). The federal law required agencies, whenever possible, to provide records in any of these requested formats—paper, computer disk, or PDF file over the Internet. It also required agencies to make certain records available online if they were available in their public reading rooms, and it took steps to eliminate the long delays faced by people making Freedom of Information Act (FOIA) requests for government documents.

Senator Patrick J. Leahy (Democrat-Vermont) and Representative Robert Goodlatte (Republican-Virginia) argued that the EFOIA should go further by encouraging agencies to revise their documents to include structured fields so that they can be more easily searched through the Internet. This means that documents could be searched by agency, author, title, date, and other useful information. Further, Leahy and Goodlatte argued that the citations of public documents within other public documents should be linked over the Internet wherever possible, and all newly created documents subject to FOIA should be searchable via the Internet, with the ultimate goal of having documents available online at the time they are filed. Federal agencies, however, have far to go to provide easily-accessible documents; only thirteen federal agencies accepted Electronic Freedom of Information (EFOIA) requests online in 2002.[51]

FirstGov.gov

In September 2000, the General Services Administration announced the creation of FirstGov.gov, the official U.S. government web portal, which provides a user-friendly and searchable site to 47 million pages of federal, state, and local government information, services, and online transactions. FirstGov.gov was funded by the Federal Chief Information Officers Council, the federal entity created in 1996, and twenty-two other federal agencies.[52] One of the key features of the FirstGov.gov portal was the powerful search engine, which searches every word of every U.S. government document, in less than a second. The search engine also covers public websites that have ".gov" and ".mil" in their primary domain suffix, which then covers the Congress, U. S. Courts, the White House and all cabinet departments, independent agencies, and a number of state websites that have adopted the ".gov" suffix. Only publicly available documents are included; no data treated by the government as private, classified, password protected, or firewall-protected is covered in the search engine.

FirstGov.gov received a design and content upgrade in March 2002, making its homepage easier to access, better focusing on online services for citizens, business, and government. The homepage focuses on services available to assist viewers; it does not focus on agencies. Nowhere on the homepage is there mention of agencies, rather the focus is on service. The Online Services for Citizens, for example, has information on how to file taxes online, apply for student loans, order consumer publications, buy postage stamps, check ZIP codes, take the foreign service examination, and apply for retirement benefits. The Citizens Services section also helps visitors compare nursing homes, locate programs to assist senior citizens in their hometowns, submit an application for a patent or trademark, and apply for veterans compensation, pensions and vocational rehabilitation benefits. In all, e-Services for Citizens list thirty-seven categories of services, with many opening up a wide variety of information.[53] Starting with 47 million pages, within a year

FirstGov.gov reached 50 million, and was predicted to have 200 million available for public viewing by 2006.

Still, FirstGov.gov has much ground to cover. The Gartner Group, among others, saw several problems with FirstGov: the sheer amount of information to be managed; the challenge of developing a portal navigation system that worked well for multiple constituencies; and working with the varied content management systems housed throughout the federal agencies, which themselves are not very well coordinated. The Gartner Group concluded that FirstGov was still going through growing pains.[54]

The Bush administration's e-government goal was to make "true government reform" by being citizen-centered rather than bureaucracy-centered, results-oriented rather than process-oriented, and market-based, rather than stifling innovation and competition.[55] Under the direction of the Office of Management and Budget, the E-Government Task force identified twenty-eight major lines of business and found that nearly 500 business lines were operating in the federal agencies—an average of nineteen agencies performing each line of business.[56] The E-Government Task force divided the federal online initiatives into four main components:

- Government to Citizen, which included USA Service (GSA, lead agency); EZ Tax filing (Department of the Treasury); Online Access for Loans (Department of Education); Recreation One Stop (Department of the Interior); and Eligibility Assistance Online (Department of Labor).

- Government to Business, which included Federal Asset Sales (GSA); Online Rulemaking Management (Department of Transportation); Simplified and Unified Tax and Wage Reporting (Department of the Treasury); Consolidated Health Informatics (Department of Health and Human Services); Business Compliance One Stop (Small Business Administration); and International Trade Process Streamlining (Department of Commerce).

- Internal Effectiveness and Efficiency, including e-Training (Office of Personnel Management); Recruitment One Stop (OPM); Enterprise HR Integration (OPM); Integrated Acquisition (GSA); e-Records Management (National Archives Records Administration); and Enterprise Case Management (Department of Justice).[57]

Despite the Bush administration initiatives, the federal government has been slow to seize upon e-government activities, while many of the states and localities have jumped in with innovative ideas and plans. "The difference between the federal government and the states is like night and day," said Janet Caldow, director of IBM Corp.'s Institute for Electronic Government, in late 2000.[58] The Gartner Group assessed electronic government initiatives, and found that roughly 60 percent of those initiatives fail or fall short of their objectives. Researchers found that e-government took more money, more effort, better and more sustained leadership than previously thought. The most difficult impediment to e-government is the structure of traditional government. According to Judith Carr of the Gartner Group, "the governance structures of many governments are not designed to support multidepartment initiatives such as e-government. . . . E-government can require new legislation, new procurement processes and new civil service rules—which are all difficult to change."[59]

One problem concerned the security of websites. A House subcommittee looked at security problems on the websites of twenty-four federal agencies. The results were alarming: the average grade for the agency websites was D–, with seven agencies failing altogether to provide web security against terrorists. Ironically, the congressional report was published one year to the day before the September 11, 2001 terrorist attacks.[60]

Technology executive Timothy J. Sprehe applauded the federal government for rallying the agencies around critical issues, but wrote that "beyond the kudos for cheerleading, the e-government strategy is an empty charade." Sprehe argued that to meet the promise of delivering information and government services required IT capital investment, and that the Bush administration and Congress were simply providing "pocket change"—$5 million spread out over all the federal agencies. In all, Sprehe called the current government IT strategy nothing more than "smoke and mirrors."[61]

Perhaps the biggest problem will be trying to overcome internal bureaucratic lethargy, turf wars, and internal cultures. One agency, the Federal Emergency Management Agency (FEMA) was trying to break through these problems by creating a single web portal for disaster assistance, called DisasterHelp.gov. FEMA's portal pulled together several systems already in use, simplified their services, and eliminated duplication. However, FEMA and other agencies trying to coordinate and harmonize technologies face another hurdle. For decades, the federal government agencies have purchased their own computer hardware and software, without any coordination among agencies, leading to a "rat's nest of technology."

The Chief Information Officers (CIO) Council, established in 1996, has served as the principal interagency forum for improving practices in design, modernization, use, sharing, and performance of federal government agency information resources.[62] The Paperwork Reduction Act of 1995 and the Clinger-Cohen Act of 1996 require federal agency heads, working through their Chief Information Officers, to better link their information technology and investment decisions, develop sound information technology policies and procedures.

Altogether, in 2001, the federal government had some 1,400 e-government initiatives underway. David L. McClure of the General Accounting Office (GAO) in testimony acknowledged that the track record of the executive branch was mixed—with some successes but too many examples of technology producing questionable results. GAO has consistently endorsed the creation of a federal CIO, but McClure acknowledged that there was no consensus, even among current federal agency CIOs, on whether there should be a centralized federal Chief Information Officer.[63]

In 2000, Congress considered two proposals to create a federal CIO and another in 2001. Lawmakers called for a central IT leadership role for a federal CIO but bills differed in how the roles, responsibilities and authorities of that position would be carried out.[64] The office of chief information officer has been created in 27 states, in major cities like Los Angeles and Phoenix, and even in smaller jurisdictions. The Canadian government has had a chief information officer since 1997, and organizations like the Progressive Policy Institute, the Council for Excellence in Government and the Gartner Group have also urged the creation of a federal CIO with cabinet rank.[65]

In December 2002, President Bush signed into law the E-Government Act of 2002, one of the most significant changes in federal information technology policy since the Clinger-Cohen Act of 1996. Among other things, the law created an Administrator for the Office of Electronic Government in the Office of Management and Budget (OMB); many lawmakers, however, preferred to have a federal CIO. The law also mapped out the government parameters from websites for managing crises, to electronic archives, and directories giving the public a road map to federal government information. The E-Government Act also earmarked money—$345 million during the first four years—to fund e-government programs. However, just a month after its enactment, the law ran into the rough waters of the Senate, where e-government funds were slashed for a second year in a row.[66]

Opportunities and Challenges

Online communications hold out the possibility of involving the interested public in a wide range of policy questions. While some dialogues are simply chat room style, with little direction and little or no follow-up or point of responsibility, others like the Environmental Protection Agency's National Dialogue on Public Involvement hold considerable promise. In July 2001, the Dialogue brought together 1,166 individuals to participate in a two-week online discussion. This experiment was to supplement the formal notice-for-comment process used in drafting regulatory language, in this case the EPA's Public Involvement Policy (PIP). As Thomas C. Beierle of Resources for the Future noted, while the citizen comments did not constitute formal public comments, "it was the first time that EPA (or perhaps any federal agency) had so highly integrated a sophisticated online participation process into its decision making."[67]

The Dialogue brought together a broad range of interest groups, citizens, government agencies, and others; 1,166 registered, but only 320 had posted messages, totaling 1,261 distinct messages over the course of the two weeks. Participants not only posted messages, but also read them: an average of about seventy messages a day per participant (and people had trouble keeping up with all the messages—some written informally, some braced in legalese and bureaucratese). As the Dialogue progressed, something of an inner circle—persons and groups with greater expertise in public participation with the EPA and other government agencies—emerged and sent the most messages. But in a follow-up survey, most participants did not feel that a small circle of players had dominated the discussion.

Despite its shortcomings, the Dialogue had some promising features: It reached out to a larger and more geographically diverse set of people and groups than otherwise would participate; a great majority (76 percent) of participants considered it a positive experience. The quality of communication was considered high; and participants were respectful of one another. It was considered a good learning experience; further, new lines of communications opened up to the EPA, which generated some good will, and encouraged some to write formal comments on the PIP. Perhaps because of the novelty, the number of EPA staffers participating in this experiment was considerably higher than otherwise would be involved.

The participants in the Dialogue were not representative of the general public. There was no participation from representatives of tribal governments and environmental justice organizations, leading the EPA to consider the continuing problems of the digital divide.

Beierle suggested that the president should establish a stakeholder task force on electronic democracy to review such initiatives and set guiding principals for future efforts, and should encourage all agencies to conduct pilot online public dialogues. Another suggestion was that Congress should provide money so that poor and minority communities could be assured equal access to the electronic democracy process.[68]

In early 2003, the Bush Administration unveiled a new portal website, www.regulations.gov, designed to assist the public in electronic rulemaking.[69] Annually, there are 4,000 new rules coming from 160 federal agencies that implement the laws passed by Congress. This new portal website will provide the public the opportunity to view all such regulatory proposals and to permit comments to be electronically submitted. Public comments to proposed rules have always been an insider's game, confined generally to those interest groups, law firms, and lobbyists who pay attention to the details of proposed changes. If the experience found at the U.S. Department of Transportation is any guide, the traffic to this new portal and the number of submissions from the public to federal rulemaking should increase dramatically. The Transportation Department found that through electronic submissions, the number of public comments soared from 3,102 on 155 rules in 1997 to 62,944 public comments on 119 rules in 2000. The regulations portal site may not change the way the regulations are considered, but it will most likely provide avenues for public comment that were not readily available before electronic communication.

Federal agencies are attempting to bring online communication closer to those with accessibility issues and for the much larger population of citizens who are poor and underserved. In December 2000, the final regulations of Section 508 of the Rehabilitation Act of 1973, as amended, were published in the Federal Register. The standards ensure that federal employees with disabilities are able to use information technology (IT) to do their jobs, and that members of the public with disabilities who are seeking information from federal sources will be able to use IT to access that information on an equal footing with people who do not have disabilities. The 508 standards require such things as text labels for graphics on web pages, desktop software that is compatible with Assistive Technology, and hardware that meets certain height and reach requirements. Each federal agency was now guided by the Federal IT Accessibility Initiative (FITAI), established by the General Services Administration and the Access Board.[70]

What do the poor and underserved want from websites? The Children's Partnership estimated fifty million Americans face Internet content barriers: twenty-one million because of lack of information, forty-four million because of literacy barriers, thirty-two million because of language barriers, and twenty-six million because of lack of cultural diversity. In its study, the Children's Partnership found that adults who were underserved wanted practical information focusing on their local community (such as local job listings, housing listings, community news); information at a basic literacy level (preparation for securing a high school equivalency degree, online resources as opposed to print materials, online learning materials with multimedia components); content for non-English speakers (such as online translation tools, online instructional material, and information in native languages); and cultural information (such as health and other vital information geared to the particular race or ethnic group).[71]

HRSA, the Health Resources and Services Administration of the U.S. Department of Health and Human Resources, was one of the agencies chosen by the federal Chief Information Officers Council to assist low income Americans by designing a federal portal to meet their needs. With a population base of ninety-seven million low income citizens, this is among the fastest growing income-based segments of Internet users. Further, market research indicated that many low wage earners who were eligible for federal programs often failed to enroll because they did not know the programs existed or that they were qualified for assistance. The Bush Administration hoped to have this federal portal as a national tool to market the many programs and services designed to improve the lives of the poor.[72]

The early indications, however, were that federal money to assist in reducing the digital divide was being reduced, not augmented. The Bush Administration's FY 2003 budget, in what the Benton Foundation called a "stark about-face," had "abandoned the decade-long national fight to bridge the digital divide."[73] The White House budget had stripped out $100 million from the FY2003 budget in public investments that were previously available for community technology grants and IT training programs—programs that were especially valuable in rural communities, for the working poor, minorities, and children.

Electronic Government and Congress

Federal, state, local, and municipal governments are moving toward a greater involvement in online communication and citizens are increasingly turning to official websites, special telephone centers, and kiosks to learn more about the services available and to better communicate with government agencies and personnel. Success is breeding further challenges, and citizens are now expecting better services and easier communication.

The federal executive branch, state agencies, and large municipal and county governments continue to pour substantial funds into improving online communication, to use them for better internal communications, to save time and labor costs, to better deliver services, and to help attract and keep businesses and jobs.

Congress, both as an institution and individual Members, can learn from the experiences of government agencies as they attempt to better communicate with and inform citizens. Congress is not in the business of granting licenses, collecting traffic fines, issuing regulations, or the wide variety of programs and services that are provided by state and local government. But Congress, like them, is in the communications business, and like local and state governments, must use the best possible technical resources to cope with the ever-increasing flow of communications. In enacting the E-Government Act of 2002, Congress took major steps in improving executive branch electronic communications.[74] As Chapters 6 and 7 will illustrate, Congress, however, still has much to do to improve its own electronic communications.

CONGRESS
RESPONDS

4

Old Communications and New

There's an institutional bias against adopting new technology.
—Rep. Brad Carson (Democrat-Oklahoma)

*Our guy doesn't legislate on who yells the loudest. He's sixty-three,
and he's used to a regular old way of communicating.*
—Press aide to a Mountain state U.S. Senator

fficiency and productivity have never been driving principles in Congress. This reality is reflected in the legislative cycle: for long stretches Congress is not in session, but on either recess, vacation or district work days; at other times, the lights are burning brightly past midnight over the Capitol Dome indicating that lawmakers are spending another long evening on the floor. At the very beginning of a congressional session, there is a flurry of activity for about a week, then the lawmakers are in recess or district work for several weeks; Easter time means at least a week's recess; August rarely finds Congress in session, and during election years, lawmakers are chomping at the bit to get home in early October so that they can run for re-election.

When in session, the legislative week is usually only three days long, from Tuesday morning through late Thursday evening. Mondays and Fridays are almost always reserved for travel back to the home district. However, like students cramming for examinations, the House and Senate often jam-pack Fridays and weekends with nearly round-the-clock sessions right before a major recess or adjournment.

The Senate, with unlimited debate, no electronic voting, and very few rules governing floor activity, proceeds at a tortoise-like pace. Anyone watching floor proceedings on C-SPAN II could be forgiven for dozing off while watching Senators leisurely deliberate and vote. Congressional scholar Charles O. Jones remarked that, "in fact, sometimes it seems that no effort is made in the Senate to force conclusions or to resolve conflicts."[1] The House of Representatives, with 435 Members, by necessity has developed a set of procedures and rules so that it can manage business, including limits on debate, requirements of germaneness for amendments, and electronic voting.[2]

The process of making laws is a slow, deliberative, often frustrating one. There are times when Congress acts quickly, such as the flurry of activity during the first 100 days of the Franklin D. Roosevelt administration in 1933; Lyndon B. Johnson's Great Society legislation in the mid-1960s; the spurt of legislation in 1981, during the first year of the Reagan administration; in 1995 during the Contract with America days; or in quickly formulating the Patriot Act after September 11. But for the most part, Congress acts much slower, taking many months, even years, for major policy to wend its way through the labyrinth to become law.

Adapting to New Technologies

The delays, redundancies, and deliberateness are part of the political dynamics of the legislative process. For much of its history, Congress has been slow to accept technological improvements and efficiencies. The young Thomas A. Edison found this out firsthand in 1869 when he came to Washington to show off his new invention, an automatic voting machine. A lawmaker would simply push a button, either aye or nay, and the vote would be instantly recorded and tabulated at the desk of the Speaker. This, Edison figured, would save lawmakers countless hours of waiting for votes to be tabulated. But Congress was not interested; this contraption interfered with the folkways, rhythms, and strategies of the legislative process. Those minutes, even hours, that were seemingly wasted while the vote was tallied by hand actually were useful tools in the slow dance of legislative deliberation: time to persuade colleagues, to develop a working coalition, or see how the winds were blowing on a close vote. As one committee chairman told the 22-year-old Edison, "Young man, that is just what we do not want. Your invention would destroy the only hope that the minority would have of influencing legislation."[3]

Forty-five years later, Representative Allan B. Walsh (Democrat-New Jersey), an electrical engineer, thought it was time to reconsider electronic voting; however, his resolution in the 63rd Congress (1914), while greeted favorably by the Rules Committee, was ignored by the full House.[4] Another half century would pass before the House of Representatives would finally adopt electronic voting. The Senate, over 130 years after Edison showed skeptical lawmakers how to speed up vote counting, still tallies votes without electronic assistance. In 2002, after much debate, the Senate began using two color tally sheets to record votes. This was hailed by Senators as a dramatic improvement in the efficiency and ease of the floor process.[5]

Congress had been relatively slow in permitting radio or television coverage of its events. As early as 1922, there were legislative proposals to permit radio coverage of the House and Senate; yet none were accepted. In 1932, Speaker of the House John Nance Garner (Democrat-Texas) refused to allow radio broadcast of the debate to repeal the Eighteenth Amendment (Prohibition), but two enterprising journalists rigged up microphones at the doorway to the House library, turned up the controls on the radio microphones, and were able to record some of the proceedings.[6] Television came to the Congress as early as 1947, to record the beginning of the 80th Congress, and camera crews were invited back periodically to provide coverage for important committee investigations, such as the 1948 House Committee on Un-American Activities investigation of Alger Hiss, the 1951 Senate Special Committee to Investigate Organized Crime, headed by Senator Estes Kefauver (Democrat-Tennessee), and the thirty-six days of coverage of the Senate Committee on Government Operations subcommittee, headed by Senator Joseph McCarthy (Republican-Wisconsin), the Army-McCarthy hearings in 1954.[7]

The Legislative Reorganization Act of 1970 allowed House committees to televise their open sessions; but the real breakthrough came in 1973, when the television networks devoted 319 hours to covering the Watergate hearings, especially the Senate Select Committee on Presidential Campaign Activities headed by Senator Sam Ervin (Democrat-North Carolina). In 1977, Speaker of the House Thomas P. (Tip) O'Neill (Democrat-Massachusetts) announced that there would be a ninety-day test period of live televised coverage of House floor proceedings. The following year, the House decided to control its own television system and began purchasing the equipment; then in March 1979, the House struck an agreement with the new cable industry enterprise, C-SPAN, to provide gavel-to-gavel coverage of House floor proceedings.

While a resolution was put forth in 1944 to permit televised floor proceedings in the Senate, there was no floor coverage until 1986, when the Senate agreed to have C-SPAN II provide gavel-to-gavel coverage. The Senate finally adopted televised coverage because of the realities of electronic communication. As Senator Robert C. Byrd (Democrat-West Virginia) bluntly put it, "Many people think Congress is only what they see on TV—Tip O'Neill and the House of Representatives—and it shouldn't be that way."[8]

The same Legislative Reorganization Act of 1970 permitted the use of electronic voting in the House of Representatives, and such a system was made operational in January 1973. There are now over forty voting stations in the House, plus electronic equipment at the floor managers' tables so that they can monitor the progress of votes, and computers in the rear of the chamber connected to the voting system used for Members. These "electronic devices" are for the smooth functioning of the institution.[9] There are no individual computers allowed on the floor, a sore subject for some Members, which is discussed in chapter seven. Cell phones are not supposed to be used, but that prohibition is not strictly enforced; and at times, a lawmaker's pager will go off on the floor while someone else is speaking. There have been periodic attempts in the Senate to adopt electronic voting, but none have succeeded.[10]

Congress was also slow in embracing computer technology. Before the 104th Congress (1995–1996), the House of Representatives was "intrinsically a 'paper-based' institution." Most documents were available only in hard copy, and those that were electronically stored such as committee documents, materials from the Library of Congress, the Congressional Budget Office, and the General Accounting Office were on separate and incompatible computer systems.[11] There was no common architecture, language, or format so that documents could be shared, distributed electronically, integrated with one another, or even viewed electronically.[12]

There were nine separate e-mail systems, and while it was possible to send e-mail between these systems, the technology did not make it easy to do so, and there was no directory of e-mail addresses in the House. "Communicating electronically among offices was clumsy and difficult, even for offices that were next door in the same building," noted a report by the Committee on House Oversight in 1997.[13] Access to most legislative information was accomplished through "primitive" mainframe computer hardware which was accessed by software written in about 1980.

Despite these institutional shortcomings, there were some halting steps to communicate online during the early 1990s. In 1993, the House and the Senate both went online with text-only Internet sites while in May 1994 Senator Edward M. Kennedy (Democrat-Massachusetts) ventured online, becoming the first lawmaker with his own website. His URL was awkward and difficult to remember (http://www.ai.mit.edu/iip/projects/kennedy/homepage.html). Thanks to some enterprising graduate students at Massachusetts Institute of Technology, Kennedy's site was created. Not until two years later did the familiar standardized names of (www.house.gov) and (www.senate.gov) appear.[14] The most important action was the passing of Public Law 103–40, which directed the Government Printing Office (GPO) to make legislative and executive branch information available through online systems, beginning with the *Congressional Record* and the *Federal Register*. In response to this, the GPO developed the ACCESS system, which first released online information to depository libraries and the public in June 1994.

In June 1993, the House of Representatives Constituent Electronic Mail System announced that seven Members had been assigned public electronic mailboxes that could be accessed by their constituents.[15] Other lawmakers soon joined in, yet e-mail was still apparently an exotic form of communication. In November 1994, for example, Senator Russell Feingold (Democrat-Wisconsin) was the only one of his state's eleven federal lawmakers with an e-mail account. Since March of that year, Feingold's office was receiving an average of eleven e-mail messages from Wisconsin residents a month, while receiving almost 10,000 regular letters, faxes, and telephone calls monthly from constituents.[16]

As more and more lawmakers began using e-mail, one of the early problems was trying to separate e-mails that came from constituents from those that came from non-constituents. E-mail spam was becoming a problem for Congress just as it was for everyone else. The House of Representatives began using an e-mail filtering system called Write Your Representative. This filter was added to the lawmakers' websites and required individuals to give their name, addresses, and ZIP codes before sending an e-mail to the Member of Congress. Through Write Your Representative, e-mail would be screened by ZIP code; only those that came from the Member's congressional district would be accepted and all other e-mails would be blocked.[17]

In the summer of 1996, Rep. Anna Eshoo (Democrat-California) was the first to try an e-mail filter through her website. She praised its efficiency and reliability, noting that with regular e-mail there were "so many glitches with what the House set up. There was an awful lot that was lost."[18] Regular e-mail, which went through the House system, left her unimpressed: "The e-mail system here . . . is less than efficient. You think of e-mail as being something that is going to short-circuit the U.S. Postal Service by days, weeks, plus all the hours left over after that. And the truth be known, it's not terrific. I mean it just gives snail mail a new meaning."[19]

For the public at large, the term "spam" meant any unwelcome, unsolicited e-mail, the electronic equivalent of junk mail. For Members of Congress, however, "spam" had a different meaning: any e-mail that comes from an individual residing in another congressional district (or state) or any e-mail that has no identifiable address. This is congressional spam and is given the lowest priority in a congressional office—usually just tossed into the electronic or circular wastebasket. Anyone who tried to send an e-mail to every Member of Congress, thinking that his or her voice would be heard by all the legislators was just wasting time and effort. As former legislative staffer Chris Casey observed, "It's a pretty safe assumption that [an e-mail] letter addressed to everybody is as good as a letter addressed to nobody."[20]

CyberCongress

On November 11, 1994, after the Republican Party bowled its way to the majority in the House of Representatives, a triumphant Newt Gingrich (Republican-Georgia), soon to become the next Speaker of the House, urged his party to enact major policy reforms as articulated in the "Contract with America." He also called for fundamental institutional changes in the House of Representatives. For decades, Republicans had chafed over their minority party status and what many thought was a condescending attitude of Democratic lawmakers who assumed that majority status was theirs in perpetuity by some political divine right. Now it was time to shake things up.

Gingrich championed the Internet and saw it as a way to cut through what he considered to be the entrenched, liberal-dominant interests of Washington and Congress. He wanted to use the Internet as an electronic town hall, to build grassroots support online for conservative causes, and create "information empowerment zones" in rural and urban areas not yet involved in online activity. Gingrich later talked about a plan for each family in America to have access to computers. The new Speaker in particular wanted more transparency and openness in the deliberations of Congress, and saw online communications as the key. He argued for changes in House rules so that congressional information would be "available to any citizen in the country at the same moment that it is available to the highest paid Washington lobbyist."[21] Gingrich's desire to have all legislation online stemmed from Republican anger over being forced to vote for a crime bill in August 1994 without knowing what was in it; the final version of the bill was being printed in the House basement when the vote took place. Under a Gingrich rule, no final vote in the House could take place until a measure was first published online.[22]

Gingrich asked the Committee on House Oversight, through its Computer and Information Services Working Group, to investigate and evaluate the current House computer facilities and capabilities. The plan that emerged, quickly known as the "CyberCongress" project, called for

> A robust, coherent, unified, multimedia computer network, with
> sufficient software and modern compatible equipment, with which
> the U.S. House of Representatives may effectively function to best
> serve the American public, the Members of the House, and other
> government institutions.[23]

The CyberCongress, using one of Gingrich's favorite phrases, called for a "third wave paradigm" built on communication, networking, and computing technologies. Using online technology, time-sensitive legislative materials, like amendment language and texts of rules and reports, would be made available to the public; communications among Members and staff would improve through universal in-boxes that allowed access to voice, e-mail, and fax messages from any location; and there would be electronic decision support systems for Members, committees and staff, such as whip counts, via pagers or messaging-based groupware.[24]

The Computer and Information Services Working Group conducted a major study calling for infrastructure upgrades of the House network, replacing outdated computer hardware and software with advanced desktop computers, developing a comprehensive security system, improving staff training and support, and developing a House presence on the World Wide Web. The study also called for the implementation of new computer applications and technologies to support the major business units of the House and collaboration among all legislative branch organizations to develop joint research capabilities to support Members and committees.[25] Along with the CyberCongress plans, the Library of Congress also weighed in with a 1996 report that noted a "continuing problem" in the fragmentation and extensive overlap of legislative information. Electronic retrieval and collection systems had been developed separately in the 1970s and needed consolidation.[26]

Newt Gingrich and Representative William M. (Bill) Thomas (Republican-California), chairman of the House Oversight Committee, directed the Library of Congress to make legislative information available to the public over the Internet. The website, christened THOMAS after Thomas Jefferson, was quickly created and unveiled in January 1995.[27] The THOMAS site was not without its early problems, however: at times it trailed by hours, even days, behind the flow of legislative business, yielding the information, but certainly not in a timely manner. Today, THOMAS includes bill summary and status information beginning with the 93rd Congress (1973–1974), text of bills beginning with the 101st Congress (1989–1990), the *Congressional Record* beginning with the 101st Congress, public policy literature files, reports of the Congressional Budget Office and the General Accounting Office, recorded votes, committee reports, and selected congressional hearings, as well as connections to other House and Senate data and other sources of legal and legislative information.

One of the most important actions came at the beginning of the 105th Congress (1997) when the House adopted Rule XI, clause 2e, which mandated that "each committee shall, to the maximum extent feasible, make its publications available in electronic form." Witnesses would be encouraged to have their official statements and accompanying documentation available in electronic format so that they could quickly be transferred to the respective committee websites.

Another important component of congressional transparency was the opening up of committee hearings to the outside public. In the 105th Congress (1997–1998), the first "cybercast" was a Senate Commerce Committee hearing on encryption policy, which was arranged in conjunction with the Center for Democracy and Technology; following that, several other committee hearings were "cybercast" over the Internet, allowing real-time remote access.[28] In the 106th Congress (1999–2000), the Committee on Agriculture began providing audio coverage of its hearings over the Internet. In preparation to support live Internet broadcasts, the Committee on Science upgraded the technical infrastructure in one of its hearing rooms: each Member's dais area included enhanced audio and data ports for computer access to the House system.

The hearing room had three wall-mounted cameras, a retractable projector mounted in the ceiling, a drop-down screen for Member viewing, flat screen monitors for the committee witnesses and audience, and a touch screen monitor at the chairman's seat to view computer generated presentations. An operator's console can control video conferencing, overhead projections, and mount presentations prepared from a computer, audio or video tape, DVD, from the Internet, or distribution of live audio/video feeds via the Committee's web page. A second hearing room is equipped to act as an overflow room, and had some of the above equipment.[29]

None of this audio-visual wizardry was out of the ordinary for any modern business, but for Congress, it was revolutionary. The Science Committee's technology and electronic sophistication stands out, but other committees, especially in the House, have been making similar investments.

During the 104th Congress (1995–1996), websites began popping up throughout the House of Representatives. In January 1995, the Committee on House Oversight first published the official House website and by the end of the session, over 222 Member offices, 27 full committees and 11 other House offices had established websites on the House web server. By the end of the 104th Congress, the House websites were being accessed approximately two million times each month.[30]

In the Senate, there was similar activity, but without the publicity found in the House. By October 1995, every Senator had some presence on the Senate Internet server; but most of the Senate sites were merely one-page billboards, generated by the Senate Computer Center. Within two years, however, all but a handful of the Senate offices had moved beyond the basic sites created for them by the Computer Center and had created their own, individualized home pages.[31]

During the 104th Congress, lawmakers had to cope with a whole new set of technology policy issues and communication realities. The Senate in June 1995 saw its first significant petition generated by e-mail. To buttress his argument against passage of a proposed Internet censorship provision of the Telecommunications Reform Act, Senator Patrick J. Leahy (Democrat-Vermont) brandished a printout of an electronic petition against the proposal. Leahy hefted the twenty-four-inch thick petition, 1,500 pages, with 112,000 signatures onto the floor of the Senate. All the names were gathered from an online petition and caught the attention of lawmakers.[32]

For many members of Congress, the Internet and electronic policy issues were a mystery; and for many, just the simple acts of turning a computer on, using e-mail, or downloading information from the World Wide Web were challenging. "A lot of people in Congress know about agriculture or know about the law, but there are almost no people in the Congress who are technology experts," said Ken Kay, executive director of the computer-industry lobby, Computer Systems Policy Project. "That handful, " Gray noted in 1995, "have had added clout."[33]

Representatives Rick White (Republican-Washington) and Rick Boucher (Democrat-Virginia) observed that many of their colleagues lacked even rudimentary knowledge about computers and online communication. This was evident during the 1995 debate over the Communications Decency portion of the Telecommunications Reform Act, the same issue that generated the first online petition. What White and Boucher heard from their colleagues convinced them that there was a steep learning curve for many lawmakers: They simply didn't understand the Internet. It wasn't just the House of Representatives; the Senate probably had a bigger problem in struggling with new technology and the policy issues that inevitably would flow from it. Many Senators don't read postal mail, let alone e-mail. Of his Senate colleagues, Senator Leahy observed in 1997, "we have a lot of people who have very strong positions on the Internet and computers . . . in the Congress who wouldn't even know how to turn on a computer if they had to. They think it's a not-working television that won't give you CNN."[34] Senator James Exon (Democrat-Nebraska), at that time leading an effort to regulate what could be discussed over the Internet, didn't use the Internet himself, nor did he have a personal computer; his Senate office lacked even an e-mail address.[35]

According to Leahy, a fellow Senator "said he had heard there were a lot of dirty pictures online. So I took him aside and showed him the Vatican's online library, the Sistine Chapel's home page, and how you can access the Library of Congress over the Internet." The result, Leahy said, was dramatic: "Once he started using the Internet, he didn't want to stop."[36] That one Senator had plenty of company: many lawmakers simply had no clue.

In the spring of 1996, Representatives Boucher and White along with Senators Leahy and Conrad Burns (Republican-Montana) created the bipartisan Congressional Internet Caucus. Their main purpose for creating the caucus was to help educate lawmakers about the promise and potential of the Internet. The task was huge, yet Representative White, who in 1995 had dubbed his colleagues as "lost in cyberspace" saw significant progress, and by mid-1997 had commented that there had been a "real sea change in Congress . . . in terms of understanding the Internet and being open to it."[37]

Internal Review and Criticism of New Technologies

To meet the demands of a CyberCongress, the House Information System, which began operations in 1971, was renamed and reconfigured as House Information Resources (HIR) in June 1995. In addition, the House created the position of Chief Administrative Officer; one of the many duties of this office was to oversee new technologies. Despite these changes, there were a number of technical and managerial problems uncovered by the Office of Inspector General (OIG) in three reports prepared during the 104th Congress (1995–1997). The OIG found "serious internal control weaknesses" through all of the House processing environments, including HIR operations and office-level systems at Member, committee and other House locations. Another report exposed a security weakness by exploiting a "back door" in the House network, permitting investigators to read lawmakers' e-mail and other data surreptitiously and send out phony e-mails by posing as Members. A third report noted flaws in the remote dial-in connections to House offices.[38]

In 1997, the Office of the Inspector General released its first comprehensive report on the operations of House Information Resources. The OIG found "serious problems" in HIR's management practices, planning and budgeting, policies, standards, procedures, and guidelines, and staffing.[39] It acknowledged that HIR and its predecessor had accomplished several important tasks in earlier years: It had reprogrammed its funds to support office automation infrastructure with desktop systems, developed site licenses for Windows 95, Netscape, and anti-virus software; established a common messaging system; had begun developing a network-centric strategy with broad band communications, high function messaging, and a highly reliable and secure Internet/Intranet Web. HIR had also helped over 250 Members, Committees and other House offices develop websites and had built a telecommunications infrastructure on Capitol Hill and in the district offices. Further, HIR had replaced the existing mainframe processor with a smaller, more economical CMOS processor, expanded its information security function, and established a good working relationship with congressional staff.

Despite this, the Inspector General's report concluded that HIR did not have a strategic plan, had not corrected certain chronic organizational problems despite restructuring and reorganizing itself four times in less than two years, and had not developed key control mechanisms, such as project standardization and tracking, performance measures, or user satisfaction analysis. The OIG report also criticized the HIR administrator for not providing effective day-to-day leadership and direction. "Historically, HIR has spent millions on major systems development efforts which have proved to be inadequate in the support of Member and House operations, had developed duplicative systems, and did not have a management process in place to make effective, informed decisions."[40] The Inspector General's report concluded that HIR was "only minimally prepared to meet the information technology challenges and demands in the short term, and is not adequately preparing the House information systems program to move into the 21st century."[41] Improvements came relatively quickly following this major report, and when the Office of the Inspector General again reviewed new technology practices in 1998, it concluded that through the appointment of a Chief Administrative Officer, there had been "significant changes in the management of operation of the critical administrative functions" supporting the House of Representatives.[42]

Computers, E-mail, and Websites

In late 1995, many computers in congressional offices were two generations old, using DOS operating systems that dated back to 1981. The e-mail system was charitably described as "creaking" and "overloaded." The Senate web server, developed in November 1995, created pro-forma home pages for at least 62 Senators, but in the Senate only half of the personal computers were capable of running the required Windows operating system.[43]

Until mid-November 1995, Senate offices could have only three staffers connected to the Internet, even though many Senate offices had forty to fifty staffers. Committees, with staff sometimes double that of personal offices, were limited to six connections. In the Senate in 1995, sixty Senators had e-mail addresses, but just two, Edward Kennedy and Barbara Boxer (Democrat-California), responded to some electronic messages with e-mail.[44]

While lawmakers and their staffs were now creating their own websites, much of what appeared on those sites was little more than self-congratulations and self-promotion. Political scientists Diana Owen, Richard Davis, and Vincent James Strickler conducted one of the earliest academic studies of the use of the Internet by Congress, finding, in 1996 that many legislators did not use the Internet effectively and those who did embrace it mostly created web pages to further advertise their accomplishments to constituents. Reporter Gebe Martinez was less kind, characterizing the Congressional websites in 1996 as "somewhat haphazard, occasionally hokey and highly political."[45]

OMB Watch, a Washington, D.C.-based research and advocacy organization, surveyed fifty House and twenty Senate websites in 1998 and found that while there had been a growing presence on the Internet, congressional offices were missing out on the opportunity to be responsive to constituent needs. Further, a 1998 joint research project conducted by Bonner & Associates and American University noted that Members of Congress were not using e-mail to communicate with their constituents, even when they had received e-mail from them.[46]

Congress is an institution that attracts extroverts, lawmakers who are usually comfortable with, or at least have adapted to, the hurly-burly of electoral politics, who have the energy and stamina to interact with a wide range of constituent groups, who don't mind the pressing of flesh and kissing babies. They are used to face-to-face interaction, comfortable with open meetings, at home with the telephone; but they usually are not hunkered before a computer screen. That is what staff do. In 2000, a Senate staffer, confided, anonymously, that she had to explain to her boss how to use a mouse and how to click onto the Internet so he could view his own website.[47]

Technology can't be forced on people, especially lawmakers. The last Member whose Washington and district offices relied on typewriters didn't leave until 1998. Rep. Joel Hefley (Republican-Colorado) in 2001 became the last Member of Congress to have a website, even though his district had the fast-growing high-tech city of Colorado Springs, and is home to the Air Force Academy, the North American Aerospace Defense Command, Air Force Space Command, and offices of MCI Telecommunications Corp. He finally put a simple site up in 2001. E-mail also gave Hefley concern. "I have two problems with e-mail," he said. "Special interest groups love to push a button and send you a message . . . and there are a lot of computer hobbyists who think it's fun to dash off a message to Congress." They want a "pen pal relationship." If we had e-mail, Hefley said, "we'd need another staffer to handle it."[48]

Vic Fazio, former Member of Congress from California, now senior partner at a Washington, D.C., law firm, said in 2000 that most Members of Congress were leery of using e-mail. "Most members are not interested in the views of those who don't vote for them or have the potential to vote for them, so when an office is inundated with messages, it is sometimes easier not to respond."[49] This was echoed by former House Majority Leader Dick Armey (Republican-Texas), an advocate of technological change. Armey described the majority of his colleagues as "living far deep down on the dark side of the digital divide." The strangest part, according to Armey, is that a great many legislators are proud of their lack of technical savvy.[50]

Congressman J. Joseph Moakley (Democrat-Massachusetts), who had served in Congress since 1973 until his death in 2001, cautioned his colleagues at a hearing on the subject of legislating in the Information Age, "But all the miraculous developments aside, Mr. Chairman, technology has its downside. It speeds up the pace of day-to-day business to the point where people feel obligated to work as quickly as they can to reload a web page. Most importantly, it separates us from our neighbors and many times it depersonalizes American life. That is where I believe technology's greatest limits lie, particularly as they pertain to the institution of Congress."[51]

While some lawmakers were hesitant or unconvinced of the importance of online communications, others quickly adapted to it. For example, then Senator John D. Ashcroft (Republican-Missouri) was quick to see several of the benefits of online communication: savings in staff time, savings in money, and particularly in opening up communications with new groups of citizens. Ashcroft in the late 1990s was one of the few legislators who answered e-mail electronically. "We've saved 250,000 pieces of paper," he noted, "and involved a whole new group of folks" in the legislative process.[52] He was also the first Senator to launch an online petition; his effort in support of term limits gathered 7,100 signatures in less than two weeks.[53]

The House of Representatives began keeping statistics on e-mail traffic in 1998, and that year the number of e-mails exceeded the number of letters and post cards. But in the next year, e-mails overwhelmed the House, with 108 million coming into congressional offices, while only 10.6 million letters and post cards were received.[54]

Part of that wave of e-mail came from popular private sites that now featured information about elections, voting, and legislative affairs. One of those, America Online's (AOL) VoteNote, was launched during coverage of 1998 elections. Within months, more than 50,000 people a day were sending e-mail messages to Congress. In 1999, AOL launched a new online service with databases of congressional and state information, linked to viewers' ZIP codes.[55] Other private portal sites followed suit with information geared toward congressional activity. Still in late 1999, there were holdouts in Congress: twenty-five Members provided no means for voters to communicate with them electronically. Another 200 Members enabled voters to contact them through Write Your Representative, but not through their own e-mails.[56]

MILESTONES IN ONLINE COMMUNICATIONS IN CONGRESS

1993	Sen. Charles Robb is the first Senator to accept e-mail and post a public e-mail address.
	Seven House members have e-mail.
	Public Law 103–40, making legislative and executive branch materials available online.
1994	Sen. Edward M. Kennedy is first to post a congressional website.
1995	Gingrich as Speaker emphasized CyberCongress.
	Forty House and twenty Senate offices had Internet connections in February.
	Rep. David Dreier inaugurates 21st Century Congress Project.
	Library of Congress THOMAS site created.
	House website, www.house.gov, debuted.
	First online petition seen on floor of the Senate.
1996	Congressional Internet Caucus created.
	Over 222 Member offices, 27 full committees, and 11 other House offices have established websites; all 100 Senators nominally have websites.
	First cybercast of a congressional hearing.
1997	Library of Congress and Congressional Research Service bring online the Legislative Information Retrieval System (LIS) for internal Congressional use.
	C-SPAN offers live video web coverage of House and Senate on the Internet.
	Sen. John Ashcroft is first Senator to launch an online petition.
1998	AOL's VoteNote is launched.
	Last Member of Congress, whose office only used typewriters, retires.
	Starr Report goes online.
	Impeachment hearings and MoveOn.org inundates Congress with e-mails.
1999	Internet Tax Hoax and the phony Bill 602-P.
2000	Sen. Peter Fitzgerald, a freshman, becomes the 100th Senator to launch a website.[57]
2001	Rep. Joel Hefley becomes the last Member of Congress to have e-mail.
	Anthrax hits Congress; postal mail grinds to a halt; e-mail soars.
2002	Still 120 House offices not rapidly adapting to new technologies.
	All personal offices in the House and Senate have websites, along with committees, leadership, caucus, and administrative sites. Total of 605 Congressional websites.
	Senate begins replacing antiquated and no longer supported cc:Mail e-mail system.
	One hundred and sixty lawmakers in both the House and Senate are members of the Congressional Internet Caucus.

The Senate was groaning under the weight of an antiquated e-mail system, which by the time the software was being replaced in late 2002 was twelve years old. The aging e-mail system even caused difficulties with communications between the Washington office and field offices back in the home states. As one exasperated staffer said, "Honestly, sometimes it seems like it would be faster to get in your car and drive the information to the home office than to use this system."[58] Nearly every Senate office seemed to have a horror story of lost e-mails, messages caught in an electronic loop and sent over and over for days on end, bogged down for days, even weeks. Senate e-mail was slow, unreliable, and just waiting for a complete collapse under the crush of millions of messages coming from constituents.

Congress has moved in fits and starts into the online information age. Systems have been integrated, old hardware and software replaced, systematic training programs established, and administrative hurdles by and large overcome. At the staff level, there is widespread acceptance of—indeed reliance on—online technology. The crush of business would simply be impossible to handle without these emerging technologies. Thousands of e-mails flow daily among and between staffs, reports are downloaded, schedules checked, communications flow between Washington and district offices, staffers can even order lunch over a special Internet site through the House food system.[59]

The House of Representatives, with its greater number of Members, committees, and staff has taken greater advantage of technological changes than the Senate, which is often two or three steps behind in implementing such changes. The House of Representatives poured $1.5 billion into infrastructure improvements from 1995–2001, and training of staff had dramatically improved.[60] In 2002, it also instituted a District Office Wellness Visits program, to help improve computer efficiency and security in every district office of House members, with software updates, desktop maintenance, and review of data communications.[61]

What seemed to be holding offices back, however, was a low priority placed on electronic communication, and the attitude on the part of some lawmakers, unaccustomed to online communication, unfamiliar with its labor and cost savings benefits, and hesitant to invest staff and personal time into full development of technology. Nevertheless, as Representative David Dreier (Republican-California) observed in 2002, it was clear that Congress has made "a remarkable transformation into the information age."[62] There was a much greater interest in online technology issues, as evidenced by the growing membership in the bipartisan and bicameral Internet Caucus; by the end of the 107th Congress (2002), some 160 lawmakers had joined.[63]

Much of that progress was due to the leadership of a few lawmakers in both the House and Senate. They had seen the importance of bringing Congress into the Information Age and in becoming expert in the complicated new media issues that confronted them.

CONGRESSIONAL LEADERS IN ONLINE TECHNOLOGY[64]

House of Representatives

- Rick Boucher (Democrat-Virginia)—co-founder of Congressional Internet Caucus
- Vernon J. Ehlers (Republican-Michigan)—helped launch 1995 CyberCongress initiative
- Christopher Cox (Republican-California)—chair, Policy Committee
- Thomas M. Davis III (Republican-Virginia)—chair, Government Reform Committee
- David Dreier (Republican-California)—chair, Rules Committee
- Newt Gingrich (Republican-Georgia)—Speaker of the House, spearheaded launch of CyberCongress initiative and THOMAS[65]
- Anna Eshoo (Democrat-California)—early advocate of electronic mail
- Robert Goodlatte (Republican-Virginia)—chair of Congressional Internet Caucus
- Zoe Lofgren (Democrat-California)—early advocate of electronic mail
- Edward Markey (Democrat-Massachusetts)—early advocate of electronic communications
- Robert Ney (Republican-Ohio)—chair of Committee on House Administration Telecommunications Trade and Consumer Protection Subcommittee
- Ellen Tauscher (Democrat-California)—early advocate of electronic mail
- W. J. (Billy) Tauzin (Republican-Louisiana)—chair of the Energy and Commerce Committee
- William Thomas (Republican-California)—helped launch THOMAS website
- Rick White (Republican-Washington)—co-founder of Congressional Internet Caucus

Senate

- Conrad Burns (Republican-Montana)—co-founder of the Congressional Internet Caucus
- Patrick J. Leahy (Democrat-Vermont)—co-founder of the Congressional Internet Caucus
- Senator John McCain (Republican-Arizona)—Commerce Committee
- Senator Ron Wyden (Democrat-Oregon)—Commerce, Science and Transportation Committee

By 2002, citizens had better access than ever before to Congress, through full coverage of floor proceedings televised by C-SPAN, audio and video coverage of selected House and Senate committee hearings through the Internet, thousands of pieces of legislation, documents and reports available online. Citizens could contact their lawmakers by e-mail, visit their official websites, and in many instances, sign up for electronic newsletters, in some instances they could join policy discussion groups, and/or participate in online polls. Millions of citizens have sent e-mail messages, visited congressional websites, and downloaded official reports and documents.

Despite this extraordinary progress, Congress still had miles to go to improve its online communications. Reynold Schweickhardt, former director of technology for the Committee on House Administration, who came from a Silicon Valley technology firm after the Republican takeover in 1995, has felt that considerable progress has been made, but that there were still about 120 offices that were not rapidly developing technology by the spring of 2002.[66] Members of Congress were facing an ever increasing number of cyber-savvy citizens who regularly used e-mail and were comfortable exploring information on the Internet; those same citizens were now demanding better and more information, faster communication time, and ready accessibility to their lawmakers. The crush of e-mail required better management, official websites needed to be better designed and more adept at conveying useful information to constituents, and Congress needed to adapt to the technology challenges of a post-anthrax world.

5

The E-mail Overload

When I first came to Congress the biggest complaint was that Congress was out of touch with the people. No one could possibly make that claim today. No Congress in history has been more in touch with its constituents.

—Rep. Vernon J. Ehlers (Republican-Michigan)

Clearly Congress is doing a much better job at taming the e-mail monster.

—Brad Fitch, Congressional Management Foundation (2002)

Current State of Congressional E-mail

t the beginning of the 107th Congress (January 2001), the Senate was faced with some severe online communication problems. Millions of e-mails were sent to the Senate during the confirmation battle of former Senator John Ashcroft to the post of Attorney General; the nomination of Gayle A. Norton for Secretary of the Interior drew unusually heavy traffic; and Federal Reserve Board Chairman Alan Greenspan's testimony before the Senate Banking Committee generated enough e-mail to back up the Senate's e-mail system for more than half an hour. Millions of electronic messages came in, but no one knows how many were bounced back to the senders or simply disappeared when the system became overloaded.

Tracy Williams, director of technology development for the Office of the Senate Sergeant at Arms, lamented that the Senate e-mail system, created in 1991, was not designed to handle the kind of volume it was receiving a decade later: "We continue to throw hardware and software at it to increase what it can handle."[1] Some Senate aides reported a five-day delay in receiving outside e-mails in early 2001. Even internal Senate e-mails, messages from a Senate personal office to Senate committee staffers, for example, were delayed for several hours to as long as a day, and interoffice e-mail sometimes backed up for hours.[2]

Newly-elected Senators were hit doubly hard. Not only did the e-mail system just creak along, but they did not have the benefit of special computer software programs, the Correspondence Management System (CMS), to help them log and respond to regular postal mail, phone calls, and faxes. The new Senators were just settling in, with new and sometimes temporary office space. They were still not staffed up to meet the crush of communications, and were without an adequate computer infrastructure and software. The reasons new Senators were left in this lurch were the continuing, protracted contract negotiations between the Senate and software vendors. One Senate staffer griped, "We are so far behind it will affect the constituent mail process for six months. And everybody knows, you don't get behind on the mail" unless you want to risk the anger of constituents.[3]

Then in October 2001 the Lotus Development Corporation stopped supporting its e-mail software, cc:Mail, the system which the Senate had depended on for more than twelve years. The timing was less than propitious: just then, the Hart Senate Office building was shut down because of the deadly anthrax spores that had infiltrated Majority Leader Tom Daschle's office. Hart building staffers had to set up temporary quarters, all postal mail was halted, and e-mail surged as the only practical way to reach Congress.

The Senate e-mail system began improving in late 2001 with the addition of four mail servers, bringing the total to twelve servers, a mix of Compaq Computer Corporation systems running Microsoft Windows NT and IMA Gateway mail translation software.[4] In addition, the Senate in early 2001 was readying a separate e-mail system for its public e-mail and its internal business e-mail so that staff corresponding with one another would not lose their ability to send messages due to a system clogged with outside e-mail.[5] By 2002 the Senate had switched over to Microsoft Outlook and Exchange, the same reliable software systems used by the House. Four years of planning and the decision of Lotus to no longer support its product meant that the Senate was finally going to have a software system that could handle the avalanche of e-mail.[6]

E-mail sent to Congress grew dramatically from 1999 to 2002. In 2001, the House and Senate received a total of 117 million messages, while the average House office received 538 e-mails a day, and the average Senate office received 880 per day.[7]

E-MAIL MESSAGES SENT TO CONGRESS[8]	
1999	51 million
2000	74 million
2001	117 million
2002 (est.)	128 million

There is a wide variety of constituent messages received in congressional offices each day, through postal letters, telephone calls, faxes, telegrams, or e-mails. Kathy Goldschmidt of the Congressional Management Foundation has noted six basic types of constituent communications:

(1) scheduling requests (the hundreds of requests that pour in annually for meetings, speaking engagements, and visits, many of them back in the home district);

(2) strange, weird, angry communications (conspiracy theories, black helicopters, aliens-coming-to-invade-us types of communications);

(3) VIP communications (letters or e-mails from very important people, who often request small but significant favors, such as a flag request for a friend, or to arrange a special meeting);

(4) Personalized constituent communications (those nicely written, compelling letters from folks back home, asking for assistance or giving advice);

(5) Weak policy-oriented campaigns (communications that aren't connected with a relevant topic that Congress is considering: perennial issues like "Notch Babies," or bringing back prayer and Bible readings in public schools, for example, which have been around for years without Congress ever resolving them); and

(6) Strong policy campaigns (organized, effective communication that take advantage of well-planned grassroots advocacy activities).[9]

Of all the communication challenges facing congressional offices, one of the most important is the ability to separate the important, relevant communications from those that are less important or only clog up the mail bags and computer terminals. Woe be to a congressional office that falls behind in answering important, constituent mail, or an office that is unable to separate the communications wheat from the chaff.

When it comes to online communications, many congressional offices have resorted to filters that automatically separate those messages from within the district from those that are not. Electronic filters help distinguish that 20 percent of e-mail that comes from constituents from all the rest.

Junk Mail and Congressional Spam

The great majority of e-mail received in congressional offices comes from outside the Members' districts or their states, and, like spammed e-mail in the private sector, it ends up in the electronic wastepaper basket.[10] Bright-Mail, a company that specializes in blocking spammed messages, noted that unsolicited e-mail accounted for 12.8 percent of the mail to its corporate clients since September 11, 2001. That was nearly double the share from the previous quarter. A spokesman for America Online said that unwanted e-mail was the number one complaint of its subscribers, and the company blocked 780 million e-mails each day, or more than 100 million more e-mails than it delivers. According to the research firm Jupiter Media Metrix, each e-mail user has received an average of 1,466 unsolicited messages during 2001, with the number expected to grow to 3,800 such messages by 2006.[11]

Congress addressed an earlier form of annoying communications in 1991 when it passed the Telephone Consumer Protection Act (PL 102–243) prohibiting unsolicited advertising via fax machines ("junk faxes"). In December 2003, Congress finally passed legislation to regulate and limit the flow of junk e-mail. Meanwhile, twenty states had enacted anti-junk e-mail laws that regulate the use of electronic spam.[12]

When Congress looks at its own e-mail, spam or unwanted e-mail takes on a different meaning from everyone else's e-mail. Granted, there will be unwanted commercial solicitations sent to Congress, but spam in congressional terms has a unique meaning: spam is e-mail sent from persons who live outside of a Member of Congress' district or outside of a Senator's state. Much of this e-mail comes from advocacy groups and those citizen activists who try to blanket Capitol Hill with messages.[13]

Many congressional offices have an unwritten policy of not answering postal mail from organized letter-writing campaigns from outside their districts or states. They do this mostly as a matter of efficient use of staff and lawmaker time. They concentrate their limited staff resources in responding to their own constituents. Given staff constraints and a crush of mail, offices would much rather spend five hours on those fifty letters sent from constituents in the district than five hours answering those 2,000 postcards generated by a mail firm and all postmarked from out of state.

Several years ago, Rep. Barney Frank (Democrat-Massachusetts) posted a message on his website that stated he did not maintain an e-mail address. He noted that a significant increase in mail volume would put too much strain on him and his staff.[14] Congressman Frank now accepts e-mail, but is refreshingly forthright about his priorities:

> Because I receive a large volume of my mail from other parts of the country, I have to restrict my responses to mail that comes from those who live in the cities and towns that make up the Fourth Congressional District of Massachusetts. For this reason, I am using the House of Representatives' Write Your Representative e-mail system, which requires people to submit geographical information in order to send a message. . . . Because of limited staff and office resources, I will not be able to respond to e-mails from outside the Fourth Congressional District. If you live in my district and you need assistance with a matter relating to the federal government, such as a problem with Social Security, or if you are seeking White House tickets or other Washington, D.C. tour information, please do not send an electronic message. Instead, please call or visit the nearest District Office where my staff can better assist you.[15]

There are two kinds of e-mail systems operating on Capitol Hill: public e-mail (with or without filters) and a web-based filtered format (like Write Your Representative). A public e-mail address for a Member of Congress (for example, congressman.smith@mail.house.gov) that uses no filters (such as ZIP code or abbreviation or name of state), invites any and all e-mail to be sent. Staff must sort through all the e-mail that has been sent to that public address. Many times it is impossible to know if the e-mail has come from a constituent or not, particularly if the sender has not included a postal address or ZIP code. This means that congressional staffers have to use special correspondence software or manually go through each e-mail, sorting out the roughly one in five messages that actually come from the Member's constituents. The average congressional staff spends three hours per week sorting through e-mail and weeding out non-constituent from constituent, while the average Senate office spends three hours per day on that sorting out non-constituent mail; only after this time can staffers devote their energies to e-mail that will be answered.[16]

With the significant increase in e-mail, lawmakers who once relied on a public e-mail address are shifting to filtered systems: 66 Senators and 226 House Members have stopped using public e-mail addresses and have gone to systems like Write Your Representative. Yet, even Write Your Representative and other filters are not foolproof. At times, staffers run across e-mail that has been specially programmed so that it is not screened out by electronic filters.

Some legislators, however, feel it important to receive all forms of e-mail, not matter how much of a barrage they might be: the role of a legislator is to be receptive to the views of everyone, no matter if they live in the congressional district. Former Senator Max Cleland (Democrat-Georgia), for example, remarked that his Senate office should answer all its communications, regardless of their origin: "We're a United States Senator. We represent not just the citizens of Georgia, but the entire country. I think that's government at its best. We bust a gut to try to get a response to everybody." Cleland even ran internal tests to make sure that his staff answered e-mail promptly.[17]

Perhaps in an ideal situation, each congressional office would have the manpower, time, and energy dedicated to receiving and responding to every e-mail communication, no matter what the origin and no matter what the subject matter. But the realities of limited budgets and manpower mean that priorities have to be set, and the top priority goes to those messages generated from within the congressional district or state.

Congressional offices have several correspondence management system (CMS) software packages at their disposal to help sort through the deluge of e-mail.[18] Filters and rules, available through e-mail management software systems like Outlook and Exchange, can define key words, such as issue topics, ZIP codes, cities, and towns. These e-mails can be placed in separate folders, then sorted further. Two private firms provide software that further assist in sorting and routing electronic mail. ACS's Intranet Quorum (IQ) and Inter-America's Capitol Correspondent software can perform a number of key tasks before e-mail is viewed by staffers: automatically download e-mail at regular intervals; separate e-mail by constituents and non-constituents; sort messages by topic; create or add to existing constituent contact records; assign form letters; and route e-mail to the appropriate staffer. Another software program, EchoMail, available only in the Senate for a trial period that ended in mid-2003, was a sophisticated system that used artificial intelligence to filter, sort, and answer mail.

Who Reads the Mail?

Congressman Richard Kleberg, back in the 1930s, didn't read constituent mail because he was both lazy and disinterested. Today, however, few Members of the House or the Senate read anything but a fraction of the enormous volume of mail that comes in. Not many legislators are sitting at their desks late at night pouring over individual letters, composing answers, and signing them. Typically, thousands of letters and e-mails come in, are answered, and returned to constituents without the lawmakers ever seeing them. Patrick Leahy remarked about his fellow Senators: "There are guys who probably haven't seen a piece of mail in years," let alone a piece of e-mail.[19] One Senate staffer remarked that his Senator had not been to the mail correspondence office, which was on the next floor up from the Senator's office, in over two years.

Correspondence systems must be automated and made as efficient as possible just to keep up with the sheer volume of messages coming in. It is also a matter of precious time. A newly-arrived Member of Congress might think that she can read every letter or e-mail, compose the proper answers, and then sign every message that goes out of the office. Soon reality sets in, and the new lawmaker, pulled in many directions by the new job, realizes that it is far better to have routine correspondence handled by the staff.[20] Making sure that all this happens in a timely fashion and assuring quality control is the responsibility of the chief of staff, legislative director, or the director of correspondence. Nevertheless, Members of the House and Senate are ultimately responsible for every piece of communication that goes out the door bearing their name. They are accountable for the content of the reply and for its prompt, courteous, and timely response.

Each Member of the House of Representatives is allotted a unified budget, called the Members' Representational Allowance, out of which virtually all of the expenses of the office must be paid. Altogether, there are approximately 11,692 personal staff employees who work for individual Members in the House. Each Member is permitted to employ eighteen permanent staffers and four additional employees, who are usually interns, part-time, shared, or temporary employees. The average fully-staffed House office has fourteen employees, with eight assigned to the Washington office, and six assigned to the district offices.[21]

Typically in the Washington office there is a chief of staff (or administrative assistant), scheduler, press secretary, office assistant, systems administrator, legislative director, and two legislative assistants. Legislative correspondence—everything from telephone calls, letters, faxes, post cards, telegrams, and e-mail—is handled by the systems administrator and the legislative assistants, with the press secretary, office assistant, and interns chipping in when correspondence becomes overwhelming. Roughly 50 percent of staff time in a typical congressional office is spent on constituent communications.

Senate personal offices, unlike the House, vary in staff size and budget according to the size of the states. The two Senators from California (population 35 million) each will have far larger staffs than, for example, the two Senators from New Mexico (population 1.7 million). The average Senate office has thirty-four staffers, with twenty-two employed in the Washington office. On the average, five Senate staffers spend most of their time on constituent communications in each personal Senate office.

In New Mexico, Senator Jeff Bingaman's personal office receives about 500 letters and e-mails from constituents in a week during slow periods, and about 2,000 letters and e-mails come in during busy times. Even in a state with a small constituency base, it takes many hands to sort, read, and respond to all the inquiries. There is a director of legislative correspondence, plus four legislative correspondents, and a mail systems operator; when things get busy, the two office receptionists help open mail and college interns help out with researching issues and sometimes trying their hand at drafting text. The legislative assistants, those staffers who deal primarily with policy issues, are responsible for providing paragraphs and information, and the legislative director is responsible for overall quality control, making sure that letters and policy statements accurately reflect the opinions and views of Senator Bingaman. A systems administrator designs and updates the website, troubleshoots technical problems, and corrects glitches in the system.[22]

Democratic Senator Dianne Feinstein from California receives about 2,500 outside messages per day, and during peak legislative periods, she receives 5,000 to 7,000 daily. The Feinstein Washington office was one of the first to use EchoMail, a software system that filters and sorts e-mail using certain key words. EchoMail recognizes the keyword "California" and its abbreviations, ZIP codes that begin with 9; out-of-state e-mail flagged by EchoMail receives an automated reply from the Senator's office stating her policy of not answering such mail. Jody Reeves, systems administrator for Senator Feinstein's Washington office, noted that about 70 percent of the e-mail that was responded to could be dispatched with pre-written policy statements and phrases.[23]

Following two years of pilot programs, EchoMail was installed in over thirty U.S. Senate offices. With the extraordinary volume of e-mail coming into Senate offices, staffers were faced with the challenge of trying to keep up with regular mail, telephone calls, faxes, and now e-mail. EchoMail automated the sorting process: It recognized preprogrammed key words and their synonyms, even looked for and recognized anger in the e-mails (by things like exclamation points). This software system has been used in the corporate world, with clients such as Calvin Klein, the Kmart Corporation, and the American Express Company. EchoMail estimated that the cost of responding to an e-mail was approximately $6.25 per message when done by humans, but that figure was cut in half when EchoMail was used, including the cost of having humans go over those e-mails that the software could not figure out.[24]

In the Senate, EchoMail was used to sort the e-mail and send it to the appropriate staffer for response. But EchoMail could also plug in the appropriate response (written by the Senate staffer), and reply to the e-mail automatically. Some offices may be nervous about relying on software and artificial intelligence to make judgments and responses, but as EchoMail or its competitors become even more sophisticated, the computer responses would become more reliable and automatic. Senator William Frist (Republican-Tennessee), who has enthusiastically supported technological improvements in the Senate, believed that EchoMail in 2001 was good enough to categorize most e-mail and send the appropriate responses without going through the extra step of having staffers check for accuracy.[25] However, the pilot program was discontinued in mid-2003.

Congressional offices can choose from a variety of correspondence management systems, from the most sophisticated (and most expensive) and efficient to the less-sophisticated but far less efficient. Nearly half of the House and Senate offices use one of the two major CMS packages, IQ or Capitol Correspondent, but the Congress Online Project[26] has found that most offices "lack the technical skill necessary" to implement the e-mail integrators. Some offices are unwilling or unable to make the significant investment necessary to upgrade their computer systems. They are thus hampered by not having up-to-date hardware, such as servers and computers, and consequently have problems with insufficient memory and storage capacity. Compounding the problem further is the lack of training and technical skills needed to fully exploit the benefits of the software systems.

Some congressional offices, however, have made the best of electronic communications, and have been willing to invest in staff training, updating of hardware and software, and inculcating a staff culture and attitude that fosters efficient communications. While other offices have since seen the value and efficiencies of e-mail communication, these are both the pioneers and the leaders in the field.

EARLY INNOVATORS IN CONGRESSIONAL E-MAIL PRACTICES

Sen. Jeff Bingaman (Democrat-New Mexico)

Sen. Conrad Burns (Republican-Montana)

Sen. Barbara Boxer (Democrat-California)

Sen. William Frist (Republican-Tennessee)

Sen. Patrick Leahy (Democrat-Vermont)

Rep. Rick Boucher (Democrat-Virginia)

Rep. Anna Eshoo (Democrat-California)

Rep. Zoe Lofgren (Democrat-California)

Rep. Thomas Tancredo (Republican-Colorado)

Rep. Charles Taylor (Republican-North Carolina)

Rep. Zach Wamp (Republican-Tennessee)

Rep. Heather Wilson (Republican-New Mexico)

Source: Congress Online Project, *E-Mail Overload in Congress*

E-mail Issues

Daniel Bennett and Pam Fielding, leaders in the private sector business of electronic advocacy, cite five problems they have found when trying to assist advocacy groups that want to communicate with Congress. The first problem is making sure the message gets through to Congress; second, helping constituents find their Member of Congress on the Internet; third, encouraging Members and staff to sort through e-mail and find communications from their own constituents; fourth, integrating the processing of e-mail efficiently into an overall congressional office communication system; and finally, using the Internet to send responses to e-mail.[27] Members and staff also have to recognize the value of e-mail as a communications tool.

Many of the problems of e-mail system overload have been solved, with new equipment, software, and infrastructure. As seen above, the Senate has upgraded its infrastructure and software systems. The House of Representatives upgraded the speed, reliability, and security of the Campus Data Network (CDN), commonly referred to as the House Backbone, during the first session of the 107th Congress, effectively doubling the speed of the House Backbone and providing, now with a Gigabit Ethernet, improvements in multimedia for streaming audio and video.[28]

One of the simplest, but first, barriers to overcome is that constituents do not know their legislator's e-mail address. Some lawmakers now include their e-mail addresses on printed stationery; others refer only to their official website. Both the House and the Senate websites (www.house.gov and www.senate.gov) maintain listings of Member websites, and the Senate includes a listing of e-mails along with the website address. Each Member office establishes its own policy on whether to use Write Your Representative, which approximately three out of four Members offices have, use an outside vendor to create a filtered e-mail system, create their own filtered system, or use a public e-mail address. The House of Representatives, through its own portal website, conveniently lists in alphabetical order all Members of the House, with a link to each of their websites, yet still chooses not to offer a listing of public e-mails.[29]

One Member of Congress has tried to solve the problem of the unknown e-mail address by making it available on all of his communications. Representative Eric Cantor (Republican-Virginia) contacted each of his constituents through a direct mail brochure, giving constituents information about his official website, and particularly information about the electronic newsletters that constituents can subscribe to. After sending this information out through his paper newsletter, constituents found out about the electronic newsletter and e-newsletter subscribers increased by 650 percent.[30] Like many of the Republican Members of Congress, Representative Cantor linked his website to the electronic policy newsletters of the House Republican Conference, and its award-winning website, GOP.gov. What Cantor was doing was following basic marketing techniques used in the commercial world: an overwhelming number of retailers with an online presence also send out printed catalogues with information and descriptions, inviting them to use their e-mail and web address.

When the Congress Online Project first surveyed congressional offices in early 2001, it found that only 10 percent of House offices answered e-mails with e-mail; a year and a half later, that number had jumped to 25 percent of the House offices.[31] The efficiencies were striking: costs went down for paper and ink; printers were used less frequently, there was no folding, no envelopes, and no external delays in sending out the responses. Staff time and office budgets were likewise spared, and constituents could benefit from having e-mail messages responded to promptly. Constituents have seen how quickly the private sector can respond to e-mail. The average United States company responds to a customer's e-mail within twenty-four hours, and in just six hours if it is an IT company.[32] Understandably, constituents want that kind of courtesy and quick response time from their elected officials as well.

Some Member offices, however, are reluctant to respond to e-mail with e-mail. They prefer to have their responses on congressional stationery, complete with the official seal and their signature. Many Members feel that letters on congressional stationery suggest that the lawmaker (and his staff) took time, showed interest, commitment and thought. As columnist David Silverberg summed it up: "E-mails convey information but paper letters convey gravitas."[33] These attitudes may change as e-mail becomes more readily seen as the communication vehicle of choice and its obvious efficiencies are realized. Perhaps the next generation of e-mail applications will feature digital congressional stationery, complete with the seal of Congress, giving at least the appearance of being regular stationery.

The other side of the issue is this: Does constituent e-mail carry the same weight and importance as postal letters? In several interviews, House staffers remarked that their bosses would pay more attention to postal letters on a particular subject than to an e-mail on the same subject. One commented, "My boss would pay far more attention to a handwritten letter coming from a constituent than to an e-mail, which was probably generated by an outside vendor." A whole industry of electronic grassroots advocacy hopes that over time whatever latent biases there are against constituent e-mail in Congress would be put to rest. Early studies suggested that the public, at least the online public, thought e-mail should be considered as an important communication vehicle. In a survey in late 1999, Juno Online Services, Inc., found that 81 percent of Juno subscribers polled felt that it was "very important" for Members of Congress to accept e-mail, and that 93 percent of the respondents felt that representatives should take e-mail as seriously as they take letters and telephone calls.[34]

One reason why lawmakers are reluctant to respond with e-mail is that they want to avoid the errant or fraudulent e-mail that bears their signature or imprint that is bouncing around to untold electronic mailboxes. They want to avoid what happened in October 2002 at the White House. The day after the Congress authorized President Bush to use force against Iraq, a mass e-mail was distributed by the executive office of the President. The e-mail referred to Senator Robert C. Byrd (Democrat-West Virginia), a leader of the opposition to Bush, as "doddering old Bob Byrd, the senile senator from West Virginia" and referred to the Hispanic Democrats in the House of Representatives as "self-centered, do-nothing, $150,000/year plus perks yo-yos."

Enraged Democrats demanded an apology and an explanation. The e-mail apparently originated with the former chairman of the Republican National Hispanic Assembly, was sent to Republicans throughout the country, including some in the White House. A relatively senior White House aide directed a young aide to forward the e-mail to Hispanic Republican activists, but it was accidentally sent to a mostly Democratic Hispanic group. The White House offered its regrets that the e-mail was mistakenly forwarded.[35]

In another instance, Senator Joseph Lieberman (Democrat-Connecticut) was compelled to post an "Internet Hoax Warning" on his official website, noting that during the latter part of 2002, a phony e-mail had been circulating bearing the Senator's name. The letter attacked the people of France for being indifferent to anti-Semitism. Through his website, Lieberman warned that he was not involved in any way with the writing or distributing of the letter, whose origins were unknown.[36]

Nothing can be more frustrating for a citizen to receive an automatic response that says something like this: "I've received your e-mail, but my office and I are just too busy to respond." This isn't confined to federal legislators. One evening I sent an identical e-mail to eight state legislators from around the country, each of whom had a reputation for being technologically savvy and sensitive to online communications. Six came right back with an automatic message, saying, in effect, we are in the midst of a hectic legislative session, and we're too busy to correspond with you. The trouble was, however, the legislative sessions in each of their states had adjourned for the year months earlier. Sometimes the constituent is lucky to get even that message, even if it is not immediately responding to the issue.

Reporters periodically have tested congressional offices to see how quickly they respond to e-mail inquiries. CyberTimes reporters from *The New York Times*, occasionally conducted surveys, sending e-mail messages to congressional offices, stating clearly that they were reporters who were testing how, if and when Members of Congress answered their e-mail. In May 1996, Cyber-Times surveyed the 232 Members with e-mail, and found that fewer than 20 percent of the offices responded within a two-week period. In October 1998, the CyberTimes reporters sent similar e-mails to 261 offices that listed public addresses on their Congressional websites. Just 14 percent responded—

nineteen legislators personally responded, and half of the returns came from automatic responses.[37] In November 2001, CyberTimes sent similar e-mail messages to 65 Senate offices listing addresses on the Senate website; twenty-seven sent back automated responses, and only seven Senate offices sent a reply within two weeks.[38]

Occasionally, there can be technological foul-ups. Senator Patrick Leahy, one of the most active and savvy Internet users in Congress, was compelled to send out a news release to constituents in May 2000, asking them to resend their e-mail messages. Hundreds of e-mail messages from Vermonters went prematurely, in Leahy's words, to "e-mail heaven" because of an unknown system failure in the Senate that was caused by a computer virus.[39] A month's worth of e-mails were being replied to and for some unknown reason were zapped. Security threats, hacking, and equipment failure can all add to the difficulties of maintaining the integrity and reliability of an electronic communications operation.

Another concern is the "pen pal" syndrome, the concern that constituents who correspond through e-mail will become pesky, frequent writers, bothering already overburdened staff with superfluous correspondence. This occasionally happens with postal mail: A constituent writes a letter, gets a quick response from his representative, and with that incentive, continues writing, time after time, becoming in effect a pen pal. With e-mail, it becomes so much easier for a constituent to do. From anecdotal evidence thus far, however, congressional offices are not acquiring e-mail pen pals.

Another concern of legislators is that an e-mail sent to a constituent might somehow be altered, then sent to that constituent's friends, the press, or a potential opponent. It is so much easier to "doctor" an e-mail than a regular letter, and the temptation, some have feared, is too great. Commercial enterprises have been able to mitigate any problem of doctoring a document by using off-the-shelf software systems like Adobe to assure that the printed word is not altered. However, again from anecdotal evidence, the potential problem of doctored e-mail replies sent by congressional offices is not materializing on the Hill.[40]

After September 11th

Not until the threat of bioterrorism struck home did many offices rethink their need to use electronic communication with constituents. When entire buildings where shut down, with police crime scene yellow tape barring congressional staffers and legislators, offices were moved to temporary quarters in other government buildings.

This put considerable strain on both the technology infrastructure on the Hill and the staffs of the House Chief Administrative Officer, House Information Resources, the Senate Sergeant at Arms, the Office of the Clerk in the House, the Secretary of the Senate, the Committee on House Administration, and the Senate Rules Committee as they tried to cope with this unprecedented emergency.

Many congressional offices landed at temporary offices in the headquarters of the General Accounting Office, a few blocks away from Capitol Hill. There they were given laptops, printers, access to the Internet, CNN, C-SPAN, and e-mail accounts.[41] Other congressional offices relocated to nearby townhouses and other temporary quarters. October 15, 2001—the day that Senate Majority Leader Tom Daschle's office was contaminated with anthrax spores—was a wake-up call for many offices. In some offices, e-mail correspondence spiked by 400 percent,[42] and many were caught flat-footed and unable to respond to the wave of electronic communications brought about by closing of offices and closing of congressional mailrooms and mail processing centers.

As his office was being locked on October 17 and he had to find temporary quarters, Rep. John Linder (Republican-Georgia) issued a plea on his Internet site: "Contact me by e-mail rather than postal mail."[43] Most other Members followed suit with similar messages to constituents and the public. Many, like Representative Brad Carson (Democrat-Oklahoma), found the shift from postal mail to e-mail to be an effective solution. Senator Barbara Boxer (Democrat-California) saw e-mail messages double to as many as 14,000 a week in the months immediately after the anthrax scare and postal mail sent to her unaffected district offices in California doubled in volume.[44]

Probably the most useful congressional website during this time was that of Senator Bill Frist (Republican-Tennessee). Frist, a medical doctor, became the point of authority in the U.S. Senate, and his leadership was reflected in his website. His homepage was filled with post-September 11 information: notice that regular mail had been suspended and that e-mail or faxes were the best way to reach the Senator; information on what to do if receiving a suspicious package or envelope; what families could do to help; how to give blood or make financial contributions; a link to America's Fund for Afghan Children; information from the Centers for Disease Control; information about anthrax; and links to sites concerning bioterrorism.[45] The Frist site became the definitive source for anthrax information, and his site which normally received 4,000 hits per week had registered over 100,000 in the week after the anthrax threat in Congress.[46] On the other hand, many congressional websites had done little to inform the public, either about the shut-down of mail, or the threat of anthrax; these sites did not link the public to federal and state public safety, health, and emergency sites. For them, the website was an afterthought, not a first- line tool of communications to an anxious public.

Another response to the anthrax attack was the creation of a pilot program in the House of Representatives to digitize postal mail. This is described in more detail in chapter seven.

Reaching Out to Constituents

Lawmakers had been experimenting with listservs and electronic newsletters for years. One of the first was Rep. Michael Forbes (Democrat-New York), who sent out this message through e-mail: *"The Federal Government is one of our biggest polluters!* As a Member of the U.S. House of Representatives from New York, I write to ask for your help. You probably become outraged like I do when you see your government working against you."* This e-mail explained why Forbes urged the closing of a nuclear reactor and sued the U.S. Navy for dumping sludge offshore. At the end of the message was an e-mail petition people could send to voice their support or disagreement with his actions. "I was shocked, to be honest with you," said Forbes, "a high number of people wanted us to know they wanted to get this [information] on a regular basis."[47] Former Senator John Ashcroft, according to one account, had turned the use of Listservs and electronic notification "into a science."[48] Some lawmakers have found that an aggressive use of e-mail in combination with their website can help anticipate the surge of inquiries that come in when policy issues become hot.

Some Member offices send out e-mail issue updates, or electronic newsletters to individuals who have asked to be placed on an electronic mailing list, or who have indicated their interest by checking a box on the lawmaker's website beside the issue update they would like to receive. Representative Zach Wamp (Republican-Tennessee), one of the biggest advocates of electronic communication, for example, provides thirteen electronic newsletters plus a notification when and where he will be visiting the congressional district.

Some will provide links from the home page of the website to information about timely issues.[49] Much of this information is prepared by the individual offices themselves, while others come from their party caucuses. Many of the Republican Members of the House link directly to information provided by the House Republican Caucus and its website, Gop.gov.

Some offices conduct online surveys on their website, usually about current topics discussed in Congress. Focus group participants have told the Congress Online Project that they want to see such online surveys and want their voices heard through such vehicles. While a growing number of congressional websites offer online surveys, too few of them clearly inform the viewer that the surveys have no scientific validity and only represent the views of those who choose to participate.

Some congressional offices direct constituent inquiries to a Frequently Asked Questions (FAQ) section of their websites and others provide comment forms and guest books on their websites so that individuals can voice their concerns or issues, without the expectation of receiving a reply from the office.

The Promise of Electronic Mail

Electronic mail sent to Congress has grown considerably during the past several years. In some offices, it now constitutes more than 50 percent of their communications volume. At certain frenzied times, such as the impeachment of President Clinton, the nominations of controversial cabinet appointees, or deliberations about war, congressional offices have been overwhelmed with e-mail and circuits have been clogged. Individual offices of Senators and Members of the House, as well as Congress as an institution have responded with mixed results to the challenges of electronic communication.

Some offices, like those listed above, have seen the challenge and made the most of the opportunities available. They have been willing to give electronic communication a high priority. Other offices have been grappling with the communication challenges, but have been reluctant to spend the necessary funds on upgrading equipment or software and, especially, have been reluctant to provide staff with sufficient training to use fully the already powerful correspondence management system software packages.

At times, the House and Senate have been slow to respond to the infrastructure needs, but they recently have been pouring enormous sums of money into technology upgrades. Congress has also been providing training, office diagnoses, assistance with web development, and other basic services.[50] If Congress were a corporation with the same highly sophisticated communication needs, there would most likely be a unified and integrated technology and communications system: all offices, divisions, and units of that corporation would use the same software and hardware, and training would be mandatory and keyed to the needs of each individual. There would be a unified set of communication expectations and protocols, and there would be a central administrative unit responsible for managing the entire operation.

Congress has some of this, through its administrative units in both the House and Senate. But at its heart, Congress is a collection of small businesses—the individual Members and committee offices—which set their own priorities and operate as they please. One congressional office may decide to spend a significant amount of funds on state-of-the-art computer technology and the most up-to-date software available. That office might be driven by a lawmaker who recognizes the advantages and efficiencies of electronic communication, who insists that staff be trained to the fullest, and that whenever possible, the costly inefficiencies of a paper-dependent office are minimized. The congressional office right next door might be using hand-me-down computer hardware, with insufficient storage and memory, breakdowns and losses of data. That office might spend enormous amounts of time manually sorting and answering correspondence, may discourage e-mail, and may pay only lip service to its uninformative website. Similarly, a committee chairman may insist on full transparency, encourage electronic communication, and push toward having as many committee activities as possible available through its Internet site. Another committee chairman may have no interest whatsoever in going beyond the bare minimum of accommodation. Effective e-mail and website usage only comes when the individual lawmakers and their senior staff are committed to them and willing to use the best practices available.

Congressional Websites

If they're only going to put on their websites all the great things they've done, it's really missing the point because what we need is a clear and accurate record of what the Representative is doing. If it's going to be just an advertisement, it's not going to really be for me.
—Focus group participant evaluating congressional websites, 2001

The best [congressional] websites . . . have done more than just take advantage of a new "tool," they have embraced a new way of thinking.
—Congress Online Project, 2002

ll Members of Congress, standing committees, leadership and institutional offices now have websites; by the beginning of the 108th Congress, January 2003, there were 610 congressional websites. To a considerable degree, congressional websites have improved markedly over the past several years. They have come far from the earlier versions, those created between 1995 and 2000, which were typically little more than self-promotional advertisements for the Member, simply extensions of their congressional newsletters.[1] Unfortunately, some congressional websites are still just that, giving biographical information, press releases, and stories about the Member, but little more.

Evaluating Congressional Websites

In March–June 2001, the Congress Online Project took a baseline snap shot of the design and features found on the 535 House and Senate personal office websites. The most common features were contact information, tourist information, how to order an American flag, and information about the Member.[2]

MOST COMMON WEB DESIGNS/CONTENT FEATURES, 2001

Feature	Number	Percentage
Office telephone numbers	515	96.26
Addresses for each office	513	95.89
Biography of Member	513	95.89
E-mail link	486	90.84
Photo of Member	477	89.16
Capitol/White House ticket info.	476	88.97
Washington, D.C. tourist info.	466	87.10
Flag ordering information	447	83.55
Press releases	436	81.50
Links to THOMAS	430	80.37

Source: Congress Online Project data

While this information was helpful, there was much that was missing. In designing and crafting their websites, congressional offices failed to understand some of the basic principles of marketing and communication research: know your audience, know what it wants, and design solutions to meet its needs.

In interviews with House systems administrators and chiefs of staff, the Congress Online Project asked who determined the design and content of websites. The typical answer was that the press secretary would decide, or the chief of staff, together with the legislative director and the systems administrator; occasionally the Senate or Member would make suggestions. In none of these interviews did we find an office that had conducted a survey or asked constituents in informal gatherings what they would like to see on the congressional websites. Every office made its own decision; some gave high priority to web communication, while others did not. What resulted was a hodgepodge of websites. No two congressional websites looked alike: some were flashy and heavily graphics-oriented; others were bare bones and simply designed; a few websites were rich in content, and others gave little information. There were congressional websites that had not been updated in months, others that contained dead links, or links to information that was two or three congressional sessions old. Some websites tried hard to be folksy, with recipes for mom's favorite bean dip or pecan pie; other sites were staid and serious, reflecting the dignity of the office.

To determine what citizens wanted to see on congressional websites, the Congress Online Project conducted a series of interviews with Internet-savvy constituents in four cities.[3] The participants were shown four congressional websites—a Republican and Democratic Member site from the House, and a Republican and Democratic Member site from the Senate—and were asked to evaluate them and to indicate what they would like to see on such sites. Citizens were most concerned about accountability: They wanted to know how their Members had voted on key issues, the rationale behind the votes, and in clear and simple language what each vote concerned. Focus group participants also wanted to know what lawmakers did in Washington: they wanted to know their daily public schedules and their schedules while back home in the districts. The citizens also wanted to have a chance to express themselves, either through online polls or through e-mail forms on the congressional websites.

The concerns of focus group participants were much the same of respondents to a nationwide online poll conducted by the Congress Online Project in early 2003. Respondents were looking to congressional websites for substantive information on issues, what their legislators felt about and voted on issues, and how citizens could readily express their opinions online. Respondents were least interested in seeing biographical information about the legislator and, unlike the focus group participants, the online respondents were little interested in viewing daily schedules.[4]

By and large, these items were missing from nearly all Member office websites. Some lawmakers directed visitors to THOMAS, the legislative database provided by the Library of Congress; but very few posted their own information on votes taken, and fewer still offered information on why they voted a certain way or provided their schedules.

In addition to conducting a baseline survey of website features, the Congress Online Project assembled a team of experts to determine Best Practices for effective congressional websites, then evaluated the 605 congressional websites then active in 2001 to determine how they had measured up to those standards.[5]

FEATURES SELDOM SEEN ON CONGRESSIONAL WEBSITES, 2001

Feature	Number	Percentage
Site in Spanish, other languages	35	6.54
Link to off-site issue information	28	5.23
Member's schedule in district	25	4.67
Links to CRS reports	19	3.55
Why Member voted certain way	8	1.50
Section 508 accessibility	10	1.87
Member's daily schedule	3	0.56

Source: Congress Online Project, *Congress Online*

The Best Practices criteria developed for the congressional websites were the following:

BEST PRACTICES FOR CONGRESSIONAL WEBSITES

1. **Audience.** The site demonstrated that the office had clearly identified its web audiences (both those seeking information from the office and those that the office wanted to target) and methodically built the site around those audiences. Those audiences included constituents, reporters, interest groups, students, and educators.
2. **Content.** The site provided content that was specifically targeted to meet the needs of the defined audiences, was up to date, attracted new visitors, and supported the goals of the office. Such materials would include legislative and issue information, demonstrations of accountability (such as how the lawmakers voted, how they could be reached, and their schedules), educational information about Congress, constituent services, references to the district or state. It would also include contact information, press information, information about the lawmaker, current national and international news, and links to relevant resources.
3. **Interactivity.** The site offered its visitors opportunities to express their views and fostered on- and off-line communications. This included subscriptions to e-mail updates or electronic newsletters, online surveys or polls, bulletin boards or chat rooms, feedback and comment forms, and staff contact information.
4. **Usability.** The design and information architecture of the site enhanced the audiences' experience by enabling quick and user-friendly access to information and services. The website should be easy to use, logically constructed, readable, consistent, and timely. It should load in no more than ten seconds, should not be distracting with too many bright colors or moving objects. Further, should provide accessibility for those with vision impairment, and include a statement on privacy policy.
5. **Innovations.** The site employed creative features that enhance a visitor's experience by making it interesting or easy to use.

Source: Congress Online Project, *Congress Online*

The results of the 2002 website evaluations, however, were discouraging.[6] Only 2.5 percent of congressional websites received a grade of "A" (or 4.00), and the average grade of all websites was "C−" (1.76).[7] The websites in the House of Representatives, which constituted nearly 80 percent of all sites, had an average grade of "C−" (1.67), while the Senate websites were slightly better, with an overall grade of "C" (2.12). Altogether, over 34 percent of the websites maintained by House individual offices and 18 percent of the Senate individual offices received either "D" or "F" scores.

Congressional offices that did not score well were falling into several patterns of mistakes: They were too concerned about promoting the lawmaker, rather than informing their audiences; they were not providing audiences with what they wanted to see; the material on the websites were outdated; they did not write for the Internet, but tended to paste onto their websites lengthy materials that were written as policy briefings; they provided superfluous information (such as local news, games, favorite recipes); the websites took too much time to load; and after trying innovative technologies, such as audio clips, they failed to follow through in maintaining them or keeping them fresh.[8]

There was no pattern of website quality based on party affiliation or chamber. Senate Democratic individual offices had the highest overall grade average ("C+" or 2.61), while House Democratic individual offices had the lowest ranking ("D+" or 1.58). Overall, the Senate sites scored better, in part because Senate offices had more funds available to them to create their websites, either doing them internally or hiring web design firms to assist them. Offices in the House, with fewer funds available, tended to rely on pre-packaged materials available from the House Information Resources office and their own internal web design capabilities.

In its 2002 evaluation, the Congress Online Project selected fifteen congressional websites that were the best examples of online communication tools. Each of these did an outstanding job in meeting audience needs, providing specific and up-to-date content, developing interactive tools, and employing creative features.

There was a second round of website evaluations completed in early 2003, and this time the changes were remarkable but also disappointing. They were remarkable because seventy-five congressional websites, not fifteen as in the year before, were now recognized for their superior efforts. Even more impressive, 50 percent of all the websites received grades of A or B, showing great improvement over the year before. (The best congressional websites of 2002 and 2003 are listed in Appendix B). The evaluations, however, also proved to be disappointing: while many offices had substantially improved their website communications, a large number of those offices which had scored poorly in 2002 continued to lag behind in 2003. Overall, however, there was improvement: the average grade point of all congressional websites had progressed from 1.76 (or a C−) in 2002 to a 2.30 (or C+) in 2003.

Many offices took up the challenge to improve the content, usability, and interactivity of their websites. They were assisted to a considerable degree by the Congressional Management Foundation, which conducted the research and evaluations for both Congress Online reports and provided valuable one-on-one training for over 175 congressional offices that requested assistance to improve their websites.[9]

The Congress Online Project found in its 2003 study that some congressional offices had dramatically improved the quality of their websites; Senate office websites were better than House office websites; and Republican websites were better than those in Democatic offices. Further, House committee websites were far better than their Senate counterparts and House Republican (majority) websites were far superior to all other committee sites. Many of the first-time award winners in 2003 had subpar or poor websites the year before; however, many other mediocre websites failed to improve. A digital divide was evident in websites: 50 percent of the 610 congressional websites had been ranked as exceptional, garnering grades of A or B; yet another 25 percent scored poorly with grades of D and F.[10]

GRADE POINT AVERAGES—CONGRESSIONAL WEBSITES, 2002 AND 2003

Office	2002 GPA	2003 GPA	Increase
House Overall (all offices combined)	1.76	2.22	0.52
House Members	1.67	2.16	0.49
House Democrats	1.58	2.08	0.50
House Republicans	1.76	2.23	0.47
House Committees	2.06	2.83	0.77
Republican (Majority)	2.20	3.37	1.17
Democrat (Minority)	1.77	2.38	0.61
Senate Overall (all offices combined)	2.06	2.57	0.51
Senate Members	2.12	2.79	0.67
Senate Democrats	2.61	3.08	0.47
Senate Republicans	2.10	2.49	0.39

GRADE POINT AVERAGES—CONGRESSIONAL WEBSITES, 2002 AND 2003 *continued*

Office	2002 GPA	2003 GPA	Increase
Senate Committees	1.62	1.81	0.19
Democratic (Majority)	1.71	1.88	0.17
Republican (Minority)	0.75	1.25	0.50
Leadership Overall (all offices combined)	2.09	2.73	0.64
Democratic Leadership	1.75	2.00	0.25
Republican Leadership	2.43	3.14	0.71
Congress Overall	1.76	2.30	0.54

Source: Congress Online Project, *Congress Online 2003*, 8.

Member Websites

The great majority of congressional websites belong to the individual Members of the House and the Senate: 539 out of the current 610 websites.[11] In 2003, ten Member websites in the House and three in the Senate were cited as the very best on Capitol Hill.

BEST MEMBER WEBSITES ON CAPITOL HILL, 2003

House of Representatives

Rep. Earl Blumenauer (Democrat-Oregon) (http://www.house.gov/ blumenauer)
Rep. John Boozman (Republican-Arkansas) (http://www.house.gov/ boozman)
Rep. Chaka Fattah (Democrat-Pennsylvania) (http://www.house.gov/fattah)
Rep. Kay Granger (Republican-Texas) (http://kaygranger.house.gov)*
Rep. Melissa Hart (Republican-Pennsylvania) (http://hart.house.gov)
Rep. John Larson (Democrat-Connecticut) (http://www.house.gov/larson)
Rep. Richard Pombo (Republican-California) (http://www.house.gov/ pombo)*
Rep. George Radanovich (Republican-California) (http://www.radanovich.
   house.gov)
Rep. Christopher Shays (Republican-Connecticut) (http://www.house.gov/ shays)
Rep. Nick Smith (Republican-Michigan) (http://www.house.gov/nicksmith)

Senate

Sen. Tom Carper (Democrat-Delaware) (http://carper.senate.gov)
Sen. Patrick Leahy (Democrat-Vermont) (http://leahy.senate.gov)*
Sen. Harry Reid (Democrat-Nevada) (http://reid.senate.gov)

Source: Congress Online Project, *Congress Online 2003:*
*Denotes site also chosen in 2002 Congress Online Project evaluations.

Representative Kay Granger

One of the best examples of personal office websites was that of Representative Kay Granger of Texas. Granger, along with Representative Richard Pombo of California, were the only House Member offices whose websites received the highest awards in the 2002 and 2003 Congress Online Project evaluations. Granger, who was elected to the House of Representatives in November 1996, was a former high school teacher, small business owner, and mayor of Fort Worth; she represents the Twelfth District, the northwest section of Tarrant County (Fort Worth) and Parker County.

The Granger website was a model for content, ease of use, interactivity, and information for constituent needs. The site contained these features:

REPRESENTATIVE KAY GRANGER WEBSITE

http://kaygranger.house.gov

Constituent Services	Help with federal agencies; assistance for businesses; educational loans; federal grants; service academy nominations and flag requests; internship information, presidential greetings, and a Washington visitors guide.
Issues	Listing of bills considered in the upcoming week and for the next day (from the Majority Whip's office); analysis of upcoming legislation (from GOP.gov), and a view of real-time floor activity.
Multimedia	Video and audio of Rep. Granger, President Bush and others.
Links	Extensive links to congressional committees, executive branch, Texas state and local government, and media.
E-Mail Sign-Up	Subscriptions to any of six separate issue areas.
Opinion Survey	Constituents asked their opinions on key issues.
Biography	Biographical statement, plus pictures.
Contact	Full information on contacting the Member, including Write Your Representative.

What Representative Granger had on her website was becoming standard fare for Congressional websites. She went several steps further than most; her site was considered among the very best in Congress because of its clarity and crispness, its ease of use, the depth of information presented, and the wide number of interesting links available. The Granger site, available in both

English and Spanish, was also impressive because it listed the names, short biographies, and responsibilities of district caseworkers and her Washington office staff. This was quite unusual in a legislative culture where staff are almost always invisible and anonymous. The Granger website also provided a handy, easy-to-read map of her congressional district.

Outstanding Features

The best congressional websites provided a wealth of material, clearly understood the needs of their primary audiences, and were designed to be interactive and easy to use.

Focus on Constituents

It is axiomatic that Member offices need to focus on the needs and interests of their constituents. This simple point, however, often was missed, as congressional websites tended to be more self-promotional than constituent-based. That changed as more offices recognized the importance of focusing on constituent needs. One of the best examples of constituent-oriented websites was that of Senator Tom Carper (Democrat-Delaware). The viewer could go to the state map, and click on one of the three Delaware counties. Pulling up New Castle County, the home of the state's principal city, Wilmington, the viewer could note both local and federal news pertaining to the area, and a long list of city, county, and private websites. There was a section called Kudos!, which listed the local area residents and their accomplishments, from winning scholastic competitions to reaching milestone birthdays.

In the Issues section of the Carper website, there was information on local interests in nine distinct issue areas. Under "Agriculture," for example, the Carper website provided links to federal agricultural and environmental agencies, plus links to download recent Congressional Research Service (CRS) issue briefs pertaining to agricultural issues of concern to Delaware farmers.

Carper's website also provided a couple of welcome, but not common touches: It encouraged viewers to help improve the website and linked to the e-mail address of his webmaster. The website also provided the names and addresses of staffers who could assist constituents with problems with federal agencies.

This attention to small things, like the Kudos! section, were details that could be handled in congressional offices or in a small state such as Delaware, but would be much more difficult and time consuming for large states like California or New York.

Senator Harry Reid (Democrat-Nevada) had a very effective section on his website explaining how he had helped citizens in the five parts of the state. Click on one section on the state map, Northern Nevada, for example, and a page for Elko, Humboldt, Northern Washoe, and Pershing counties listed all of the recent activities of Senator Reid, including press releases. Reid also tailored information resources for selected audiences: children, media, senior citizens, students, veterans, and women.[12]

Casework Information

Constituents could easily be frustrated when trying to figure out which federal, state, or local agency was responsible for handling a problem. Many times constituents had little understanding of the basics: Was this a problem that should have been handled by a federal agency? If so, which agency? Was this really an issue or problem that it could handle? How did one communicate with the right person?

Congressional state or district field offices handle these kinds of questions as a routine matter. To ease the flow of constituent relations, some Senate and House offices are now posting timely, easily understood information so that constituents could arm themselves with basic information about casework and federal or state agencies.

One of the best examples of this information was found on the website of Senator Jeff Bingaman of New Mexico. In simple, easily understood language, the web page entitled "How I Can Assist You" explained what casework was ("a problem or concern an individual has with a federal government agency") and gave examples (Social Security disability or difficulties with the federal income tax). The site took the viewer through several steps: first, to determine whether the question or issue was something which the Senator's office could provide assistance with, together with examples of state issues over which the Senator had no jurisdiction (such as child custody, divorce, criminal trials, or state taxes); second, the site provided a list of quick answers to frequently-asked-questions about casework (such as "I am trying to reach the IRS. It used to be in the phone book, but now I can't find it. What is the local number?" or "I have become disabled and am unable to work. What happens after I apply for Social Security?")

Third, the casework site provided links to the federal agencies, then the site helped a constituent open a case with one of the Senator's five state offices (completing a Personal Authorization Form, gathering the necessary paper-work, and links to downloadable forms from several agencies). Finally, the site gave the contact numbers, addresses of his five state offices, including a picture of the front of each building and the pictures of the caseworkers who could help). As forward-thinking and helpful as this site was, it could have been improved by being in Spanish as well as in English.

This exceptional level of information, written from the vantage point of the constituents who may know very little about how to obtain assistance, made the Bingaman website a model that many offices could easily emulate. Other very good casework sections came from the websites of Senator Patrick Leahy, who gave detailed information on getting assistance from federal agencies, from Representative John Boozman (Republican-Arkansas) whose site was open and easily accessible to constituents; and Representatives Kay Granger (Republican-Texas); Nick Smith (Republican-Michigan); and Steve Rothman (Democrat-New Jersey); each of whom offered step-by-step casework guides for citizens. Representative George Radanovich (Republican-California) provided a "Life's Events" section on his website, which listed online government services for every stage in a viewer's life: from birth, school, taxes, and retirement. Senator Sam Brownback (Republican-Kansas) let viewers make appointments with him and his staff online.[13]

How Did They Vote?

One of the key conclusions of focus group analysis was that citizens wanted their lawmakers to be accountable to them; and most important, citizens wanted to know how lawmakers voted on key issues. But few Members provide this information: just 37 percent of the House Member office sites and 14 percent of the Senate Member office sites provided information about voting records.[14]

Representative Lynn N. Rivers (Democrat-Michigan) did an admirable job in providing roll call information on her official website. For example, for the week of June 17, 2002, her website listed fifteen separate roll call votes, the vote total in the House, and her vote (with a graphic showing a thumbs-up or thumbs-down). Hyperlinked to each bill title was the information about the bill itself, provided by THOMAS. Her site was both timely and complete: The information provided was less than two days old, and her site allowed viewers to go back two years, on a weekly basis, to see how she voted.[15] Representative Rivers went a step further by providing a web page that previews legislation that is scheduled for floor consideration in the week ahead.

The website of Representative Jennifer Dunn (Republican-Washington) provided another example of publishing roll call votes, although the votes chosen were selective (only one vote listed for several of the weeks), and were not up to date (the last weekly summary was three months old when checked). Representative Dunn linked these votes with explanations of her voting decisions. For example, the relatively complicated 245(i) Extension Act, a part of the Immigration and Nationality Act, was explained in clear, simple language, and Representative Dunn gave her reason for voting using the same measured, clear writing.[16] Representatives Chaka Fattah (Democrat-Pennsylvania) and Judy Biggert (Republican-Illinois), and Senator Bill Frist (Republican-Tennessee) explained their positions on various policy issues and why they voted for or against key pieces of legislation.[17] Senator Dianne Feinstein (Democrat-California), Representative Frank Wolf (Republican-Virginia), and Representative Christopher Shays (Republican-Connecticut) also provided full voting histories on their respective websites, in easy to understand language, categorized by topic.[18]

The creation of web pages that give complete voting histories of the Member or Senator certainly take staff time to create, update and maintain, but they are the one key feature that constituents want to see. Even more helpful would be web pages, like Representative Dunn's, that explain in simple terms what the vote was about and why the legislator voted a certain way, and web pages, like Representative Rivers', that gave a listing of upcoming roll call votes. None of this information was difficult for a congressional staff to obtain, and listing of votes and rationale for voting should be a part of the information Members compile in any event.

For even those legislators who balk at compiling their own records and displaying them on their official websites under the pretense of too much staff time involved, all they had to do was follow the practice of Representative Earl Blumenauer (Democrat-Oregon), who, on his voting page, provided links to five outside website sources: the Office of the Clerk of the House, which listed all official roll call votes, Capitol Advantage's Congress.org, C-SPAN's Congressional Votes Library (powered by Capitol Advantage), Project Vote Smart, and the THOMAS legislative site.[19] Such links could be provided with no cost of time or effort by the legislator's staff.

One complaint was that legislators do not want to give ammunition to potential campaign challengers by providing ready-made research on their voting record. This, however, was a false rationale. As a former candidate and opposition researcher, I could simply say that any researcher worth his or her salt could easily obtain far more complete information about voting records, impact of votes, cost of programs, and other vital information from sources not even remotely connected to the legislator's official website.

Content and Issues

The best congressional websites were rich in content, providing valuable and useful information to constituents, the media, and others who view their pages. Senator Dianne Feinstein (Democrat-California) excelled in this regard, providing a near-encyclopedic amount of material on her website, including downloadable legislative brochures. Senator Patrick Leahy (Democrat-Vermont) provided exceptional depth in his coverage of issues and legislative priorities. Senator Carl Levin (Democrat-Michigan), gave viewers a wide range of issue information. His website had links to twenty-seven issue areas on its home page, ranging from current issues (campaign finance reform, Medicare, targeting terrorism), to his committee work (Armed Services Committee, Governmental Affairs Committee, and Great Lakes Task Force), to other issues like gun safety, hate crimes, and trade with China. The website of Senator Tom Harkin (Democrat-Iowa) did a particularly good job in targeting specific issue areas of interest to his Iowa constituents, including twenty-one separate issues. Senator Kay Bailey Hutchison (Republican-Texas) had sixteen pages devoted to issues on her website.[20]

Several websites emphasized the legislative expertise that the lawmakers had developed. Representative Chaka Fattah (Democrat-Pennsylvania) emphasized his priority in education issues, Representative Christopher Shays (Republican-Connecticut) focused on campaign finance reform, while Representative Mike Honda (Democrat-California) concentrated on veterans issues. Senator Fred Thompson (Republican-Tennessee) paid particular attention to state issues on his websites.[21]

Schedules

When the Congress Online project team conducted a series of focus groups of citizens, it discovered that few of the eighty participants knew what Members of Congress did on a day-to-day basis.[22] Some of their immediate impressions were distinctly negative images of Congress: pictures from C-SPAN, showing just a handful of Members present on the floor, information in their newspapers about Congress being in recess (and presumably its Members relaxing) for long stretches frequently throughout the year, and the most damning impression of legislators on some junket to an exotic location, being escorted by a high-priced lobbyist.

This is not how legislators typically spend their time. Most work extremely long hours, with hyperactive schedules that shuttle them back and forth between their home districts and Washington every week. Unfortunately, this information was not conveyed to the public, at least not on many Member websites. Some Members listed "schedule" on their website homepage, but then linked it to the official calendars of the House and Senate, without further attention paid to it. When focus groups were shown one such House website, and "schedule" was clicked on, up came "Recess. House not in Session." This led to knowing laughs and cutting comments from the participants, because that information reinforced the simplistic view that legislators were just taking it easy. However, when another House website was displayed, and "schedule" was clicked on, up came a long list of events and activities that the legislator was involved with back home during the district time. Focus group participants were quiet, or agreed that that was what a Member of Congress should be doing. Few Members of Congress made their schedules available on their websites, either because they (or their staffs) simply had not thought of doing it, they feared it would be used as opposition research by an opponent, they did not want meetings to be made public, or they felt there were significant security implications.

Representatives Lynn Woolsey (Democrat-California), Melissa Hart (Republican-Pennsylvania), John Boozman (Republican-Arkansas), Tom Allen (Democrat-Maine) and Senator Larry Craig (Republican-Idaho) have determined to be more accountable to the public and make their daily public schedules available, listing upcoming committee hearings, public events that they would be attending, and selected office appointments.[23] The sites were far from perfect, but they give much more information about the day-to-day activities of legislators than many of their colleagues.[24]

Electronic Newsletters

Many legislators now send out electronic newsletters, usually developed around common themes, such as education, environment, children's issues, and the like. Such electronic newsletters fall under the same House franking regulations as regular mass mailings. [25] Representative Tom Allen (Republican-Maine) gave nearly seventy choices of e-mail issues that constituents can receive by checking the appropriate box on his website. Appropriately, he called this page "Staying in Touch."[26] Senator Harry Reid (Democrat-Nevada) offered twenty choices of e-mail subjects and also had a page inviting citizens to tell their personal stories and to get involved. Other good examples of e-mail newsletters come from Representatives Mike Pence (Republican-Indiana), Kay Granger (Republican-Texas), Melissa Hart (Republican-Pennsylvania), Mike Honda (Democrat-California), Richard Pombo (Republican-California), and Senators Barbara Boxer (Democrat-California) and Mary Landrieu (Democrat-Louisiana).[27]

Senator Debbie Stabenow (Democrat-Michigan) took this several steps further by creating on her Senate website a new way to encourage citizens to participate in government. The feature was called the "Prescription Drug People's Lobby," and Senator Stabenow attempted to create an online community of individuals interested in legislation, in staying informed about the issue of Medicare, prescription drugs, and other health issues. On her web page featuring the prescription drug issue, viewers could learn about the most recent legislation, sign up for future e-mails concerning prescription drugs, and share their own stories about the burdens of high-cost drugs. Through this simple device of an Internet site, Senator Stabenow was creating her own constituency, not just of voters in Michigan, but from around the United States.[28]

Interactivity

A number of lawmakers directly ask constituents their opinions about federal law and policies, usually through an online poll on their website. Many of the online polls on congressional websites would be scoffed at by professional pollsters. Such polls were inherently unscientific and only represented the voices of those who have decided to vote. In no way would they be considered representative of the opinions of the entire constituency. The online poll posted on the website of Senator Harry Reid (Democrat-Nevada) was an example: "Which economic stimulus proposal do you think will have more of a positive effect on the economy, one that provides investment tax breaks to the wealthiest Americans, or one that targets tax relief to working, middle-class Americans?" The poll itself was fundamentally faulty because its choices lead viewers to a particular answer ("tax relief" for "working, middle class" Americans rather than "tax breaks" for the "wealthiest.") The poll also permitted individuals to post answers multiple times. When such online poll results were displayed on congressional websites, the results should also indicate that the poll only reflected the preferences of those who bothered to vote. Yet, many congressional websites failed to mention this simple, but key fact.

Senator Reid's website, through his "Get Involved" section, encouraged citizens to e-mail him, subscribe to his electronic newletters, or request a video conference session or an Internet chat. Reid also encouraged constituents to tell their story, and refreshingly, to give feedback on the content and design of his website. Representative Blumenauer offered a section called "Effective Advocacy," teaching citizens how to communicate effectively with elected officials; he also provided links to voter registration information and local advocacy groups.

In an example of bipartisanship, Senators Joseph Lieberman (Democrat-Connecticut) and Fred Thompson (Republican-Tennessee) launched a website to gather public input on federal e-government initiatives. They had hoped that the Internet site, called the E-Government Project, would help them gather public responses to help them write better legislation dealing with e-government.[29] Citizens were asked to weigh in on a variety of issues, such as whether to have a federal chief information officer and how best to improve the organization of government information. The website presented a policy idea: the National Academy of Sciences would conduct a study specifically focused on e-government and any disparities in Internet access, to determine, among other things, what should be done to ensure that e-government does not widen any gap in Internet access. Then, the site asked for viewer response and feedback.

Representative Henry Waxman (Democrat-California) set up an "Enron Tip Line" on his congressional website, inviting prospective whistleblowers to share information. In its first few weeks, however, the site had recorded 2,000 responses about Enron, in addition to 2,000 responses from "right-wing antagonists and the occasional anti-Semite."[30] This reflected one of the downsides of an open invitation to the public: Unless filters were applied, anyone could respond to a hotline or online poll; and often, there were no restrictions on the number of times an individual may respond.

Student/Educational Information

Some congressional websites have recognized that they perform an important educational function for the general public through information about casework and solving problems, and for students and children in understanding how government works. Many congressional websites now have a "Kid's Page" or a "Student's Page" designed to help students, their parents, and teachers better understand how Congress and the federal government work, along with information about the symbols and importance of democratic institutions. In focus groups, the Congress Online Project found that this feature was particularly appreciated, especially by teachers and parents.

One of the best examples came from the website of the Clerk of the House of Representatives, called "Kids in the House."[31] Teachers and parents were given lesson plans about Congress, information about visiting the Capitol with student groups, links to various government-sponsored sites of interest to children and families, and a glossary of terms. Children had puzzles and games about Congress, an interactive coloring book, and a feature called

Build-a-Bill, allowing students to fill in bill titles, sponsors and co-sponsors, the text of their own bills which they could create and would appear in much the same form as a bill printed for House use.[32]

Problems Persist

While there had been considerable progress made in the development, design, and content of many congressional websites, still problems abound. Fully one-half of the congressional websites were doing no more than a mediocre job of communicating with the public. Many of the websites rated "poor" or "fair" gave only bare bones information about the services the Member could provide. Some websites rated as "failing" were hopelessly out of date, confusing in their navigation or had no real navigation at all, or were perpetually "under construction." Most disappointing as a group were the Republican committee websites in the Senate, which ranked the lowest of any group both in 2002 and 2003.[33]

Bilingual Sites and Accessible Sites

Few offices provided bilingual websites. In early 2001, just thirty-five Member sites were bilingual, usually offering Spanish-language versions for some of the webpages. Some offered pages in other languages as well. One of the key reasons why so few Member websites are bi- or multilingual is the sheer difficulty and time constraints of maintaining such sites. It takes considerable staff time to translate and update web pages, and many staffs are stretched so thin that only the home page and some second-language specific pages can be offered.

Representative W. J. (Billy) Tauzin, from the Third District of Louisiana, offered himself as "*Votre Ambassadeur Cadien au Congrès*" ("Your Cajun Ambassador to Congress"), with parts of his official website in Cajun French.[34] Congressman James Langevin (Democrat-Rhode Island) went further, offering his website in eight different languages. He did this by linking his official website to AltaVista's Babel Fish Translation System; however, the resulting translations were too often garbled or inelegant.[35] The House Education and Workforce Committee became the first panel to create a Spanish-language website so that viewers could read President George W. Bush's "No Child Left Behind" educational initiative.[36]

Congress appears to be making good progress on the accessibility of website information to those with disabilities. Representative Langevin, the Bipartisan Disabilities Caucus along with the Chief Administrative Office James E. (Jay) Eagen III began in 2002 to push for greater use of accessibility standards among Member and committee websites.[37] The Congress Online Project

142 • Congress Online

concluded in a 2003 report that a full 75 percent of congressional websites had either "good" or "very good" accessibility when compared to the federal accessibility standards.[38]

Timely Information

Websites should stay fresh and up to date. Some Congressional websites have been updated daily, with timely news or information posted within hours. Others had not been touched for months, or had links to THOMAS for sessions long past, rather than the current Congress. Another problem occurred at the beginning of each new Congress, with freshman lawmakers delayed in creating a web communication presence. For example, a full two months into the 108th Congress, in March 2003, several freshman Senators still had not been able to develop and publish their own websites. The Senate had provided them with a one-page filler, which gave a short biography, but nothing further had been added. New Senators Saxby Chambliss (Republican-Georgia), Norman Coleman (Republican-Minnesota), Elizabeth Dole (Republican-North Carolina), Lindsay Graham (Republican-South Carolina), John E. Sununu (Republican-New Hampshire), and James Talent (Republican-Missouri) had only short biographical listings, and some did not even mention that theirs were temporary websites. Freshman Senators John Cornyn (Republican-Texas) had a "transition site," while Lamar Alexander (Republican-Tennessee), Lisa Murkowski (Republican-Alaska), Mark Pryor (Democrat-Arkansas), and veteran Senator Frank Lautenberg (Democrat-New Jersey), returning after a four-year absence, managed to develop and publish their new websites.

Committee and Leadership Websites

The websites maintained by the standing committees and the leadership positions varied greatly in quality. The best were extraordinary in the range and breadth of material presented, while the worst of such committee sites were barely acceptable as communication tools.

BEST COMMITTEE AND LEADERSHIP WEBSITES, 2003

House Committee on Energy and Commerce (majority) (http://energycommerce.house.gov)*

House Committee on Government Reform (minority) (http://reform.house.gov/min)

House Republican Conference (http://www.GOP.gov)*

Source: Congress Online Project, *Congress Online 2003*

*Denotes site also chosen in 2002 Congress Online Project evaluations

House Committee on Energy and Commerce

The House Committee on Energy and Commerce had an extraordinary range of jurisdiction, including telecommunications, health care, energy, the environment, consumer protection, and trade. Under the direction of Representative W. J. (Billy) Tauzin (Republican-Louisiana), the Committee has produced an exceptionally comprehensive website, filled with important information about the committee, those who testify before it, and the activities of the full committee and subcommittees. Equally impressive, the Minority (Democratic) website was also an excellent example of a committee online communication tool.[39]

Energy and Commerce provided a wealth of information, permitting viewers to download witness testimony and hearing transcripts (although these may have been sixty to ninety days old), with printed transcripts, officially called the Printed Hearing Record, downloadable from the 106th Congress (1999–2000) to the present. Viewers could also receive committee schedule updates by e-mail, and download committee publications.

The Energy and Commerce site gave the viewer an opportunity to not only contact the committee, but also to ask questions, point out problems, or comment on the website design. Further, the website provided a Tip Line, encouraging viewers to submit information on waste, fraud, or abuse by the federal government or by private business. Viewers could do this anonymously or provide full contact information.

The website provided a clear, easily designed listing of legislation that had cleared the Committee, together with supporting documents, committee mark-ups with amendment language and votes; it also provided an upcoming schedule of meetings and legislation to be considered. Hearing transcripts were available, together with audio and video archives of past hearings.

Energy and Commerce set the standard for committee online communications. It was easy to use, filled with committee news, speeches, official letters sent to agency heads, mark-up actions, and an up-to-date document menu. In addition, all committee meetings and mark-up sessions were webcast.

House Republican Conference (GOP.gov)

The House Republican Conference website (GOP.gov) set the standard for leadership sites. It was extraordinarily rich in information and billed itself as the online clearinghouse for Republican news.[40] The Congress Online Project characterized this site as setting standards "so high that it is clearly unmatched in Congress."[41] GOP.gov provided a central clearinghouse for Republican information on every bill that would be considered on the floor of the House, including the bill's status, background, cost estimates, press releases, and other information. The site index was particularly impressive: at a glance were the names, titles, and hyperlinks to all House leadership offices, the communication web pages of each of the committees together with links to each of the communication pages of all Republicans in the House, sorted by either name or by state.

The site could also be tailored to the interests and concerns of the visitor. Viewers can subscribe to one of many targeted e-mails that reach over 75,000 subscribers a year. News releases from most Republican Members were posted on GOP.gov as well. Further, viewers could follow daily and weekly floor briefings. These weekly floor briefings provided what GOP.gov considered to be an in-depth analysis of legislation that was scheduled for the week, including bill highlights, background information, cost estimates, arguments for and against controversial legislation, and other information.

The site also provided a section called "War on Terrorism: Homeland Security Central," which gave the Republican point of view on homeland security issues, press releases, summaries of legislation, reference materials, plus links to many useful executive branch sites dealing with terrorism threats. Many Republican individual Member offices had links to the War on Terrorism site in addition to many other products from GOP.gov. The site also had major issue sections on Social Security, national security, education, and tax relief issues.

The site provided a GOP.gov Dialogue, giving subscribers to GOP.gov (which could be anyone) a chance to ask a question, post a comment, or merely vent. It also contained a relatively new feature, Capitol Beat, a resource-rich web presence for Republican staff, featuring the Republican's message of the day, a search feature, quick and easy access to constituent letters, media guide, issues central, and daily and weekly floor briefings; there was also a Recess packet, with event ideas, and other activities so that Republicans can maximize their impact while back home.

What Is Not on Congressional Websites

The House of Representatives had set certain restrictions on what cannot be on a Member's website. Websites may not include political or campaign information, nor could they be connected to the websites of political parties. In May 1996, more than a dozen members of Congress were cited for using their websites to point to overtly political Internet sites, but since then, there have been few instances where this provision has been violated.

Websites also could not include grassroots lobbying or seek support for a Member's position, nor could the Member websites generate, circulate, solicit, or encourage the signing of petitions, although some Members had done this. The Member websites could not include any advertisement for a private individual, firm, or corporation, or imply that the government endorsed or favored specific commercial products or services. Further, when creating a URL name for the official website, it had to include "house.gov" and could not include a slogan, like "FightingTedSmith.house.gov."[42]

Senate Internet Usage Policy prohibited Senators from maintaining material that was purely personal and unrelated to official business activities on Member websites. Some Members come close to the line when they include biographical information about their family and folksy items about their favorite recipes or favorite stories. Also prohibited was any article or account which was complimentary or laudatory of a Senator on a purely political or personal basis, any reports on how and when a Senator, spouse or member of the family spent personal time, or any transmission of holiday greetings.[43]

Other material was not available on congressional websites because of congressional policy or the personal preference of individual Members or committee chairs. Working drafts of bills and amendments were usually unavailable, although enterprising lobbyists could obtain these, if not have a hand in drafting them. Also generally unavailable were chairmen's marks, the final version of the draft bill language used in committee. Working drafts were not posted to THOMAS, because current policy required THOMAS not to post an update until the text had been processed in final form by the Government Printing Office.[44]

Also missing were the transcripts and witness statements found in many congressional hearings. Some committees, especially in the Senate, have audio feeds, which could be downloaded through C-SPAN, and some post witness testimony and hearing remarks. THOMAS, the Library of Congress website, did provide transcripts of testimony, but it often took months for the information to become available online. Lobbyists, lawyers, and others who follow congressional activity closely could purchase such timely materials from private sources and have them available within hours. Those without the funds or unwilling to pay them simply have to wait. Newt Gingrich's 1994 declaration to have congressional information online "available to any citizen in the country at the same moment that it is available to the highest paid Washington lobbyist" was far from being fulfilled.

Since 1952, Congress has had exclusive control and custody of all Congressional Research Service (CRS) products. For several years, Congress had considered, but rejected, the idea of making all CRS reports available to the public. The expert research staff of the CRS publishes hundreds of reports each year, all for the benefit of Members of Congress. Members frequently gave away CRS reports to constituents who requested them, but, by and large, they were not widely known nor used by the public. A visit to the CRS website (www.crs.gov) would give citizens no help whatsoever. On the screen would appear the message that access was denied: "You are not authorized to view this page. HTTP Error 403—Forbidden." But access to CRS reports was not forbidden to all. Several private publishing firms obtain printed copies of CRS reports from Member offices and sell them to the public. In addition, former Members are permitted to obtain copies free of charge; these were quite valuable reference sources for the some 150 former Members who became lobbyists.

In 1998, the chairman of the Senate Rules Committee Senator John Warner (Republican-Virginia) and ranking member Wendell Ford (Democrat-Kentucky) made CRS products available over the committee's website and encouraged others to do the same. During the 108th Congress (2003–2004), however, no CRS reports were available through the Senate Rules and Administration Committee website, although there are well over 150 such reports posted on the House Rules Committee website. Several lawmakers, most notably Rep. Christopher Shays (Republican-Connecticut) and Senator Thomas Daschle (Democrat-South Dakota), have posted hundreds of CRS reports on their websites, making them available to the public. Probably one of the simplest reasons why lawmakers were reluctant to release all CRS reports to the public over a CRS or other congressional website was that they saw them as another little perk that they could give away to their constituents. In defense of that argument, Daniel P. Mulhollan, director of the CRS, argued that open access to CRS products would obstruct the Member-constituent relationship: "Wholesale direct dissemination of CRS products to the public would bypass this longstanding relationship by denying constituents the benefit of their Member's additional insights, party viewpoints, or regional perspectives on CRS analysis."[45]

Shays, who began making CRS reports available to the public in September 2000, together with Senators John McCain (Republican-Arizona) and Patrick Leahy (Democrat-Vermont) were lead sponsors of legislation to make CRS materials available to the public. This legislation, however, never made it out of committee.[46]

In conjunction with a report issued by the Project on Government Oversight which advocated release of CRS reports to the public, Senators McCain and Leahy, joined by Senator Tom Harkin (Democrat-Iowa), reintroduced a resolution in February 2003 to make CRS materials available to the public, and to have other selected documents, such as Member's receipt of honoraria and travel reimbursements on the Internet, as well as urge all committees to report bills, reports, and official transcripts of hearings available to the public over the Internet.[47]

Other important, public documents are not readily or quickly available to the public. All Members, officers, and staff of the House of Representatives must file with the Clerk of the House reports that detail their travel-related expenses reimbursed by non-government sources and charitable contributions made in lieu of honoraria. These Gift and Travel reports are public documents, but are only available from the House Legislative Resource Center in the Capitol itself, and not available online. The same policy applied to Legal Expense Fund disclosure forms; Franked Materials (mass mailings) forms; and Financial Disclosure forms for Members, officers, certain staff, and candidates for the House of Representatives. All of these public documents are available, but none can be viewed online and in real time. Nor can Lobby Filing Disclosure forms be viewed, other than in person at the House Legislative Resource Center. In the Senate, however, the viewer can go to the Senate home page (www.senate.gov) and download the lobbying disclosure forms from the Senate Office of Public Records, from 1998 to the present. The viewer can select the information by registrant name, client name, lobbyist name, amount reported, and date the lobbying information was posted. For 2002, for example, the viewer can see the fifteen organizations that spent more than $5 million for lobbying purposes, headed by the U.S. Chamber of Commerce, which spent $7,940,000. Another click will download the 230–page report filed by the Chamber of Commerce in July 2002.

Transparency certainly has its limits: Not everything that Congress does, or that individual Members say, should be made public. Matters of national security cannot be divulged, nor internal communications and confidential information between Members and their staff. Yet Congress has an obligation, as the people's legislative houses, to be as forthcoming as possible, and have available through online communication whatever it has made available to the public. As long as a committee hearing is open to the public, the information found at that hearing—the witness statements, a transcript of the questions and answers between lawmakers and witnesses—should be available to the widest possible audience. They should not be available just to those lawyers, lobbyists, and others who can crowd into a hearing room. If working documents—proposed amendments, working drafts of legislation, chairman's marks, and later committee reports—were available to the public, they should at the same time be made available online for everyone to view.

There should be no excuse for a policy stating that a public report would be available to the public, but could only be viewed physically at the House or Senate records offices or wait for them to be available through the Government Printing Office. If the information is made public, and available to the public, then it should be disseminated as widely as possible.

The bright light of transparency, of course, could lead to greater attempts at secrecy. Some civic groups have found that when all local city council meetings were forced to be held in the public, there was a heavy temptation on the part of council members to conduct the real business out of the public arena, in non-public, unofficial meetings, where no minutes were kept, and no record of decisions made. There was nothing to suggest that many of the decisions arrived at between lawmakers and lobbying interests would ever be open to the public or that records of such meetings would be kept; the most old-fashioned form of influence, words spoken (or even unspoken) between lawmakers and interested parties will never change. Hearings and official statements often were simply part of a larger choreographed set-piece between lawmakers (and their staff) and witnesses. Nevertheless, if information was available in any form to the public, it should be available to all. The information should be no more than a click or two away, should be easily retrievable even by the individual with little sophistication in mining the raw data of legislation.

Probably those who would take most advantage of such a transparency would be the well-connected lawyers and lobbyists themselves. They have been the greatest beneficiaries of the web casting of hearings, reports available online, and instant knowledge of legislative activity. But such information would also be available to a diligent press, those special interests that could not afford to have staffers or lobbyists watching over legislative activity and physically located in Washington, and the attentive public. C-SPAN has collected a curiously loyal following over the years—the "C-SPAN junkie"—viewers drawn to congressional debates, personalities, and legislative action. A Congress truly online, with real-time audio and video feeds of committee and subcommittee hearings and a full range of public documents and votes readily available, may be of little interest to the general public, but on specific issues and concerns, it could be a welcome information resource for both the curious and informed citizen.

A Congressional Portal

Both the House of Representatives and the Senate maintain their own public Internet sites. The House completely redesigned its website (www.house.gov) for the opening of the 108th Congress (January 2003), making it easier for constituents to use the Write Your Representative feature, expanding the search capabilities for Member, committee, and leadership information, and providing a convenient drop-down menu for Member and Committee websites. The House Information Resources web development team also added links to FirstGov.gov, the executive branch web portal, and made design features to provide visually and physically challenged individuals with better access to House.gov.[48]

House.gov provided easily found information on House floor and committee schedules, plus weekly and annual congressional calendars; it linked directly to a full-text, searchable version of the United States Code, voting information through the office of the Clerk of the House, links to THOMAS, and information about the legislative process. Further, the House site linked to all House committee and Member websites and gave multiple listings of lawmakers' addresses and committee assignments; it even provided downloadable mailing labels with Member addresses. (There was no such information, however, on committee or personal staff.)

The Senate official site, www.Senate.gov, provided much of the same information as the House website, but not as comprehensively or in the same easily accessible manner. Both the House and the Senate gave ample information for tourists and guests, but especially attractive for students and tour groups was the Senate's virtual tour of the Senate side (only) of the Capitol building. Viewers could see a floor plan of the Senate side, plus five key locations, the National Statuary Hall, the old Senate chamber, the old Supreme Court chamber, the President's room, and the current Senate chamber. Each of these virtual tours had a 360 degree panoramic display of the rooms, together with information about the history of each room, the artwork contained in them, and the historical events that occurred there.[49] The Senate website has a much stronger connection with its history and works written about the Senate than did the House.

While both the Senate and particularly the House provide very useful material on their institutional websites, the first time viewer would have difficulty finding an official site devoted simply to Congress as an institution. A logical place for viewers to go, searching for a U.S. Congress portal would be www.congress.gov. This, however, was the website of the Legislative Information System (LIS), the internal legislative data system for use only by staff and lawmakers. Constituents clicking on www.congress.gov would be taken directly to THOMAS, the public legislative data website found at http://loc.gov/thomas. A further search would take the viewer to Capitol Advantage's website (www.congress.org) or to the House of Representatives home page (www.congress.com), or the Congressional Network (www.congress.net), another private site.

There is, however, no portal website for the entire Congress, which would give the viewer an overview of both the House and Senate, the committees, personal offices, administrative offices, and services. FirstGov.gov has attempted to do this for the much larger and much more complex federal executive branch, and its aim was to provide information easily, quickly, with a user-friendly portal page that offered needed information with no more than three clicks. Under its section called Online Services for Citizens, individuals could click on sections for Online Tax Filing, Disaster Help, Student Loans, INS Case Status, and many more categories. A congressional portal could do much the same: provide in easily accessible and understandable terms basic information about legislation and lawmaking, devoid of technical jargon and terminology. A portal site could, for example, be able to answer simple questions, with no more than two or three clicks: What laws were passed last year that dealt with elementary education? Which committees have jurisdiction over environment issues? How can I buy a souvenir paperweight from Congress? Senator Jones introduced some legislation dealing with campaign finance reform; is there a companion piece of legislation in the House?

Although the focus in Congress is on individual Members, committees, and leadership, there should be a central focal point, a congressional web portal that will help individuals, particularly those less familiar with legislative complexities and idiosyncracies, to navigate through the power centers and nooks and crannies of representative democracy. Many individual Member, committee and leadership websites provide extraordinary amounts of highly useful information. A congressional portal could draw that information together and provide that missing piece, a coherent first look at Congress as an institution.

PART

3

ONLINE
DEMOCRACY
AND
COMMUNICATION

Challenges and Opportunities

*Our mail looks like it's been dropped in the toilet
and dried in an oven.*
—Congressional staffer on irradiated mail

*It's ridiculous that we can't have laptops on the House floor . . .
It would make things run that much more efficiently.*
—Rep. Jesse Jackson, Jr. (Democrat-Illinois)

Spending More Time in the District

any Members of Congress spend an increasing number of hours commuting back and forth between their home, district offices, and Washington. Life for lawmakers has become far more peripatetic, with many, especially in the House, choosing not to move their families to Washington, instead bunking down in a studio apartment or sharing a frat-house arrangement with other legislators, and coming home as soon and as often as possible. A growing number of legislators have been keeping close to home, emphasizing constituent services and personal meetings with individuals and groups. All this is time-consuming, grueling, but necessary, work.[1]

Legislators also have increased the number of district-based staff dedicated to assisting constituents. Stephen E. Frantzich observed that in the late 1970s, less than 10 percent of congressional staffs were in district offices; by the mid-1990s, around 40 percent of congressional staff worked in district offices.[2] Fifteen years ago, a congressional office may have had a total of fifteen staffers, with five in the district offices and ten in Washington; by 2003, seven or eight of those fifteen staffers were in the district. Some 97 percent of all congressional caseworkers work in district offices.[3] Casework has been growing over the past several years, with 53 percent of the House offices and 42 percent of Senate offices receiving between 1,000 and 5,000 cases each year, and nearly a third of the Senate offices reporting more than 7,500 cases annually.[4]

This shift to the district offices has been smoothed by technology. The telephone has always been central to instant communications, and by the mid-1980s, a new generation of fax machines had been developed and Washington offices were then able to receive from their district offices newspaper clippings, messages and reports each morning. This modest technological advance, followed by e-mail and the Internet meant that there could be an almost seamless flow of information between constituents, Washington, and district offices.

Thanks to technology, more resources can be pointed toward district offices. Congressional staff have direct access to federal agency documents, they can contact state and local officials more readily, and help constituents through a myriad of casework problems without resorting to assistance from a Washington source.

Technology has made it possible for legislators to stay in touch with organizations and constituents through video conferencing. It would never be a true substitute for being there in person, but video conferencing could certainly ease legislative multitasking. Members who could not visit with constituents back home during the middle of the week, or during a weekend crammed with other events, could turn to video conferencing, for at least a welcome from the Member, a few remarks, even for hours of video conference attendance. Artfully done, the lawmaker could communicate effectively with far more constituents. However, it could not turn into communications solely through the air waves: nothing replaces the personal touch, the handshake, the personal acknowledgment of friends at a meeting. The balance must always be weighed: personal touch versus efficiency of communication.

Access to Committee Hearings

In June 2000, a new for-profit business, HearingRoom.com, was launched, promising to provide over the Internet real-time audio and video streaming of committee hearings and those mark-up sessions that were open to the public. Founder Phil Angell planned to use voice-recognition software and the Internet to deliver near real-time information from committee hearings. Angell explained: "What this is really about is the speed of getting the information out. Media gets the info out like a jack rabbit, business like an antelope, yet Congress is a tortoise. We're creating a business that is like putting a jet pack on the turtle."[5] HearingRoom.com's plans were ambitious: to provide access to all of Congress's 192 committees and subcommittees, which share forty-four hearing rooms in the House and twenty-six in the Senate. This private service came at a price: $1,000 per hearing, discounted to $150 per hearing for bulk users. Transcripts with audio links would be available in several hours after the hearings, at a cost of $500, and dropped to $250 for next-day service. For corporations, law firms, and trade associations, with sometimes millions of dollars riding on the language of pending legislation, this seemed like a bargain: valuable information would be instantly available over the Internet.[6]

Gary Ruskin, director of the Congressional Accountability Project, a public-interest watchdog group affiliated with Ralph Nader, however, strongly disagreed. In a mass e-mail, Ruskin made his case: "Congressional hearings are public information. We taxpayers paid for these hearings. We ought to be able to read them, on the Internet, for free."[7]

HearingRoom.com paid to have all of the House hearing rooms wired for audio pickup (the Senate committee rooms were already wired). Two other services, Federal News Service and Federal Document Clearing House, sold transcripts of congressional hearings, but were not able to provide the instantaneous Internet reporting promised by HearingRoom.com. What seemed like a vital service for a decidedly niche market, however, lasted only until early 2002, when HearingRoom.com closed down.

In 2001, C-SPAN began offering CapitolHearings.org, a website which allowed citizens to listen to Senate hearings live online, without charge. The Senate produced the audio feeds from its twenty-six committee hearing rooms, and C-SPAN encoded and streamed the hearings via this website.[8]

The House Committee on Science was the first congressional committee to offer live web casts of its hearings. Further, the Committee on Science archived past hearings for users to view.[9] Some, but certainly not all, committees began offering web casts of their hearings. J. H. Snider found fourteen out of nineteen House committees having at least some of their activities online—usually prepared witness testimony, with full transcripts available later, sometimes up to a year later.[10] There is no central authority or policy requiring committees to make use of online technologies. The decision on priorities of communication, funds expended, commitment to transparency, and commitment to using the Internet rest with the majority party, and is primarily in the hands of the chairman and senior staff. Some committees, like the House Energy and Commerce Committee, have a high commitment to online communication, while others are much less enthusiastic.

60-Day Rule

Senate internal rules require that official websites cannot be updated within sixty days before an election. The Senate rule prohibited use of web pages for "personal, promotional, commercial or partisan political/campaign purposes." The Senate *Ethics Manual* stated

> During the 60-day period immediately preceding the date of any primary or general election (whether regular, special, or runoff) for any national, state or local office in which the Senator is a candidate, no Member may place, update or transmit information using a Senate Internet Server . . . unless the candidacy of the Senator in such election is uncontested.[11]

In 2002, the 60-day rule presented something of a communications disadvantage for Senator Tim Johnson (Democrat-South Dakota), who was in a pitched re-election battle against Republican House Member John Thune. Senator Johnson was required, under Senate rules, to make no changes whatsoever on his official website from April 3 until June 4, 2002, because he faced an opponent in the Democratic primary. Representative Thune, who did not have a primary opponent, was under no such restriction because the House did not have a similar 60-day rule. The Senate rule, put in place in 1996 when websites were in their infancy, basically followed the rule for mass mailings—that Senators could not flood mailboxes with mass mailings sixty days before an election.[12]

Even further, Senators were prohibited during the months of September and October in congressional elections from posting information on their official websites that might be construed as helping a colleague get re-elected. The Senate ethics rule, also developed in 1996, stated:

During the 60-day period immediately before the date of a biennial general Federal election, no Member may place or update on the Internet Server any matter on behalf of a Senator who is a candidate for election, unless the candidacy of the Senator in such election is uncontested.[13]

Only when a Senator was unopposed in a primary, or in the far less likely event, in a general election, could the official website be changed. Senator Wayne Allard (Republican-Colorado), like other Senators, posted prominently on the homepage of his website: "U.S. Senate Internet Services Usage Rules and Policies prohibit the Senator's website from being updated 60 days prior to any state assembly, primary or general election. This site will be updated after the Colorado State Assembly, July 1, 2002."[14]

One of the problems that the 60-day moratorium created was that a congressional website might look stale if it is not changed and updated. To get around the problem of a homepage looking static for 60 days, or in some cases, 120 days, some inventive offices, like Senator Tom Harkin's (Democrat-Iowa), randomly recycled previously posted material.[15]

No one knows how much difference it would make to have updated official business available on a congressional website. In the Johnson-Thune senate race, the margin of victory for Senator Johnson was a bare 528 votes out of 337,506 cast. In such razor-thin elections, any variable, even the 60-day ban, could come into play.

House of Representatives rules stated that Members cannot send mass mailings, that is, more than 500 pieces in a single Congress, of "substantially identical material" 90 days before *any* election for *any* public office in their state. This ban, however, was modified in late 2003 to permit House Members to continue sending e-mails to constituents who had agreed to subscribe to their e-mail lists.[16]

Ari Schwartz, of the Center for Democracy and Technology, argued that the Senate Rule viewed congressional websites as one-dimensional: "It seems that the Senate views the web only for self-promotion rather than ongoing and interactive communication between elected officials and constituents." "Imagine," Schwartz argued, "if the panel put forward a rule forbidding senators and staff members from using the Senate phones within 60 days of an election for fear of campaigning."[17]

Websites for Members of Congress are meant to convey official business only; they are not meant to be vehicles for re-election. For that purpose, lawmakers rely on campaign websites, which are built, maintained, and funded by campaign contributions, not taxpayer monies. Further, they may have no link to the official congressional sites. Campaign websites have no such 60-day rule and their sole purpose is to help the candidate get elected.

A Congressional Chief Information Officer

As seen in Chapter 3, there had been considerable discussion over the creation of a cabinet-level officer, a federal CIO, to oversee the management and technology of the executive branch. The E-Government Act, signed into law in December 2002, established the office of Administrator for the Office of Electronic Government, in the Office of Management and Budget. A number of lawmakers had wanted to create a more high-profile position, both for the executive branch and a similar position for the Congress.

The House of Representatives relied on the Committee on House Administration for internal technology issues. House Administration oversaw the work of the office of the Chief Administrative Officer (CAO), which was responsible for maintaining and upgrading the technology infrastructure in the House. The Senate equivalent was the Sergeant at Arms office. The Chief Administrative Officer had offered major technology initiatives in a comprehensive multi-year blueprint and various pilot projects. In this sense, the Chief Administrative Officer and House Administration have been trying to push for new technology, while a number of Members, especially new and younger legislators have been calling for more improvements.[18]

State governments have taken the lead in creating cabinet level CIOs; by March 2001, twenty-five states had CIOs in place who reported directly to the governor, and twenty-four states had CIOs who reported to a staff, legislative, or cabinet-level officer.[19] If there were to be a CIO for the House or Senate, or even more boldly, for the entire Congress, it would require several things, according to David L. McClure, the Director of Information Technology Management Issues, at the U.S. General Accounting Office.[20] It would require the full cooperation of the House and Senate. This would not be an easy thing to accomplish, given the history and cultures of the two bodies, and their unwillingness to share information. In addition, the CIO would have to have high standing within the Congress, reporting to leadership in both the House and Senate. The office would need to have institutional credibility to come up with short and long range solutions and recommendations, and be taken seriously as the central source in the legislative branch. The CIO must be able to measure results, changes, and accountability and there would have to be a focus on meeting congressional needs, not just satisfying technology demands. Finally, there would have to be attention paid to human capital, with the mandate to recruit, train, and retain a competent workforce.

Communicating after September 11th and Anthrax

Handheld Wireless Technology

A year before the September 11th terrorist attacks, the Committee on House Administration considered distributing handheld wireless e-mail units to lawmakers and senior staff; the committee decided to wait, however, following the advice from technology experts, before recommending wholesale purchase of these devices. Many staffers and some Members, however, were already sporting BlackBerry wireless e-mail units, developed by Research in Motion, Ltd. (RIM), a Canadian technology firm. When the terrorists hit, Representative Robert Ney (Republican-Ohio), chair of the Committee on House Administration, with a BlackBerry strapped to his belt, found that the only way he was able to communicate with his family and staff was through this wireless e-mail system. Ney, whose committee was responsible for overseeing the physical security of the Capitol, promptly ordered BlackBerry units, one for each of the Members of Congress and for senior staff. The committee's then-technology director, Reynold Schweickhardt, stated that the BlackBerry program was "an effort to seed the House with Members who would use the technology" and influence others. Immediately following the October 15, 2001 anthrax attack in Senator Daschle's office in the Hart Senate Office Building, and the evacuation of six congressional office buildings, BlackBerrys were widely used for basic communication needs.[21] "The response has been dynamic," noted Chairman Robert Ney, "BlackBerrys are the thing on the Hill now."[22] By January 2003, Congress had invested nearly $6 million in Black-Berry technology, including distributing 3,000 handsets to lawmakers and their senior staff in both chambers.[23]

The wireless e-mail units have been invaluable for staff and lawmaker communication, both for emergencies and for routine business. BlackBerrys have added another, perhaps unintended, level of communication. Members, sometimes barely able to pay attention during lengthy or tedious committee hearings, would e-mail their offices, telling staff that they were bored and wanted something to do; staffers watching floor debates could e-mail their bosses that another lawmaker had just said something from the podium that was factually wrong and here were the correct figures; or a Member over in one corner of the House floor could e-mail another Member fifty feet away to tell her how idiotic he thought the last speaker was. The Congress is indeed a gregarious institution and handheld wireless units made it just that much easier to add another level of communication.

Until January 2003, House rules stated that there were to be no electronic devices on the floor of the House. Members were not supposed to have their BlackBerrys, cell phones, or pagers turned on. But they did, often surreptitiously, fearing the disapproving glare of the Speaker of the House. For some, it was like giving school boys a secret way to communicate with each other without the teacher finding out. When it first convened as the 108th Congress, in January 2003, the House adopted a rule that officially permitted legislators to use Palm Pilots and other PDAs, pagers, and BlackBerrys on the House floor; but not cell phones and laptops.

By the end of 2002, about 100 Members of the House still had not adapted the BlackBerry as a communication tool. This number undoubtedly will dwindle, with newer and younger Members coming into the chamber, and with the technological advances and the eventual ordinariness of handheld devices.[24]

Irradiated Mail and Digitized First-Class Mail

By mid-summer 2002, Congress had still not fully recovered from the anthrax attack of October 15, 2001. The Senate Hart Office Building, four House Member offices and the first floor of the auxiliary Ford building were displaced by the anthrax attack for fifteen weeks, not opening until late January 2002. As a preventative measure after October 15th, all pieces of incoming postal mail addressed to ZIP codes that began with 202, 203, 204, and 205 (serving only the federal government in Washington) were sent to irradiation facilities in Bridgeport, New Jersey, run by Ion Beam Applications, Inc., or to another facility in Lima, Ohio, owned by Titan Corporation. Roughly 300,000 to 350,000 pieces of mail a day had to be irradiated.[25] Several more days were needed to fumigate the mail; it would eventually arrive at congressional offices after a two-week delay. Before anthrax, mail on the average took five days to be processed. Once the irradiated mail reached the intended congressional office, much of it had deteriorated dramatically: paper became like parchment or was fried to a crisp, some of it smelled, and some pieces literally disintegrated when staffers tried to open them. Further, the irradiated mail was making postal workers and congressional staffers sick. There were reports of nausea, rashes, headaches, and a metallic taste that pervaded the air. Four months after the anthrax attack on the Capitol, at least 104 Hill staffers reported suffering adverse reactions to the irradiated mail.[26]

In the House, delivery of first-class mail and flats resumed in early

December 2001; and delivery of packages from national shippers resumed on a limited basis in early January 2002, and was limited to packages from known sources.[27] The delays were unsettling. Mail sent to the House and arriving on April 30, 2002, had been postmarked on the average 121 days earlier.[28] Even in the most efficient of congressional offices, it would take another three days to a week to process and answer incoming mail. Tests had revealed that sixty-five bags of mail (out of 572) were contaminated by anthrax-tainted letters mailed to Senators Tom Daschle and Patrick Leahy.[29]

Following the anthrax scare, many Hill staffers who normally handled the incoming mail were undoubtedly relieved to handle only e-mail, faxes, or telephone calls. Further, constituents, afraid of what they were hearing about Washington's vulnerability, were probably just as relieved to receive an e-mail from their Representative rather than a letter. Reynold Schweickhardt stated that the first priority was to get first-class mail up and running again, figure out how to handle boxes and packages, and then examine how to present hard mail in electronic form.

Pitney Bowes Management Services, a division of Pitney Bowes, Inc., managed roughly 1,300 mail rooms for corporate and other clients worldwide, also had been handling all incoming, outgoing, and internal mail processing for the House of Representatives since February 1996.[30] In 1998, the House Inspector General issued a report recommending that Pitney Bowes, in conjunction with the Capitol Police, develop an overall security and disaster recovery/contingency plan; the focus of that plan, however, was unauthorized access and destruction of mail, rather than biological tampering.[31]

Mail received by Congress was unique, and the House of Representatives was a most unusual client. Instead of a unified corporate structure, with fixed mail procedures and office protocols, the House of Representatives was comprised of 435 separate personal offices plus many other administrative, leadership, and committee offices, and each with its own demands and schedules. Furthermore, the mail going to the House or Senate was much less secure than that going to corporate clients or even to private individuals, according to David T. Nassef of Pitney Bowes. From Pitney Bowes figures, 83 percent of mail coming into corporate mail rooms or private homes was secure, because it is pre-postmarked, while in Congress 90 percent was not secure, because it was usually sent in an envelope or package using postage stamps, at times without a return address. Pitney Bowes noted that metered mail was "far more secure" than stamped or permit mail because of the meter identification number on each piece, which was traceable to the location, even the specific floor of a building. As a Pitney Bowes report noted, "Terrorists sending hazardous mail content have used stamps, which are the postal equivalent of cash."[32]

Private industry had accepted digitized mail for many years, primarily to improve efficiency rather than enhance security. Insurance companies, for example, with complicated forms and information now use digitized mail, because they need to process each item quickly, efficiently, and in a cost-effective manner.

In late summer 2002, a dozen lawmaker and committee offices volunteered for a pilot program to have their incoming mail electronically scanned, then delivered to them online.[33] Private contractors would receive the unopened, non-irradiated mail, and within 24 hours would scan the contents and send digitized files to the House computer network. Staffers would then download the mail addressed to their offices. Under the pilot program, the physical letters would be subject to decontamination and quarantine before eventually being delivered to the respective House offices.[34]

While promising greater security and efficiency, the idea of digitizing mail worried some lawmakers and their staffs. Foremost was the concern that someone other than the legislator's staff assistants would be opening mail, and sensitive materials or personal information would be opened by a private vendor before being digitized. Vendors answered that all this was done on a rapid mechanical basis, with no snooping on the part of employees wanting to see what people were writing to their legislators. Written into the request for bids by the House chief administrative officer was a requirement that the vendor provide a secure environment for mail processing with procedures to protect against unauthorized disclosure of information.[35]

Another matter concerned one of the most popular requests made to legislators' offices, the ordering of an American flag to be flown over the Capitol. Often those requests were accompanied by personal checks. Certainly this problem has been long ago solved by private companies who sold items online; eventually Congress would resolve these internal issues through electronic means as well.

House and Senate officials decided in February 2002 that packages from FedEx, UPS, and other shippers could not be delivered directly to House and Senate office buildings for safety considerations. The packages would have to go to an offsite facility of Pitney Bowes, before being sent to a laboratory for testing for anthrax and other biological agents. This added at least another three days to services that specialized in the overnight market niche. Some congressional offices tried to work around this by having packages sent to the homes of staffers, even though this was being strongly discouraged by congressional officials.[36]

Digital Information

In 1995, the House approved the distribution of laptop computers to all new Members.[37] The computers would give newly-elected lawmakers access to congressional Intranet information so they could keep up on legislative activity during the two months between their election and taking the oath of office. This sounded promising, but Congress forgot to tell the new Members-to-be that they could not take those same laptops to the floor of either the Senate or the House of Representatives. On the first day of the 104th Congress (January 1995), with all its promises of a CyberCongress and third-wave high-tech paradigms, the House of Representatives amended its internal rules adding a new set of prohibitions: "Neither shall any person be allowed to . . . use any personal, electronic office equipment (including cellular phones and computers) upon the floor of the House at any time." When printed in the *Congressional Record*, the analysis section explained why the change was made: "It is the purpose of this new rule to avoid the disruptions and distractions that can be caused by the sounds emitted from such equipment." On the floor, there was neither debate nor discussion of this provision.[38]

In the Senate, the corresponding rule stated that "The sergeant at arms shall be authorized to admit into the Senate chamber such mechanical equipment and/or devices which, in the judgment of the sergeant at arms, are necessary and proper in the conduct of the official Senate business and which by their presence shall not in any way distract, interrupt or inconvenience the business of members of the Senate." Senate Sergeant at Arms Gregory Casey in 1997 noted that this regulation could be justification for allowing notebook computers for taking notes, but not to be connected to the outside world.[39]

In 1997, freshman Senator Mike Enzi (Republican-Wyoming) wanted to bring his laptop onto the Senate chamber. While he was a state senator in Wyoming, Enzi had used a laptop during four legislative sessions. He had come to rely on his laptop to write speeches, take notes, write down issues during debate, and look up documents. He relied on it in Wyoming because as a state senator there, he had no staff to help him out.

Casey studied the matter for three months then told the Senate Rules and Administration Committee that the use of laptops did not violate current Senate rules provided they were not networked to computers outside of the chambers (such as linked to a lobbyist's e-mail). But in the Senate, where electronic voting still does not exist, traditions die hard. Senator Dianne Feinstein (Democrat-California) spoke against Enzi's request: "Most people wouldn't allow their sons or daughters to bring their laptops to the dinner table." In rejecting Enzi's request, Senator Wendell Ford (Democrat-Kentucky), allowed that he did not want to "be an old fogy" or appear to be "standing in the way of progress and technology," but he had determined that Enzi's request was "a little ahead of its time." The other members of the Rules Committee agreed.

In 1997, two-thirds of the state legislatures were online, with lawmakers furnished with laptops or PCs.[40] In 2002, Senator Enzi tried again: He understood the question of Senate decorum, in fact, he once offered to cover his notebook in mahogany. His bigger concern, however, was in doing his job more efficiently. "During the closure of the Senate office buildings [in late 2001] . . . if we could have then taken those notebook computers on the floor, we would have had access to all that information right at our fingertips as the Senate continued its legislative work," he argued.[41] In the Senate some traditions die hard, and neither Enzi nor any other senator has laptop access on the floor.

In the House, there might have been the logistical problem of where to put the laptops, since there are no individually assigned desks, such as found in the Senate, although there are long tables available for the respective floor managers. Perhaps by the time the laptop issue is resolved, technology will have passed it by, and handheld wireless devices, the now ubiquitous Black-Berry or its next generation, would make the issue moot.

While both chambers of Congress prohibit the use of laptop computers, some state legislatures, at first reluctantly, then enthusiastically, have embraced computer access in their chamber. Indiana was the first state legislature to install computers, in 1994.[42] By 1999, when Representative David Dreier (Republican-California) held the third of his hearings on the 21st Century Congress project, twenty-nine state legislatures were already offering laptop access in their chambers, and by 2002, forty-two chambers in thirty-eight state legislatures had laptops or personal computers installed.

By 1999, lawmakers in the Nevada state legislature were able to use their laptops anywhere within the legislature building, using a powerful FM wireless system.[43] Nevada lawmakers were now on their third generation of laptops, and according to Allan Smith, information systems manager, only one of the sixty-three legislators had turned back his latest version wireless IBM ThinkPad.[44] It was not simply having laptops available, but what could be accessed from them. In Nevada, the laptops have access to the Internet, all bills, amendments, resolutions, the state's bill tracking system, e-mail from the public, access to other legislators, the word processing from their own staff, and specialized reports.

In Minnesota, virtually all legislators use laptops. State Representative Gene Pelowski recalled how he was able to use his laptop while in the House chamber, fire off a couple of e-mails to local firefighter groups, and then download their answers, and use that information in floor debates about pending legislation. He observed, "It's very rare now when we're going in for hours at a time where people don't bring [their laptops.]"[45]

Allowing Members to receive e-mail on the floor from outside lobbyists, however, might run up against the House prohibition against lobbying on the House floor and would undoubtedly meet with resistance in the Senate.[46]

Learning from State Legislatures

Despite the improvements made in online communication in recent years, Congress can still learn from others. One place to turn is to state legislatures. Interest in citizen online access to legislative materials goes back to the time when the Internet was in its infancy. One of the first to understand this was Debra Bowen, a newly-elected member of the California State Assembly, who in 1993 introduced a bill that would require an account of bills introduced, votes taken, committee analyses, debates and other legislative matters to be posted on the Internet by the close of each legislative business day. Further, her bill directed the Office of Legislative Counsel to make available online the California constitution, state code, and daily floor schedule and committee agendas. Bowen's legislation was signed by Governor Pete Wilson, making California the first state to offer much of its legislative information free of charge over the Internet.[47]

California and other state legislatures began posting current public information on the Internet and creating websites for their institutions and for individual lawmakers. State legislature websites were going through many of the growing pains experienced by congressional websites. OMB Watch, a Washington-based non-partisan organization, surveyed state legislature websites and online communication in late 2000, and gave a decidedly mixed review.[48] It found that while 92 percent of the legislative websites provided contact information for legislators, only 12 percent provided the means to address concerns directly to leglislators online. OMB Watch also found that more than half of the states provided no information on legislative calendars, committee or floor schedules, or a legislative session report. Most of the state legislatures provided information on majority and minority leadership, but not the oversight, ethics, or legislative branch research bodies. Further, OMB Watch found that no state provided clearly identifiable compliance with commonly accepted web accessibility design principles for those with disabilities.

Since that report, several pioneering state legislatures have made it easy and convenient for citizens to learn about state government. The National Conference of State Legislatures noted that seventeen states offered streaming video of their legislative proceedings, with fourteen states offering audio-only webcasts. The state of Louisiana encouraged citizen comments for cutting wasteful spending in the state budget; Florida provided a free service to monitor activities and performance of 300 state agencies and programs. Minnesota provided streaming video describing legislative rules and processes.[49]

The Nevada state legislature invited the public to register their yes or no on bills that were being considered.[50] For the 71st Session (2002), there were a total of 35,402 opinions registered by the public on a list of bills that was thirty-nine pages long. Most bills had only a small handful of citizens registering their "vote," but two pieces of pending legislation on changing public employee retirement benefits received over 2,500 votes each, and a bill to recognize reciprocal beneficiary relationships had a total of 4,133 votes recorded, with the great majority against the legislation. None of these electronic tallies had any binding effect on the state legislature nor was there any pretense that the opinions represented the entire citizenry, but it gave legislators a sense of which issues were of interest to the attentive public.

The Texas Legislature, through its Texas Legislature Online (TLO), provided an easy-to-use format for tracking legislation, including a personal bill list, searching legislation by using a general subject index, or popular name, or bill geared to a certain location in the state. TLO gave an easily understood glossary of legislative terms, explaining "adjournment sine die," "ex officio," "Supplemental House Calendar," and "voice vote" along with many other legislative terms. It also provided a comprehensive listing of all legislative events for the day, providing monthly calendars, schedules, and links to the House and Senate Chamber broadcasts.[51]

Nebraska had its Blue Book, the official reference manual, available online, while the New Jersey Legislature invited citizens to register online to testify at one of the joint public hearings of the Senate Budget and Appropriations Committee and the Assembly Budget Committee on the proposed state budget.[52]

Florida State Senate Website

The award-winning Florida State Senate website[53] offered an interesting contrast to those found in Congress. This website combined the virtues of simplicity and uniformity with rich content. The clean homepage served as a portal, making it an excellent overview of what appeared in the rest of the website: links to each senator, committees, publications, session summaries, budget requests, bill text and search capability; it also had links to frequently-asked-questions, legislative employment, lobbyist information, material for children, video of the sessions, and publications and subscriptions. Further, there were links to the Florida House of Representatives, the state executive agencies, and Florida laws, statutes, and constitution.

One of the interesting features was the uniform design of the web pages. The Senators' pages all looked the same and had the same content categories. Consequently, Senators were neither vying against each other for the best looking site nor were they embarrassed for not having relevant or up-to-date information. In the upper left hand corner of each Senator page was a simple, dignified official picture of the Senator (no pictures of the lawmaker kissing babies or dressed in fishing gear holding up his catch). Underneath the picture was a link to all legislation sponsored and cosponsored by that lawmaker. Immediately below was complete contact information: capitol office, district office, address, telephone, and e-mail. Then came a feature rarely seen on congressional websites: a list of staff assistants who work for the Senator.

Many Members of Congress fail to mention their party affiliation or bury it somewhere in their biographical statement. The Florida state Senators have their party affiliation uniformly listed on their Member page, right below the name of the district each represents. Also, each Senator's page had a link to a map, showing where the district was located, another feature seldom seen in congressional websites.

Directly below the district information was a listing of committee member-ships, with links to each of those committees. Each committee page was also uniform in design and features, with a link to each of the committee members, the committee staff, current calendar, and a helpful link to information called "Learn how the Committee Process Works." The biographical section provided space to list legislative service (prior elected service, when elected to the Senate), affiliations (such as membership in service organizations), then occupation, education, date of birth, religious affiliation, and recreational activities. None of this was unusual, but the contrast with congressional sites was striking: Every Florida Senator had bare-bones information, there were no lengthy, self-serving statements or biographical flourishes. On the other hand, standardization and uniformity can be fairly boring. The Florida Senators are not given the chance to present themselves creatively or go beyond the bounds of the standardized web page template.

At the bottom left hand corner of each Senator page was a link to "Effective Communication with your Legislator," which spelled out in simple language the importance (indeed responsibility) of participating in the democratic process. The page gave general tips on how to write effective letters to lawmakers, with simple, but solid information on how to communicate, how to address lawmakers, correspondence courtesy and other information.

Another part of the Florida State Senate website contained detailed and searchable information on lobbyists. The information went back to the 1999 legislative session, covered both legislative and executive lobbyists, and could be accessed by name, location, and by principal lobbyist. Selected at random was Fred W. Baggett; his address and telephone number were given along with the five organizations which listed him as principal lobbyist. There was a hyperlink to each of these organizations; the viewer could then tell who else was hired to lobby for those organizations. The "location" link let the viewer know that fifteen lobbyists registered for the 2003 session were based in Atlanta, Georgia; and there was a link to each one of those lobbyists. There was an alphabetical listing of all organizations who have hired lobbyists and links to those lobbyists. Lobbyists and others could also use this website to find registration and other required forms, view a directory of lobbyists, plus guides to legislative and executive branch lobbying.

Those who want to know the latest information about Florida legislation could check Senate (or House) bills, by number or title; this information was clearly spelled out, and easy to understand. The information went back to the 1997 session. This legislative data was not as comprehensive as that found in the Library of Congress website, THOMAS, but it was far easier to understand and to use. Further, the viewer could read the summary reports and materials, from each of the standing committees and from the Senate as a whole, going back to the 1997 session. All of these materials were easily accessible, as PDF files, from one page.

Congress can go much further in using online technologies to benefit the essential communication between citizens and representatives. It can look to the best examples from state legislatures, which have incorporated computing portability, wireless technology, and other devices to assist legislators conducting business. It can further look at the degree of transparency and ease of use that appears in the best of state legislative website communications. Congress can also turn to the best examples of federal, state, and local government website design and implementation to incorporate best practices for communicating with the public.

However, all this has to be balanced with the central understanding that electronic technologies, no matter how sophisticated, time-saving, or efficient, are just one set of tools among many, needed to communicate with the various audiences of the legislative branch.

Congress and the Deliberative Process

We should keep in mind, first and foremost, that Congress literally means 'a coming together,' and if you lost that you will lose the very essence of our representative and deliberative democracy.

—Donald R. Wolfensberger

Let's push technology to the limits. Envision a true virtual Congress where our legislators live in their home districts and engage in polemic video conferences, proselytizing and pontificating in front of snazzy 21-inch flat-panel monitors, their every twitch recorded by a motion-detecting video camera.

—David Fine

ongress is now in its third decade of using advanced technology to improve its internal operations, speed up communications, ease the burdens of increasing workloads, and better connect with constituents and the outside world. Each of the new technology systems employed by Congress has required some initial adjustment, but now have become natural and settled features of legislative life. For a long time, Congress was reluctant to televise its proceedings; many Members were averse to giving out their fax machine numbers or their e-mail addresses; and many were slow to appreciate the communications value of the Internet and websites. While the pace of change and acceptance has been at times slow and haphazard, Congress, as an institution, and individual lawmakers are coming to appreciate far more than before the value of online communications.

Lawmakers, many of whom initially were reluctant to do so, are now sporting BlackBerry portable e-mail devices next to their electronic pagers. Some are urging rule changes to permit laptop computers and other electronic devices onto the chamber floors. Lawmakers have climbed a steep learning curve, and have carved out a whole new field of public policy in electronic communications; some have become expert in this field, and many now can at least understand the issues and language. The Congressional Internet Caucus was created to give lawmakers basic training in electronic communications issues; membership now tops 160 Members. There has been a marked improvement in the quality and content of congressional websites. While there still are holdouts—lawmakers who have little familiarity with the Internet and its potential—there are no certified electronic Luddites roaming the halls of Congress. If Members are unsure of themselves in this growing field of electronic communication, staff are not. They have for the most part embraced electronic communication wholly and enthusiastically, as a matter of convenience and efficiency in their own work, but also as a matter of survival in coping with the demands of their work and those of their constituents.

The online communications plans announced at the start of the 104th Congress were perhaps overly optimistic, too ambitious, and too full of enthusiasm. They were launched during the go-go days of the dot.com revolution and swept along with the hype associated with it. The challenges facing an increasingly electronic Congress were formidable. There was above all a necessary, but difficult, cultural shift: Newt Gingrich and his allies in the House were trying to undo the operational norms of secrecy, decisions made behind closed doors, and information closely held. The new emphasis on transparency was an extraordinary change, and many lawmakers—both Democrats and Republicans—were reluctant to shed light on their activities. Gingrich's mandate to make documents and information available to the public at the same time they were obtainable by high-paid Washington lobbyists was a revolutionary, and lofty, goal.

There has been much progress in making information more readily available, thanks to C-SPAN, the Internet, and e-mail, but Gingrich's mandate has still to be realized. Many documents and transcripts are available to any citizen with access to a computer, printer, and the knowledge of how to obtain them. But many key items, like real-time transcripts of committee hearings, were available for hefty fees—only to those law firms and interests who could afford such add-on services. There is considerable distance to go before committee hearings, reports, and transcripts are available the way Gingrich envisioned them; and certainly miles to go before chairman's marks and committee mark-up language are available. Some lawmakers will insist that these are internal, working documents, that necessarily must be kept private while the committee or subcommittee deliberates. That position is sound, provided it is adhered to. But when internal working documents, such as these, are shared with a handful of interested outside parties, giving them the advantage of knowing the committee's thinking, and helping themselves in shaping the content and debate, then the spirit of the Gingrich mandate is violated. If documents and information are available to one; they should be available to all. That point would only come when committees adopt internal rules that require all working documents, testimonies, and working legislation to be made available, free of charge in real time. If a committee is reluctant to release its internal documents because it feels that these are works in progress, then they cannot be released to anyone. This is a tough ask: no matter what the impulse toward transparency, there is too strong a pull toward pressure applied and decisions made behind closed doors, through sharing of confidential documents with favored interests, and conversations not recorded.

The technology infrastructure also had to be improved so that Congress could cope with advanced communication systems. Both the House and the Senate have spent billions of dollars on capital improvement aimed at improving the backbone of technology services. House Information Resources, the administrative office that supports much of the technology, has undergone a transformation during the past decade, improving in fits and starts, and now provides training, web design and templates, and hardware and software support for Washington and district offices to meet the challenges of communication. The Office of the Senate Sergeant at Arms similarly has gone through a technological transformation, resolving some of the most difficult issues of providing enough capacity and software to cope with the crush of e-mail. The remaining weak links in congressional online communication, however, are not rooted in antiquated software, slow servers, or inadequate infrastructure. They lie in the cultural reluctance to accept fully and integrate online communications; a lack of commitment; insufficient training; and a shortage of skilled personnel.

In this extraordinary Internet world, with so much information now available, constituents may find themselves both pleased and dismayed. They may be pleased to find at their fingertips information that, up until this point, was difficult, if not impossible to obtain: reports, documents, press releases, and links to other sites. From the best of congressional websites, citizens can sign up for electronic newsletters on subjects specifically of interest to them; they can view a Member's voting record and on the rare occasion can find out why the lawmaker decided to vote that particular way. They can find out when the lawmaker will be back in the home district, or follow the step-by-step process on how to obtain help from a federal agency. Citizens can also participate in online policy preference polls. Those polls have no scientific validity, but they do afford citizens the chance to voice their opinion. Websites can give a real-time audio and visual peek into the workings of committees, community meetings held in a lawmakers district, or addresses given by the Member. The best websites also perform an educational function, for both students and adults alike. Lawmakers recognize that they are doing more than simply casting votes and solving casework issues; they are also providing information for a whole new generation of students eager to learn about civic responsibility, American values and traditions, and the workings of democratic institutions.

Unfortunately, there is a long way to go and much that Congress still can do to promote online communication. One of the most important concerns is that information is simply too complicated. There is no central web portal for Congress, although there are separate Senate and House website portals, which can explain to citizens the basics of the immensely complicated world of Capitol Hill. Even the simplest question cannot be answered on the existing portal sites. When does Congress meet? What do the committees do? What does a Member do all day? I'm concerned about environmental clean-up of the Great Lakes; who handles that in Congress and what has been done recently? Private, media, and commercial sites that cover Congress do a far better job of explaining these simple questions than Congress itself.

Too often Member websites will direct visitors to THOMAS, the comprehensive legislative website created by the Library of Congress. THOMAS is quite useful, but it is cumbersome to use, difficult to navigate and, particularly for the first-time visitor, too daunting to be of any particular use. As one close observer of congressional technology put it, THOMAS "intentionally lacks public access to valuable information to which the public has a right."[1] Even professional Congress watchers, whose business is to keep up with the daily activities on the Hill, find THOMAS laborious to use.

Further complicating the issue is the sheer difficulty of navigating a website. Frequent Internet users might find congressional websites relatively effortless to navigate, but those who use the Internet less often or are intimidated by online communications, may find websites complicated, daunting, and simply too much to cope with. Successful web design means not only providing relevant, useful content, but also ease of use, with clearly understood directions and links.

From the pioneering studies done by the Congress Online Project, best practice standards have been established, benchmarks set, and congressional websites have been examined over a two-year period. The first-year results were not particularly hopeful, with very few congressional websites receiving what were considered A or B grades; by the next year, 2003, however, a full one half of the websites received those grades. This in itself was a remarkable turn-around, demonstrating a sea-change in thinking and understanding about web-based communications. Lawmakers became more committed to online communication, congressional staff learned much from other offices and could see what the best offices were doing, and many turned for help to outside vendors experienced in public communication.

The anthrax attack has led Congress to seriously consider a program of isolating and digitizing incoming mail, making such mail more readily accessible now in digital format, free of the risks of contamination, but losing much of its touch and personality. The handwritten letter on lined paper, the looping script on flower-lined stationery, or the heft of a letter printed on embossed corporate stationery—all these might be homogenized into a digital format. Much will depend on the success of pilot demonstration projects.

A Virtual Congress

Neither House, during the Session of Congress, shall, without the consent of the other, adjourn for more than three days, nor to any other place than that in which the two Houses shall be sitting.

—Article 1, Section 5, U.S. Constitution

September 11th and anthrax have led to larger issues, the most interesting of which is the idea of a "virtual Congress," where lawmaking activity is conducted while the lawmakers are not physically in Washington. Congress already has dipped its toe into "virtual" lawmaking activity. After Senator Trent Lott (Republican-Mississippi) famously put his foot in his mouth at Strom Thurmond's birthday party, Senate Republicans informally decided on their new leader and subsequently the Majority Leader of the Senate, by a conference call. Senators, scattered throughout the country and elsewhere, were connected by a telephone conference call to agree that Senator William Frist (Republican-Tennessee) would be their next leader. This, however, was unofficial—but highly serious—business; a party caucus, rather than a formal vote on the floor of the Senate. No one raised an issue with it, and it served the purpose of the Republican Senators to resolve the matter quickly and without the inconvenience of bringing them back to Washington.

Members of Congress have also been using telephone and video conferencing to connect with constituents back home. When a legislator cannot leave Washington because of voting or other responsibilities, it can become a convenient substitute to have a telephone or video conference hook-up with constituents assembled at a meeting. Representative Jo Ann Emerson (Republican-Missouri), for example, in 2000 used video conferencing to hook up with a seventh grade class in her congressional district to discuss Congress and civics education, and sent letters to each of the school superintendents in her district to determine if they had an interest in, and capability to, participate in such interactive video or Internet conferences.[2] Certainly, this long-distance relationship is a short-term solution; no Member of Congress would ever shift over to teleconferencing as a permanent solution to a busy calendar. Constituent groups want, and expect, the Member to be with them in person; they are often disappointed when a staffer shows up in the Member's stead, and feel there is no substitute for the legislator himself. Constituent relations are the life blood for a successful Member, form a part of the unofficial, unwritten, but absolutely vital function of a Member.

Another example of a "virtual Congress" is the use of video conferencing in official committee hearings. The first such was held in 1996, in conjunction with the House Rules Committee "21st Century Congress Project," and included witnesses participating long distance through video conferencing and allowed individuals to submit questions and comments through e-mail.[3] But Congress has been reluctant to push widespread use of video conferencing. As the Democratic Leadership Council has noted, Congress is "already a generation behind much of the private sector in using information technologies to conduct business in the absence of physical meetings."[4]

Congress may find that video conferencing has considerable potential in bringing witnesses, the public, and lawmakers closer together. It might be possible, even desirable, to have witnesses from around the world testify before a congressional panel while not being physically present. The federal judiciary has tried such an experiment, when, for probably the first time, a witness testified in early 2002 from Amman, Jordan, via a satellite link to a U.S. courtroom in Knoxville, Tennessee.[5] Such video conferencing, through broadcast equipment or through an Internet connection, could encourage more congressional witnesses to participate, without having to come to Washington. This was particularly true during the 2003 war with Iraq. L. Paul Bremer III, the top U.S. civil administrator in Iraq, for example, addressed a House committee and a Pentagon news conference by video phone from Baghdad in June 2003.[6]

The harder questions start coming, however, when lawmakers sitting on a full committee or subcommittee might want to vote remotely on a measure. The reasons for wanting to vote remotely certainly could be considered reasonable and plausible: The Member cannot physically be present for the vote at the subcommittee, or committee, because he is ill, missed a flight connection, had another important activity away from the Capitol, was attending another committee meeting at the time, and so forth. At one time, Members could have their committee votes recorded by using the proxy system. The subcommittee chairman, for example, would have the votes of absent Members in his pocket, and would present them as proxy votes. This led to having committees, with just a minimum number for a quorum, say seven Members present; twenty-five votes were recorded, eighteen of those by proxy. The Republican-controlled House of Representatives, under Newt Gingrich, banned proxy voting in the 104th Congress, while the Senate allows proxy voting in committees unless a committee adopts rules prohibiting such practice.[7]

September 11th seemed to have changed the mood of many Members. Rep David Dreier (Republican-California) noted in testimony in May 2002 that Congress had "closed the door on even limited trials" of remote voting, such as requests for remote committee attendance during a family medical emergency, "for the simple reason that this would invariably lead to pressures to widen the circumstances under which such requests are accepted."[8]

Terrorist threats and catastrophe scenarios have gotten lawmakers to do some serious thinking about the horrible circumstances. The U.S. Constitution permits state governors to appoint replacements for Senators who die in office; those newly appointed Senators serve out the term of office of the individual they replaced. That appointment may be within weeks, even days, of the death of the Senator. In the House of Representatives, a Member who has died is then replaced by a lawmaker chosen by special election, called by the governor, usually three or four months after the death. Arguing that the current system would take too long, especially if a catastrophic situation were to occur, Rep. Brian Baird (Republican-Washington) has proposed a constitutional amendment that would allow state governors to appoint temporary replacement legislators if more than a quarter of the Members of Congress were killed or incapacitated.[9]

If there were a catastrophe at the U.S. Capitol building complex, would it be better to have a system of online communication with Members far flung in their home districts, or for the Congress to meet physically at another location? In the wake of the anthrax attack, Members of Congress and scholars met at a panel discussion sponsored by the American Enterprise Institute in late 2002, ghoulishly entitled "What if Congress Were Obliterated?" and others have given serious thought to this question.[10]

During the Revolutionary War, the British army forced the Continental Congress to flee from Philadelphia. Congress and the White House both were burned in 1814, as Admiral George Cockburn's British forces captured Washington, forcing President Madison and Members of Congress to flee.[11] At the height of the Cold War, Congress developed elaborate plans to use a hidden bunker at the Greenbrier Resort in West Virginia as a place for lawmakers to be evacuated during an emergency. The knowledge that the United Airlines flight 93 which crashed in a field in Somerset County, Pennsylvania, on September 11th was most likely targeted to hit the U.S. Capitol (or the White House), focused lawmaker's attention on the reality of their vulnerability.

Rep. James Langevin (Democrat-Rhode Island) in the 107th Congress introduced two pieces of legislation dealing with such emergencies, one to require the National Institute of Standards and Technology (NIST) to investigate the feasibility and cost of implementing a computer system for remote voting and communication; the second directing the Comptroller General to join with the National Academy of Sciences to conduct a study regarding an emergency electronic communication system for Congress.[12] Both Baird and Langevin are newcomers to Congress, and their ideas and proposals, while important and timely, probably will not see the light of day, except when taken up by more senior lawmakers in their appropriate committee jurisdictions.

James H. Snider of the New America Foundation has argued for an electronic Congress, one that can meet remotely over the Internet in times of national emergency. One of his main concerns is security of Congress and the lawmakers, and his primary argument is "really quite simple: it's simply not prudent to put all your eggs in one basket."[13] Snider further has argued that among the positive effects of permitting remote voting and deliberation via the

Internet is that a remote Congress "would be a better documented and publicized" Congress, more so than ever in American history.

Another voice recommending that Congress seriously consider an electronic alternative is the Democratic Leadership Council (DLC). It has argued that we should begin thinking about an "electronic Congress," which would permit legislators to convene, hear testimony, and actually vote online. In a report, entitled "Legislating By Any Means Necessary,"[14] the DLC has argued that a website could easily be built to facilitate "virtually all of the business" normally conducted on the floors of the House or Senate or in committees—from debates and mark-ups, to votes. During a national emergency, Members could log on to this site from wherever they may be using a simple password or some kind of human verification, like a fingerprint or iris print. Congressional staffers would have access as well, but the site would be a read-only site to the public, so citizens could watch much as they now do on C-SPAN. This scheme, DLC argues, is "not as far-fetched as it might initially seem."

Others, particularly Members of Congress, are not so sure. "I think [a virtual Congress is] the dumbest thing I've ever heard," said Senator Conrad Burns (Republican-Montana), co-chair of the Congressional Internet Caucus. "Do you want to turn Washington over to the bureaucrats with no one to act as a check on them and give the White House a free hand?"[15] Representative Dreier argued that even the physical destruction of the Capitol would not be a justification for remote voting, because the Members of Congress could still meet in one location, assuming that there was not a simultaneous disruption of the nation's transportation system. He noted further that "[n]o technology, no matter the clarity of the speaker phone or the resolution of the video display, can provide for the essential *human* atmosphere required to develop the interpersonal, collegial relationships that are at the heart of [Congress.]"[16]

The argument becomes more of a power struggle with the executive branch or the logistics of where Congress would meet if not in Washington. Professor Stephen Frantzich has raised important concerns: "The initial question [of a virtual Congress] is not one of technology, but one of philosophy and politics."[17] Further questions have to be answered: Who should be allowed to participate? When should an e-Congress meet? Are the staff and the public permitted to participate? How is the deliberative process established and maintained? How will official records be accessed and maintained?[18]

It may make perfect sense to have such a web-based mechanism in place from the standpoint of national security, but it would run up against some enormous cultural and institutional barriers, in an establishment that is deeply bound to its own culture and traditions. Members cannot vote on floor matters from their offices, they must be physically present; they are forbidden to let other Members carry their voting cards onto the floor and vote for them by proxy. They can vote by proxy in certain committee deliberations, but that is as far as it goes. Congress has banned the use of cell phone and laptop computers on the floor.

The overwhelming tradition and culture in Congress depend on face-to-face communication, whether in committee, on the floor, in party and leadership caucuses, in the other corners and corridors of legislative power: It is the Johnson Treatment—the infamously successful Lyndon Johnson with his face two inches from a Senate colleague arguing his point; it is Speaker of the House Tip O'Neill with his bearlike arm draped around a colleague making a last-minute convert; it is a heated argument in the House Republican Caucus meeting, or a silent nod from one Senator to another on how to vote on a tough issue. The Congress is becoming more technologically savvy, it is using online communications far more often, Members are brandishing their pagers, Palm Pilots, and BlackBerrys—but in the end, the Congress is a profoundly personal organization, based on both collegiality and enmity, personal exchange, and face-to-face lawmaking. It is not built for speed and efficiency, and as maddeningly slow as the legislative process may be, its multi-check-points, duplications and inefficiencies, at times, have served the national well.[19]

The Internet and e-mail are simply tools for helping lawmakers, their staffs, and constituents better communicate with one another; they do not possess magical powers. As Donald R. Wolfensberger had written, the Internet is "not a solution to our educational problems, any more than educational radio and television were. And it is not a solution to our governance problems, any more than telegrams, telephones, or television were."[20]

Communicating Across the Digital Divide

Veteran lawmaker Lee Hamilton (Democrat-Indiana), who served for thirty-four years in the House of Representatives, wrote that it "makes me wince" when Congress is accused of being "out of touch" with the American people. Hamilton argued that "most Members of Congress feel a deep sense of oblig-ation to reach out to the public."[21] As we've seen, lawmakers reach out in many formats: participating in radio of television call-in shows, cutting radio "actualities" for use by local radio stations; video conferencing; meeting constituents in a variety of settings, such as small group meetings, town hall events, or individually. Lawmakers write op-ed letters, send out news bulletins, blanket their districts with newsletters, and respond with personal letters. The methods of communication have multiplied, but the admonition given by Speaker William Bankhead in 1938 to newly-elected Members still applies: No matter how you vote, stay in touch with your constituents. Certainly websites, electronic newsletters, and e-mail have added immeasurably to that mix of communications.

What of those citizens on the other side of the digital divide? Even today, some 40 percent of citizens do not use e-mail. Over time, that figure will undoubtedly drop, but there will still be a persistent minority of individuals untouched by e-mail, the Internet, and electronic communication. Lawmakers must be able to communicate with them, and they with their lawmakers by the old-fashioned, non-technical means of letters, post cards, telephone, and face-to-face conversation.

America continues to suffer from poor voter turnout, low civic participation, and a high sense of mistrust of and citizen isolation from elected officials. As promising and important as online communications are, lawmakers should never forget that it takes a wide variety of communication tools to reach every person, and that the simplest of messages, written in pencil, grammatical mistakes and all, should receive the same attention as any e-mail text.

Today, online communication benefits those who are already well-informed. In a society that values communication, immediate access to resources, and the ability to mobilize like-minded citizens or interests, online communication adds immensely to the power of those already plugged in. Washington lobbyists, journalists, opinion-makers, and professional Washington watchers flock to the Internet and e-mail, using online communication as a major source of information retrieval. For them, the Internet has become an essential tool of reliable and timely information.

When looking at the general public, there are signs of a disturbing coalescence of Internet usage and civic awareness. We are in danger of reaching a point where those who use e-mail and Internet sites for business or pleasure are roughly the same persons who participate in civic affairs, turn up at citizen meetings, and who vote. Regular use of e-mail or the Internet does not a good citizen make, but we may find a strong correlation between those who vote and those who are savvy to electronic communication. Those who are not connected tend to be those who do not participate, and the greater emphasis we place on online communication, the better chance there is that the non-computer literate and e-mail phobes will be left further and further behind.

Online communication should be encouraged and expanded; as a matter of public policy, this country should encourage the wider and broader use of online communication by all people, making computer software and online access affordable, easy to operate, and widely available especially through libraries, kiosks, and other public spaces. At the same time, elected officials, especially Members of Congress, must be receptive to and aware of constituent needs and demands through whatever form of communication they choose to express themselves.

Appendix A

Research Methodology and Best Practices

The Congress Online Project undertook several research projects to help it develop the Best Practices model for Congressional websites and to evaluate those sites.

Research

Focus Groups with Constituents. Eight focus groups were conducted with constituents in Washington, D.C., Richmond, Virginia, Phoenix, Arizona, and Philadelphia, Pennsylvania, from January–March, 2001. Thomas Opinion Research, Manassas, Virginia, conducted the focus group research on behalf of the Congress Online Project. The findings of the research were reported in *Constituents and Your Website: What Citizens Want to See on Congressional Websites,* available at (http://www.congressonlineproject.org/focus groups.htm).

Interviews with Congressional Staff. More than 100 Senate and House management, administrative, and technical staff were interviewed.

Industry Research. We identified and analyzed website standards and best practices in a wide range of industry sectors.

Survey of Political Reporters. We asked a relatively small sample of government and political reporters, both inside and outside the Beltway, to give their impressions and expectations of congressional websites.

Survey of Advocacy Groups. We interviewed practitioners in the field of electronic advocacy, conducted an online survey of advocacy groups, and reviewed the literature about electronic advocacy and public affairs.

Review of Non-congressional Websites that Provide Congressional Information. We examined a range of public, private, and non-profit sector websites that provided access to information about Congress and Members of Congress.

Review of Previous Evaluations of Congressional Websites. We collected and analyzed the findings and recommendations of previous evaluations of congressional websites.

Building Blocks

These building blocks were identified and used as the benchmarks to evaluate the congressional websites. The building blocks are listed in order of their importance.

1. **Audience.** The site demonstrates that the office has clearly identified its web audiences (both those seeking information from the office and those that the office wants to target) and methodically built the site around those audiences.

2. **Content.** The site provides content that is specifically targeted to meet the needs of the defined audiences, is up-to-date, attracts new visitors, and supports the goals of the office.

3. **Interactivity.** The site offers its visitors opportunities to express their views and fosters on- and off-line communications.

4. **Usability.** The design and information architecture of the site enhances the audiences' experience by enabling quick and user-friendly access to information and services.

5. **Innovations.** The site employs creative features that enhance a visitor's experience by making it interesting or easier to use.

Evaluation Process

The Congress Online Project twice evaluated all congressional websites. The first evaluation, covering 605 websites, was conducted from August–October 2001; the ensuing report, *Congress Online: Assessing and Improving Capitol Hill Websites*, was released in January 2002. The second round of evaluations, covering 610 websites, was conducted from August–November 2002; the second report, *Congress Online 2003: Turning the Corner on the Information Age*, was released in March 2003. There were several steps in the evaluation process:

1. *Benchmarking and Grading.* Every website was subject to a detailed analysis and given a numerical score. This evaluation was conducted by the members of the Congressional Management Foundation team, headed by Kathy Goldschmidt. The top 25 percent of sites—those that had received grades of A or high Bs—were then further evaluated.

2. *Fine Tuning.* In this round, the websites were evaluated not by the fundamental components for a successful website, but on elements that would considerably enhance those sites. The best sixty-two sites were then sent to the Expert Panel.

3. *Expert Panel Review.* This panel determined which among those submitted to them would be Gold Mouse Award winners, that is, websites with a rating of "A+." The panel also gave recommendations for the Silver and Bronze Mouse Awards. In the end, the Congressional Management Foundation added several other sites for inclusion in the Bronze Award category. The expert panel consisted of John Aravosis, president, Wired Strategies Internet Consulting (2003 evaluation only); Graeme Browning, author of *Electronic Democracy: Using the Internet to Transform American Politics* (2002); Janet Caldow, Director of the IBM Institute for Electronic Government (2002, 2003); Michael Cornfield, Associate Research Professor, Graduate School of Political Management, The George Washington University (2003); Max Fose, partner, Integrated Web Strategy (2002, 2003); Kathy McShea, president, Emerald Strategies (2002, 2003); Chris Porter, founder and CEO, Your-Congress, Inc. (2003); Joiwind Ronen, Director of Intergovernmental Technology Leadership Consortium, the Council for Excellence in Government (2002, 2003); John Sampson, Federal Government Affairs Manager, Microsoft Corporation (2003); and James Vaughn, Director for Government and Political Programming and Products, America Online (2003).

Source: Congress Online Project, *Congress Online: Assessing and Improving Capitol Hill Websites* (Washington, D.C.: Congress Online Project, 2002). Written by Kathy Goldschmidt, Nicole Folk, Mike Callahan, Richard Shapiro, and Brad Fitch, all of the Congressional Management Foundation, and the Congress Online Project, *Congress Online 2003: Turning the Corner on the Information Age* (Washington, D.C.: Congress Online Project, 2003). Written by Nicole Folk and Kathy Goldschmidt, with contributions by Rick Shapiro, Brad Fitch, and Mike Callahan. Both reports are available at (http://www. congressonlineproject.org).

Appendix B

Best Websites in Congress

The Congress Online Project awarded fifteen "Gold Mouse" awards to the best Congressional websites and twenty "Silver Mouse" awards to the next best websites in 2002. The following year, the Congress Online Project awarded sixteen "Gold Mouse," twenty-three "Silver Mouse," awards and a new category, "Bronze Mouse," awards to thirty-three recipients.

Congress Online Gold Mouse Awards, 2002–2003

Senate Member Sites

Senator Jeff Bingaman (Democrat-New Mexico) (http://bingaman.senate.gov) (gold-2002; silver-2003)

Senator Barbara Boxer (Democrat-California) (http://boxer.senate.gov) (gold-2002; bronze-2003)

Senator Tom Carper (Democrat-Delaware) (http://carper.senate.gov) (no award-2003, gold-2003)

Senator Kay Bailey Hutchison (Republican-Texas) (http://hutchison.senate.gov) (gold-2002; silver-2003)

Senator Patrick Leahy (Democrat-Vermont) (http://leahy.senate.gov) (gold-2003; gold-2003)

Senator Harry Reid (Democrat-Nevada) (http://reid.senate.gov) (no award-2002; gold-2003)

House Member Sites

Rep. Earl Blumenauer (Democrat-Oregon) (http://www.house.gov/blumenauer) (no award-2002; gold-2003)

Rep. John Boozman (Republican-Arkansas) (http://www.house.gov/boozman) (no award-2002; gold-2003)

Rep. Chaka Fattah (Democrat-Pennsylvania) (http://www.house.gov/fattah) (no award-2002; gold-2003)

Rep. Kay Granger (Republican-Texas) (http://kaygranger.house.gov) (gold-2002; gold-2003)

Rep. Melissa Hart (Republican-Pennsylvania) (http://hart.house.gov) (no award-2002; gold-2003)

Rep. Mike Honda (Democrat-California) (http://www.house.gov/honda) (gold-2002; silver-2003)

Rep. John Larson (Democrat-Connecticut) (http://www.house.gov/larson) (no award-2002; gold-2003)

Rep. Mike Pence (Republican-Indiana) (http://mikepence.house.gov) (gold-2003; silver-2003)

Rep. Richard Pombo (Republican-California) (http://www.house.gov/pombo) (gold-2002; gold-2003)

Rep. George Radanovich (Republican-California) (http://www.radanovich.house.gov) (no award-2002; gold-2003)

Rep. Christopher Shays (Republican-Connecticut) (http://www.house.gov/shays) (no award-2002; gold-2003)

Rep. Nick Smith (Republican-Michigan) (http://www.house.gov/nicksmith) (silver-2002; gold-2003)

Standing Committees

Senate Budget Committee (majority) (http://budget.senate.gov) (gold-2002; silver-2003)

House Committee on Energy and Commerce (majority) (http://energycommerce.house.gov) (gold-2002; gold-2003)

House Committee on Energy and Commerce (minority) (http://www.house.gov/commerce_democrats) (gold-2002; gold-2003)

House Committee on Rules (majority) (http://www.house.gov/rules) (gold-2002; no award-2003)

House Government Reform Committee (minority) (http://reform.house.gov/min) (no award-2002; gold-2003)

Leadership Offices

Speaker of the House (http://www.speaker.gov) (gold-2002; no award-2003)

Office of the House Majority Whip (http://majoritywhip.house.gov) (gold-2002; silver-2003)

House Republican Conference (http://GOP.gov) (gold-2002; gold-2003)

Congress Online Silver Mouse Awards, 2002–2003

Senate Member Sites

Senator Sam Brownback (Republican-Kansas) (http://brownback.senate. gov) (no award-2002; silver-2003)

Senator Larry Craig (Republican-Idaho) (http://craig.senate.gov) (no award-2002; silver-2003)

Senator Dianne Feinstein (Democrat-California) (http://feinstein.senate.gov) (silver-2002; silver-2003)

Senator Bob Graham (Democrat-Florida) (http://graham.senate.gov) (silver-2002; silver-2003)

Senator Tom Harkin (Democrat-Iowa) (http://harkin.senate.gov) (no award-2002; silver-2003)

Senator Mary Landrieu (Democrat-Louisiana) (http://landrieu.senate.gov) (silver-2002; silver-2003)

Senator Carl Levin (Democrat-Michigan) (http://levin.senate.gov) (silver-2002; no award-2003)

Senator Don Nickles (Republican-Oklahoma) (http://nickles.senate.gov) (silver-2002; no award-2003)

Senator Debbie Stabenow (Democrat-Michigan) (http://stabenow.senate.gov) (no award-2002; silver-2003)

Senator Fred Thompson (Republican-Tennessee) (http://thompson.senate. gov) (silver-2002; silver-2003)

House Member Sites

Rep. Tom Allen (Democrat-Maine) (http://tomallen.house.gov) (silver-2002; no award-2003)

Rep. Judy Biggert (Republican-Illinois) (http://judybiggert.house.gov) (no award-2002; silver-2003)

Rep. Chris Cannon (Republican-Utah) (http://www.house.gov/cannon) (silver-2002; no award-2003)

Rep. Brad Carson (Democrat-Oklahoma) (http://carson.house.gov) (silver-2002; no award-2003)

Rep. Wayne Gilchrest (Republican-Maryland) (http://gilchrest.house.gov) (no award-2002; silver-2003)

Rep. Mark Green (Republican-Wisconsin) (http://www.house.gov/markgreen) (silver-2002; no award-2003)

Rep. Steve Rothman (Democrat-New Jersey) (http://rothman.house.gov) (no award-2002; silver-2003)

Rep. John Thune (Republican-South Dakota) (http://johnthune.house.gov) (silver-2002; no award-2003)

Rep. Heather Wilson (Republican-New Mexico) (http://wilson.house.gov) (silver-2002; bronze-2003)

Committee Websites

Senate Energy and Natural Resources Committee (majority) (htp://energy.senate.gov) (no award-2002; silver-2003)

Joint Economic Committee (majority) (http://www.house.gov/jec) (silver-2002; no award-2003)

House Agriculture Committee (majority) (http://agriculture.house.gov) (no award-2002; silver-2003)

House Armed Services Committee (majority) (http://house.gov/hasc) (no award-2002; silver-2003)

House Committee on the Budget (majority) (http://budget.house.gov) (silver-2002; bronze-2003)

House Committee on Resources (majority) (http://resourcescommittee.house.gov) (silver-2002; bronze-2003)

House Education and the Workforce Committee (majority) (http://edworkforce.house.gov) (no award-2002; silver-2003)

House Science Committee (majority) (http://www.house.gov/science) (silver-2002; bronze-2003)

House Small Business Committee (majority) (http://www.house.gov/smbiz) (silver-2002; no award-2003)

House Committee on Standards of Official Conduct (majority) (http://www.house.gov/ethics) (silver-2002; no award-2003)

Leadership Websites

House Democratic Caucus (http://housedemocrats.house.gov) (silver-2002; no award-2003)

Senate Republican Conference (http://src.senate.gov) (no award-2002; silver-2003)

House Republican Policy Committee (http://policy.house.gov) (no award-2002; silver-2003)

Congress Online Bronze Mouse Awards, 2003

Senate Member Sites

Senator Jean Carnahan (Democrat-Missouri) (http://www.carnahan.senate.gov) (no award-2002; bronze-2003)

Senator Mark Dayton (Democrat-Minnesota) (http://dayton.senate.gov) (no award-2002; bronze-2003)

Senator Christopher Dodd (Democrat-Connecticut) (http://dodd.senate.gov) (no award-2002; bronze-2003)

Senator Bill Frist (Republican-Tennessee) (http://frist.senate.gov) (no award-2002; bronze-2003)

Senator Ernest Hollings (Democrat-South Carolina) (http://hollings.senate.gov) (no award-2002; bronze-2003)

Senator Herbert Kohl (Democrat-Wisconsin) (http://kohl.senate.gov) (no award-2002; bronze-2003)

Senator Jon Kyl (Republican-Arizona) (http://kyl.senate.gov) (no award-2002; bronze-2003)

Senator Charles Schumer (Democrat-New York) (http://schumer.senate.gov) (no award-2002; bronze-2003)

Senator Arlen Specter (Republican-Pennsylvania) (http://specter.senate.gov) (no award-2002; bronze-2003)

Senator Paul Wellstone (Democrat-Minnesota) (http://wellstone.senate.gov) (no award-2002; bronze-2003)

House Member Sites

Rep. Cass Ballenger (Republican-North Carolina) (http://www.house.gov/ballenger) (no award-2002; bronze-2003)

Rep. Eric Cantor (Republican-Virginia) (http://cantor.house.gov) (no award-2002; bronze-2003)

Rep. John Doolittle (Republican-California) (http://www.house.gov. doolittle) (no award-2002; bronze-2003)

Rep. Porter Goss (Republican-Florida) (http://portergoss.house.gov) (no award-2002; bronze-2003)

Rep. Gil Gutknecht (Republican-Minnesota) (http://www.gil.house.gov) (no award-2002; bronze-2003)

Rep. Amo Houghton, Jr. (Republican-New York) (http://houghton.house.gov) (no award-2002; bronze-2003)

Rep. Walter Jones, Jr. (Republican-North Carolina) (http://jones.house.gov) (no award-2002; bronze-2003)

Rep. Jim Matheson (Democrat-Utah) (http://www.house.gov/matheson) (no award-2002; bronze-2003)

Rep. John Mica (Republican-Florida) (http://www.house.gov/mica) (no award-2002; bronze-2003)

Rep. George R. Nethercutt, Jr. (Republican-Washington) (http://www.house. gov/nethercutt) (no award-2002; bronze-2003)

Rep. Lucille Roybal-Allard (Democrat-California) (http://www.house.gov/ roybal-allard) (no award-2002; bronze-2003)

Rep. Bernard Sanders (Independent-Vermont) (http://bernie.house.gov) (no award-2002; bronze-2003)

Rep. Thomas Tancredo (Republican-Colorado) (http://www.house.gov/ tancredo) (no award-2002; bronze-2003)

Rep. Lee Terry (Republican-Nebraska) (http://www.house.gov/terry) (no award-2002; bronze-2003)

Committee Websites

House Budget Committee (minority) (http://www.house.gov/budget) (no award-2002; bronze-2003)

House Financial Services Committee (majority) (http://www.house.gov/ financialservices) (no award-2002; bronze-2003)

House Government Reform Committee (majority) (http://reform.house. gov) (no award-2002; bronze-2003)

House Judiciary Committee (majority) (http://www.house.gov/judiciary) (no award-2002; bronze-2003)

Source: Congress Online Project, *Congress Online: Assessing and Improving Capitol Hill Web Sites* (Washington, D.C.: Congress Online Project, 2002). Written by Kathy Goldschmidt, Nicole Folk, Mike Callahan, Richard Shapiro, and Brad Fitch, all of the Congressional Management Foundation, and the Congress Online Project, *Congress Online 2003: Turning the Corner on the Information Age* (Washington, D.C.: Congress Online Project, 2003). Written by Nicole Folk and Kathy Goldschmidt, with contributions by Rick Shapiro, Brad Fitch, and Mike Callahan. Both reports available at (http://www. congressonlineproject.org).

Other Government Websites

Federal, state, and local government websites cited in the text.

Federal Executive

FirstGov.gov (http://www.FirstGov.gov)
Chief Information Officers Council (http://www.cio.gov)

State Government

State of California (http://www/ca.gov/state/portal.myca)
State of Delaware (http://www/delaware.gov)
State of Georgia (http://state.ga.us)
State of Georgia, Secretary of State (http://www.sos.state.ga.us)
State of Illinois, Illinois Criminal Justice Information Authority
    (http://www.icjia.org)
State of North Carolina, NC@Your Service (http://www.ncgov.com)
State of Maine (http://www.state.me.us)
State of Maryland, eMaryland Marketplace (http://www.emaryland
    marketplace.com)
State of Michigan (http://www.michigan.gov)
State of New Jersey (http://www.state.nj.us)
State of Nebraska (http://www.nol.org)
Commonwealth of Pennsylvania (http://www.state.pa.us)
State of Tennessee (http://www.tennesseeanytime.org)
State of Utah (http://www.utah.gov)
Commonwealth of Virginia (http://www.state.va.us)
Commonwealth of Virginia, Division of Motor Vehicles
    (http://www.dmv.state.va.us)
State of Washington (http://access.wa.gov)

Local Government

City of Austin, Texas (http://www.ci.austintx.us)

City of Bellevue, Washington (http://ci.bellevue.wa.us)

Village of Blacksburg, Virginia, Electronic Village (http://www.bev.net)

City of Boston, Massachusetts (http://www.cityofboston.gov)

City of Boulder City, Colorado (http://www.ci.boulder.co.us)

County of Boulder, Colorado (http://bcn.boulder.co.us)

City of Cedar Rapids, Iowa (http://www.cedar-rapids.org)

City of Chicago, Illinois (http://www.cityofchicago.org)

City of Colorado Springs, Colorado (http://www.colorado-springs.com)

City of Conyers, Georgia (http://www.conyersga.com)

City of Costa Mesa, California (http://www.cityofcostamesa.com)

City of Des Moines, Iowa (http://www.des-moines.ia.us)

Douglas County, Nevada, Clerk's Office (http://www.cltr.co.douglas.nv.us)

Village of Downers Grove, Illinois (http://www.vil.downers-grove.il.us)

City of Durham, North Carolina (http://www.ci.durham.nc.us)

Fairfax County, Virginia (http://www.fairfaxcounty.gov)

City of Hampton, Virginia (http://www.hampton.va.us)

Hampton Roads, Virginia (http://smartregion.org)

City and County of Honolulu, Hawaii (http://www.co.honolulu.hi.us)

City of Houston, Texas (http://www.cityofhouston.gov)

City of Indianapolis, Indiana (http://www.indygov.org)

City of Louisville, Kentucky (http://www.louky.gov)

New York City, New York (http://home.nyc.gov/portal)

City of Miami-Dade County, Florida (http://www.miamidade.gov)

City of Mobile, Alabama (http://www.cityofmobile.org)

Montgomery County, Maryland (http://www.co.mo.md.us)

City of Plano, Texas (http://www.planotx.org)

City of Richardson, Texas (http://www.cor.net)

City of Roanoke, Virginia (http://www.ci.roanoke.va.us)

Salt Lake City, Utah (http://www.ci.slc.ut.us)

City of San Francisco, California (http://www.bayareagov.com)

City of San Jose, California, Permits Online (http://www.sjpermits.org)

City of Seattle, Washington (http://www.cityofseattle.net)

City of Tampa, Florida (http://www.tampagov.net)

City of Virginia Beach, Virginia (http://vb.gov.com)

Judicial Branch

Arkansas Judiciary (http://courts.state.ar.us)
North Dakota Supreme Court (http://www.court.state.ne.us)
Utah State Courts (http://www.utcourts.gov)

For a comprehensive listing of government websites and information from government sources, see Greg R. Notess, ed., *Government Information on the Internet*, 4th ed. (Lanham, Maryland: Bernan, 2001).

Appendix D

Citizen-Oriented Websites

Websites of citizen-oriented organizations cited in the text.

AARP (http://www.aarp.org)
Benton Foundation (http://www.benton.org)
California Voter Foundation (http://www.calvoter.org)
Capitol Advantage (http://www.capitoladvantage.com)
Center for Congress, Indiana University
   (http://www.congress.indiana.edu)
Center for Responsive Politics (http://www.opensecrets.org)
Conservative HQ (http://www.conservativehq.com)
Democracy Network, League of Conservation Voters
   (http://www.dnet.org)
Democracy Online Newsletter (http://www.e-democracy.org/do)
Digital Sunlight (http://www.digitalsunlight.org)
E-The People (http://www.e-thepeople.com)
Environmental Defense Action Network (http://www.actionnetwork.org)
FEC Watch (http://www.fecwatch.org)
Grassroots Enterprise (http://www.grassroots.com)
Klaas Foundation for Children (http://www.klaaskids.org)
Minnesota E-Democracy (http://www.e-democracy.org)
MoveOn.org (http://www.moveon.org)
National Library on Money in State Politics
   (http://www.followthemoney. org)
OurForests.org (http://www.ourforests.org)
Pandora's Box: The Secrecy of Child Sexual Abuse
   (http://www.preventabuse-now.com)
Project Vote Smart (http://www.vote-smart.org)
Public Disclosure, Inc. (http://www.publicdisclosure.org)

Speakout.com (http://www.speakout.com)

StopDrLaura.com (http://www.stopdrlaura.com)

Web White and Blue 2000
   (http://www.markle.org/news/WWBEvaluation.pdf)

Win Without War (http://www.winwithoutwarus.org)

Women's Sports Foundation (http://www.womenssportsfoundation.org)

YourCongress.com (http://www.yourcongress.com)

Congressional Website Statistics
535 House and Senate Personnel Offices, 2001

Most Common Website Design/Content Features

Feature	Number	Percentage
Office telephone numbers	515	96.26
Addresses for each office	513	95.89
Biography of Member	513	95.89
E-mail link/link to WYR	486	90.84
Photo of Member	477	89.16
Capitol/White House ticket info.	476	88.97
Washington, D.C. tourist info.	466	87.10
Flag ordering information	447	83.55
Press releases, by date	436	81.50
Links to THOMAS	430	80.37

Website Differences Between the House of Representatives and Senate

Feature	House Percentage	Senate Percentage
Web form to contact office	18.85	58
FAQ section	6.67	26
Links to often-requested resources	10.34	44
Links to further information/resources	57.24	26
Highlight legislative accomplishments	41.61	78
Information on 10+ legislative issues	29.92	40
Links to THOMAS	84.14	64
Allow search of THOMAS from site	19.08	3

Seldom Seen on Websites

Feature	Number	Percentage
Site in Spanish, other languages	35	6.54
Link to off-site issue information	28	5.23
Member's schedule in district	25	4.67
Links to CRS reports	19	3.55
Why Member voted certain way	8	1.50
Bobby compliance	10	1.87
Member's daily schedule	3	0.56

Data compiled by Lisa Wallenda, graduate student, Master of Arts in Legislative Affairs program, the George Washington University, March–June 2001; data assembled by Kathy Goldschmidt, Congressional Management Foundation.

Project Vote Smart

National Political Awareness Test

Selected questions from the 2000 presidential questionnaire.

Abortion Issues

Indicate (✓) which principles you support (if any) concerning abortion.

_____ a. Abortions should always be illegal.

_____ b. Abortions should be illegal when the fetus is viable, with or without life support.

_____ c. Abortions should always be legally available.

_____ d. Abortions should be legal only within the first trimester of pregnancy.

_____ e. Abortions should be legal when the pregnancy resulted from incest or rape.

_____ f. Abortions should be legal when the life of the woman is endangered.

_____ g. Abortions should be limited by waiting periods and notification required as decided by each state government.

_____ h. Prohibit the dilation and extraction procedure, also known as "partial birth" abortion.

_____ i. Prohibit public funding of abortions and public funding of organizations that advocate or perform abortions.

_____ j. Support funding for research on the drug RU-486.

_____ k. Support "buffer zones" by requiring demonstrators to stay at least five feet from abortion clinic doorways and driveways.

_____ l. Provide funding for family planning programs as a means to decrease the number of abortions.

_____ m. Will your Supreme Court nominees share your principles on abortion? _____ yes _____ no _____ undecided.

Campaign Finance Issues

Indicate (✔) which principles you support (if any) concerning campaign finance issues.

_____ a. Support public taxpayer funding for congressional candidates who comply with campaign spending limits.

_____ b. Eliminate publicly financed matching funds for presidential campaigns.

_____ c. Increase the amount individuals are permitted to contribute to federal campaigns.

_____ d. Strengthen and enforce legislation that encourages full and timely disclosure of campaign finance information.

_____ e. Prohibit Political Action Committee (PAC) contributions to candidates for federal office.

_____ f. Provide free or low-cost television advertising to candidates who agree to voluntary campaign spending limits.

_____ g. Ban unregulated soft money campaign contributions to political parties or committees.

_____ h. Prohibit non-U.S. citizens from making soft money contributions to national parties or party committees.

_____ i. Require full disclosure of funding sources of issue advocacy commercials which appear within 60 days of an election.

_____ j. Make campaign spending limits mandatory for all federal candidates.

_____ k. Require union to get members' permission before using union dues for political advocacy.

_____ l. Remove all contribution limits on federal candidates and parties, but require complete and immediate disclosure via the Internet.

_____ m. Require congressional candidates to raise over half of their campaign money from the home state.

Gun Issues

Indicate (✓) which principles you support (if any) concerning gun issues.

_____ a. Ban the sale or transfer of semi-automatic guns, except those used for hunting.

_____ b. Maintain federal restrictions on the purchase and possession of guns.

_____ c. Ease federal restrictions on the purchase and possession of guns.

_____ d. Repeal federal restrictions on the purchase and possession of guns by law-abiding citizens.

_____ e. Allow citizens to carry concealed guns.

_____ f. Require manufacturers to provide child-safety locks on guns.

_____ g. Increase penalties for the possession of any illegal guns.

_____ h. Hold gun owners responsible for crimes committed with their guns by children age 16 and under.

_____ i. Raise the minimum age for ownership of handguns from 18 to 21.

_____ j. Require three business days for background checks of gun buyers at gun shows.

_____ k. Strengthen enforcement of current regulations on guns.

_____ l. Require a license for gun possession.

Notes

Introduction

Epigraph quote from C. Estes Kefauver and J. Levin, *A Twentieth-Century Congress* (New York: Duell, Sloan and Pearce, 1947), 171–172, retold in Donald R. Matthews, *U. S. Senators and Their World* (New York: W. W. Norton and Company, 1973), 220. Speaker Bankhead gave this advice to Kefauver (Democrat -Tennessee) as he entered his first year of service in the House of Representatives.

1. Robert A. Caro, *The Years of Lyndon Johnson: The Path to Power* (New York: Alfred A. Knopf, 1982), 221,226; Matthews, *U.S. Senators Their World*, 79. In 1935–1935, Members of Congress earned $8,500. Since 1995, the House of Representatives replaced its old system of separate allowances (such as franking, clerk-hire, office expenses) with a single account, the Members' Representational Allowance (MRA), which averaged $987,000 per office in 2000. *Setting Course: Congressional Management Guide.* 107th Congress edition (Washington, D.C.: Congressional Management Foundation, 2000), 30. As of January 2003, Members earned $154,500. Air-conditioning came to the House in 1928, the Senate in 1929, and to the White House the following year.
2. Matthews noted that "old-timers around the Senate can remember when twenty letters one day was 'big mail.'" *U.S. Senators and Their World*, 219.
3. Caro, *The Path to Power*, 222–224. The Kleberg office was able to have an additional assistant because a $130-per-month patronage job as mailman in the House Post Office traditionally "belonged" to the Fourteenth District, at 229.
4. David M. Kennedy, *Freedom from Fear: The American People in Depression and War, 1929–1945* (New York: Oxford University Press, 1999), 433. On Coughlin, see Donald Warren, *Radio Priest: Charles Coughlin, the Father of Hate Radio* (New York: The Free Press, 1996). While isolationist views dominated the mail, 70 percent of public opinion favored Roosevelt's proposed legislation. Robert A. Dahl, *Congress and Foreign Policy* (New York: Harcourt, Brace and Company 1950), 34 cited in Matthews, *U.S. Senators and Their World*, 222–23, n. 12.
5. "20 Million Americans See Starr's Report on Internet," *CNN.com,* September 13, 1998, available at (http://www.cnn.com/TECH/computing/9809/13/internet.starr).
6. Congress Online Project, *E-Mail Overload in Congress: Managing a Communications Crisis* (Washington, D.C.: Congress Online Project, March 2001), 2–3; written by Kathy Goldschmidt. The Congress Online Project website is (http://www.congressonlineproject.org). Also Gail Russell Chaddock, "Behind Vote on Ashcroft, A Signal," *Christian Science Monitor*, February 2, 2001, 4.
7. Department of Commerce, Economics and Statistics Administration and National Telecommunications and Information Administration, *A Nation Online: How Americans*

Are Expanding Their Use of the Internet (2002), available at http://www.esa.doc.gov/508/esa/nationonline.htm). The survey, using data from the September 2001 U.S. Census Bureau *Current Population Survey*, included 57,000 households and more than 137,000 individuals across the United States. Forrester Research, a leading electronic communications research firm, noted in a late 2001 report that more than half of all Americans use e-mail, for an average of one-half hour each day. Jupiter Media Metrix, another research firm, predicted that by 2006, 140 million Americans would be "active" e-mail users, up from the 87 million e-mail users in 2001. Rachel Konrad and Paul Festa, "E-Mail a Savior Amid Anthrax Scare," *CNET News.com*, (October 16, 2001, available at (http://news.com.com/2100-1023-274516.html).

8. A study by the Pew Internet and American Life Project found that fifty-seven percent of those American adults who did not have access to the Internet had no intentions of using it. The holdouts were mostly aging Baby Boomers and senior citizens. By contrast, young Americans who do not now have Internet access are planning to use it soon. Within a generation or so, Internet penetration will approach the levels enjoyed by the telephone, which is used by 94 percent of Americans and television, which is used by 98 percent of Americans. Amanda Lenhart, *Who's Not Online: 57 Percent of Those Without Internet Access Say They Do Not Plan to Log On* (Washington, D.C.: Pew Internet and American Life Project, September 21, 2000), available at (http://pewinternet.org). See also, Theda Skocpol and Morris Fiorina, eds., *Engagement in American Democracy* (Washington, D.C.: Brookings Institution Press, 1999).

9. See Pew Internet and American Life Project home page for a daily Internet activities chart, available at (http://www.pewinternet.org/reports/chart.asp?img=Daily_A 1 .htm).

10. Jason Miller, "Survey Finds E-Government a Hit," *Government Computer News* (January 9, 2002), available at (http://www.gcn.com/vol1_no1/e_gov/17740-1.html). The 2001 National Technology Readiness Survey of 418 adults was conducted by the Robert H. Smith School of Business, University of Maryland and Rockbridge Associates, Inc., Great Falls, Virginia. "The percentage of people using the Internet to obtain government information, pay taxes, apply for permits and conduct other business is surprisingly high, especially at the state and local level," noted Roland Rust, director, Center for e-Services, University of Maryland. "E-service appears to be an increasingly attractive alternative to standing in line at a government office."

11. Elena Larsen and Lee Rainie, The *Rise of the E-Citizen: How People Use Government Agencies' Web Sites* (Washington, D.C.: Pew Internet and American Life Project, April 3, 2002), available at (http://www.pewinternet.org/release/index.org).

12. Andrew Leigh and Robert D. Atkinson, *Breaking Down Bureaucratic Barriers: The Phase of Digital Government* (Washington, D.C.: Progressive Policy Institute, November 2001), Appendix II. The Internal Revenue Service website is found at (http://www.irs.gov).

13. February netScore, ComScore Networks, press release, March 11, 2002, available at (http://www.comscore.com/news/feb).

14. *Getting Serious Online* (Washington, D.C.: Pew Internet and American Life Project March 2002), available at (http://pewinternet.org/reports/toc.asp?Report=55).

15. William Matthews, "Survey Says Congress Should Get Online," *Federal Computer Week*, December 13, 1999, available (http://fcw.com/articles/1999/fcs_12131999_survey.asp). However, a May 8, 2002 survey by Mindshare Internet Campaigns, based on the responses of 90 offices, found that constituents preferred to receive responses by regular mail from Members of Congress by a margin of five to one. "Study Finds Congressional Offices Prefer Snail-Mail to E-Mail More than 5 to 1 for Constituent Contact." Report available at (http://mindshare.net/2002–05-17.13.phtml).

16. See Burdett A. Loomis, "The Congressional Office as a Small (?) Business," *Publius: The Journal of Federalism*, Summer, 1970, 35–55.

17. Congress Online Project, *Congress Online 2003: Turning the Corner on the Information Age* (Washington, D.C., 2003), 72–73. Written by Nicole Folk and Kathy Goldschmidt, with contributions by Rick Shapiro, Brad Fitch, and Mike Callahan. Available at (http://www.congressonlineproject.org).

18. See Richard Fenno, *Home Style: House Members in Their Districts* (Boston: Little, Brown and Company, 1978).

19. Stephen Frantzich, "Computers and the U.S. Congress: A Forty Year View," an unpublished paper presented at the Democratic Governance and ICT Conference, Copenhagen, Denmark, January 2003.

Chapter 1: New Tools for the Active Citizenry

Epigraph from Brandeis, "What Publicity Can Do," *Other People's Money* (1932), 92; first published in *Harper's Weekly*, December 20, 1913 and Digital Sunlight website, (http://www.digitalsunlight.org). Digital Sunlight is a project of the California Voter Foundation.

1. For example, Michael L. Sankey, Peter J. Weber, and James R. Flowers, Jr., *Public Records Online: The National Guide to Private and Government Online Sources of Public Records*, 3rd rev. ed. (New York: Facts of Demand Press, 2000), Carole A. Lane, *Naked in Cyberspace: How to Find Personal Information Online*, 2nd ed. (Medford, New Jersey: Cyber Age Books, 2002). According to Sankey et al., at 8, there are over 165 private companies that offer online databases on public record information. This phenomenon of open records has led to the inevitable counter movement of citizens who want to hide their identity. For example, J. J. Luna, *How to Be Invisible: A Step-by-Step Guide to Protecting Your Assets, Your Identity, and Your Life* (New York: St. Martin's Press, 2000).

2. Focus group surveys conducted for the Congress Online Project by Thomas Opinion Research, January–March 2001, in Washington, D.C.; Richmond, Virginia; Phoenix, Arizona; and Philadelphia, Pennsylvania.

3. Ralph Nader, "Congress Hides Their Votes," *The Nader Page*, November 14, 2001, available at (http://nader.org/interest/111401.html). Nader cited Reps. Christopher Shays (Republican-Connecticut) and Frank Wolf (Republican-Virginia) as the only two Members of Congress who provided this information. (See chapter six for further information and other lawmakers who post their voting records.)

4. Project Vote Smart website (http://www.vote-smart.org) and Congress.org website (http:// www.congress.org).

5. Richard Kimball, Project Vote Smart website (www.vote-smart.org/letter/phtml). Project Vote Smart's board of directors has included former presidents Gerald R. Ford and Jimmy Carter, former Speaker of the House Newt Gingrich, presidential candidate George McGovern, and other public officials and good government types. To become a board member, an individual is required to join along with "a political enemy." True to this philosophy, one of the founding members of Project Vote Smart was Barry Goldwater, Kimball's political rival. It is staffed by a corps of volunteers, many college students, who agree to work full-time from two weeks to two years, and liken their experience to that of the Peace Corps. Project Vote Smart now operates from Philipsburg, Montana.

6. Project Vote Smart website (http://www.vote-smart.org/nosell.phtml).

7. Center on Congress, Indiana University, available at (http://congress.indiana.edu).

8. YourCongress.com is available at (http://www.yourcongress.com).

9. C-SPAN website (http://www.c-span.org). C-SPAN radio is only available in the Washington, D.C. metropolitan area, but is available on the C-SPAN website.

10. Senate hearings are found at (http://www.capitolhearings.org); HearingRoom.com operated from mid-2000 to January 2002.

11. U.S. Congress House Committee on Government Reform. *Joint Statement by Chairman Tom Davis, Committee on Government Reform and Rep. Adam Putnam, Subcommittee on Technology, Information Policy, International Relations and the Census, on Electronically Databasing Committee Hearings with Text Searchable Applications,* March 13, 2003, available at (http://reform.house.gov).

12. *Washington Post* online version is found at (http://washingtonpost.com), *The New York Times* is (http://nytimes.com); The CNN website is (http://www.cnn.com) and the ABC News website is (http://www.abcnews.com).

13. Congressional Quarterly 2002 promotional materials.

14. Rebecca Fairley Rainey, "Election Regulators Clear the Way for Online Debates," *The New York Times* (October 29, 1999). Available at (http://www.nytimes.com/library/tech/99/10/cyber/articles/29campaign.html).

15. League of Women Voters press release, "Voters and Candidates Flock to the League of Women Voters' Democracy Network (DNet) During Election 2001," November 9, 2001. Democracy Network website is (http://www.dnet.org); League of Women Voters website is (http://www.lwv.org). DNet was created by Tracy Westen and others at the Center for Governmental Studies in Los Angeles in 1993, originally for use for cable television networks, but became web-based in 1997. DNet then became property of Grassroots.com, an Internet political site, of which Westen became chairman. Grassroots.com developed a joint venture with the League of Women Voters, which prompted complaints from rival web companies who argued that the arrangement gave Grassroots.com unfair help from the League's network of volunteer staff. Grassroots.com changed its business focus, gave sole control over DNet to the League of Women Voters in 2001 and changed its name to Grassroots Enterprises. See Ross Kerber, "Grassroots to Give Web Project to League of Women Voters; Backs Away from Joint Venture," *Boston Globe,* February 12, 2001, C3.

16. Web White & Blue 2000 was a nonpartisan consortium of seventeen of the largest Internet and traditional news organizations. The Web White & Blue 2000 evaluation is found at (http://markle.org/news/WWBEvaluation.pdf).

17. "4,802 Candidates Pass National Political Awareness Test," Project Vote Smart website, (http://www.vote-smart.org/press/quality.html).

18. Carol Goar, "The Wisdom to Choose Project Vote Smart," *Toronto Star,* February 11, 1996, F6.

19. Project Vote Smart website at (http://www.vote-smart.org/press/quality.html), Appendix IV.

20. Alan Bernstein and Melanie Markley, "Campaign '94," *Houston Chronicle,* November 7, 1994, A15. When Senator Jim Sasser (Democrat-Tennessee) was up for a difficult, and ultimately unsuccessful, re-election campaign in 1994, Project Vote Smart warned the Sasser campaign that it would publicize the Senator's failure to fill out the NPAT survey. This led to an angry confrontation, with Sasser's press secretary who allegedly threatened Project Vote Smart's tax-exempt status. The Sasser spokesman later backed down from denying he ever said such a thing, once a tape recording was produced, and then re-iterated the Senator's policy of not responding to any questionnaires. "Senate Aide Admits Threatening Group's Tax Exempt Status," *Los Angeles Times,* September 25, 1994, A30.

21. Ben White, "Issues Survey Gets Cold Shoulder From Several Contenders," *The Washington Post*, January 17, 2000, A4.

22. Project Vote Smart website (http://www.vote-smart.org/press/quality.html).

23. Charles Lewis, "Revealing State Secrets," *Columbia Journalism Review*, May–June 1998, available at (http://www.cjr.org/year/98/3/state.asp).

24. Follow the Money website (http://www.followthemoney.org). The National Institute on Money in State Politics, based in Helena, Montana, is a non-partisan, non-profit organization, headed by Samantha Sanchez and Jeff Malachowsky. The National Institute is funded by variety of foundations, including The Carnegie Foundation, Ford Foundation, Open Society Institute, The Pew Charitable Trusts, and the Joyce Foundation. There are at least fifteen state-oriented sites that cover individual state campaign finances. See Leslie Wayne, "Following the Money, Through the Web," *The New York Times*, August 26, 1999, A1.

25. Lewis, "Revealing State Secrets." David M. Poole headed the project, along with Robert Holsworth of Virginia Commonwealth University. The newspapers who combined resources for this project were the Newport News *Daily Press*, the *Richmond Times-Dispatch*, the *Roanoke Times*, *The Virginian-Pilot*, and *The Washington Post*. The Virginia Public Access Project website is (http://www.crp.org/vpap).

26. TRKCINC's predecessor was Public Disclosure, Inc. Political MoneyLine's website is (http://www.tray.com/FECinfo).

27. The list of 187 records includes the Department of Justice, FEC, and other federal, state, and municipal agencies of major fines ($25,000 or more). This information can be viewed at (http://www.tray.com/cgi-win/x_vce.exe).

28. Open Secrets website (http://www.opensecrets.org).

29. FEC Watch is found at (http://www.fecwatch.org). Another useful site is Campaign Finance Information Center (http://www.campaignfinance.org), which is run by Investigative Reporters and Editors, Inc., and is geared primarily toward reporters who cover campaign finance and elections stories.

30. Michael X. Delli Carpini and Scott Keeter, "The Internet and an Informed Citizenry," 129–153, at 148 in David M. Anderson and Michael Cornfield, eds., *The Civic Web: Online Politics and Democratic Values* (Lanham, Md.: Rowman & Littlefield Publishers, Inc., 2002).

31. See discussion on "Minnesota E-Democracy Project," at Benton Foundation website (http://www.benton.org/Library/State/edemocracy.html) and Steven Clift, "E-Democracy: Lessons from Minnesota," 157–165 in Anderson and Cornfield, eds., *The Civic Web*.

32. League of Women Voters DemocracyNet, press release, "Election 2002: DNet Traffic Surpasses 2000 Presidential Election" (November 13, 2002), available at (http://www.dnet.org/news_document.dnet?NewsEventID=11095&siteid=3).

33. Steve Brandt, "Minneapolis E-mail Forum has Become a Force in City Politics," *Minneapolis Star Tribune*, available at (http://www.startribune.com/462/773948.html).

34. Steven Clift, Democracy Online Newswire, October 22, 2001, available at (http://www.e-democracy.org/do).

35. Clift, Democracy Online Newswire, October 22, 2001.

36. Brandt, "Minneapolis E-mail Forum." The Minneapolis forum continues to operate with 900 members in 2004 alongside new local forums in St. Paul and Winona, Minnesota.

37. Bill Workman, "Political E-Gadflies," *San Francisco Chronicle*, February 5, 2001, A13. Jeannette Sherwin's website is (http://www.oaklandnews.com); the Sonoma Town Hall Coalition website is (http://townhallcoalition.org); and Alice Barnes' website is

(http://www.sanbrunobart.com), which informs the reader that "B.A.R.T. also stands for Belle Air Residents for Truth."

38. Rebecca Fairley Raney, "Suits Target Carte Blanche Posting," *Online Journalism Review*, February 7, 2002, available at (http://ojr/usc/edu/content/story.cfm?request=697).

39. Web address for E-The People is (http://www.e-thepeople.com). E-The People worked with over 400 online newspapers, television stations, and Internet portals; E-The People in 2002 became a non-profit organization, merging with Quorum.org.

40. MoveOn.org website (http://www.moveon.org).

41. MoveOn.org website (www.moveon.org/coverage.htm), citing articles from the *San Francisco Chronicle*, October 15, 1988, and *The Washington Post*, October 9, 1988.

42. (www.moveon.org/documentation.htm).

43. Katie Hafner, "Mobilizing Online for Gun Control," *The New York Times*, May 20, 1999, G5.

44. The Issue Forum is hyperlinked to (http://www.actionforum.com).

45. Scott Harris, "MoveOn.org is Doing Just That," *The Standard*, March 14, 2001, available at (http://www.standard.com/article/display/ 0,1151,22858.html).

46. Win Without War website (http://www.winwithoutwarus.org). Among the thirty-two committees were the Council for a Livable World, Evangelical Lutheran Church of America, Greenpeace, NAACP, National Organization for Women, and the Sierra Club. Susan Shaer, Women's Action for New Directions, and Robert Edgar, National Council of Churches, were co-chairs.

47. Juliet Eilperin, "'Virtual March' Floods Senate with Calls Against an Iraq War," *The Washington Post*, February 27, 2003, A22.

48. Website address was (http://www.stopdrlaura.com). Remarks by Aravosis at the 2002 Politics Online Conference, May 20, 2002, at the George Washington University, Washington, D.C., and quoted in Donna Ladd, "StopDr.Laura.com," *Salon.com* available at (http://www.salon.com/tech/log2000/03/01/drlaura).

49. Peter S. Goodman, "Congress to Block Imaginary Internet Tax Bill," *The Washington Post*, May 10, 2000, E1; Mark Stencel, "E-Mail Hoax an Issue in N.Y. Senate Debate," *The Washington Post*, October 8, 2000 available at (http://washingtonpost.com/ wp-dyn/articles/A34390–2000Oct8.html). The original hoax e-mail is available at David Emery, "Bill 602P–U.S. Postal Tax on E-Mail," May 5, 1999, (http://urbanlegends. about.com/science/urbanlegends/library/blemtx2.htm).

50. Melody Simmons, "Internet Helped Activist Push Land Mine Ban," *Baltimore Sun*, October 21, 1998. On Jody Williams, see Stephen Frantzich, *Citizen Democracy: Political Activists in a Cynical Age* (Lanham, Md.: Rowman and Littlefield, 1999). See also, Daniel Bennett and Pam Fielding, *The Net Effect: How Cyberadvocacy is Changing the Political Landscape* (Merrifield, Va.: e-Advocate Press, 1999); Jennifer Lee, "How Protesters Mobilized So Many and So Nimbly," *The New York Times*, February 23, 2003, WK-3. On "smart mobs," see Howard Rheingold, *Smart Mobs: The Next Social Revolution* (New York: The Perseus Press, 2002).

51. Website address (http://www.protest.net). Henshaw-Plath quote from Bob Tedeschi, "Protest Portal Unites Activists Under One URL," *The New York Times*, September 2, 1998, available at (http://www.nytimes.com/library/98/09/cyber/articles/02protest. html).

52. See Dennis W. Johnson, *No Place for Amateurs: How Political Consultants Are Reshaping American Democracy* (New York: Routledge, 2001), ch. 9.

53. David S. Broder, *Democracy Derailed: Initiative Campaigns and the Power of Money* (New York: Harvest Books, 2001) and Peter Schrag, *Paradise Lost: California's Experience*,

America's Future (New York: The New Press, 1998); see also, Johnson, *No Place for Amateurs.*

54. Tracy Westen, "Electronic Democracy (Ready or Not, Here It Comes)," Advisory Committee to the Congressional Internet Caucus, 2001 Briefing Book, available at (http://www.netcaucus.org/books/egov2001). Westen is also vice-chair of Grassroots Enterprise.

55. The Democracy Symposium met in Williamsburg, Virginia, in February 2002 to resolve issues and create a "Legislature of the People." Funding for this Symposium was provided in part by the People's Lobby in memory of its founders, Edwin and Joyce Koupal, available at (http://66.136.171.185/index.html).

Chapter 2: The Rise of Electronic Advocacy

Epigraph quote from McCurry in Rebecca Pollard, "Digging Deep: Grassroots Lobbying," *Influence Online*, March 20, 2002, available at (http://www.grassroots.com/inthenews/influence_online_032002.html); quote from Seiger, personal interview, January 13, 2003, Washington, D.C.; quote from Rehr in Elizabeth Drew, "Bush's Weird Tax Cut," *The New York Review of Books,* August 9, 1991.

1. The term comes from Jeffrey H. Birnbaum and Alan S. Murray, *Showdown at Gucci Gulch: Lawmakers, Lobbyists, and the Unlikely Triumph of Tax Reform* (New York: Vintage, 1987); see also, Jeffrey H. Birnbaum, *The Lobbyists: How Influence Peddlers Work Their Way in Washington* (New York: Times Books, 1994).

2. On corporate grassroots activities, tactics, and case studies, see Edward A. Grefe and Martin Linsky, *The New Corporate Activism: Harnessing the Power of Grassroots Tactics for Your Organization* (New York: McGraw-Hill, 1995).

3. P. J. Huffstutter, "Lawmakers, Internet Fail to Click," *The San Diego Union-Tribune,* January 1, 1996, A1. At the time of this quotation, Seiger was with the Center for Democracy and Technology.

4. Keith Koffler, "Hired E-Guns Roam the Web," *CongressDaily,* February 9, 2000.

5. Michael Totty, "Politics on the Web Has Gone Mainstream," *The Wall Street Journal,* April 15, 2002, C1, available at (http://online.wsj.com/public/article_print/0,4287, SB1018650866755190720m00.html).

6. Totty, "Politics on the Web Has Gone Mainstream."

7. American Society of Anesthesiologists, AnesthesiaSafety.Net, available at (http://www.anesthesiasafety.net). Like any good advocacy campaign, the Anesthesia Safety.Net thanked those who sent letters and asked them to send thank you notes to President Bush and Health and Human Services Secretary Tommy Thompson.

8. Cost comparisons and other information from e-Advocates, Washington, D.C., May 2002.

9. Pollard, "Digging Deep: Grass-Roots Lobbying." Kevin Donnellan was AARP's director of grassroots and elections.

10. Website address of AARP is (http://www.aarp.org).

11. Whitney Wilcox, "Reassessing Your Communications Initiatives: Lessons from Environmental Defense," Benton Foundation (December 2001), available at (http://www.benton.org/Practice/Features/ed.update.html). The web address is (http://www.scorecard.org).

12. Environmental Defense Action Network web address is (http://actionnetwork.org). Ohio SOAP Network web address is (http://actionnetwork.org/Ohio.SOAP/home.html).

13. Available at (http://www.hogwatch.org) and the Poop Counter at (http://www. hogwatch. org/html/java/counter.html).

14. Wilcox, "Reassessing Your Communications Initiatives."

15. Eric Pianin and Helen Dewar, "In Nuclear Waste Site Debate, Visions of Transport Disaster," *The Washington Post,* July 8, 2002, A3.

16. Eric Pianin and Helen Dewar, "Senate Approves Storage of Nuclear Waste in Nevada," *The Washington Post,* July 10, 2002, A1.

17. Jeffrey H. Birnbaum, "How Microsoft Conquered Washington," *Fortune* (April 20, 2002), 96.

18. FIN web address is (http://www.microsoft.com/freedomtoinnovate/howhelp.asp). FIN also provides an electronic newsletter, links to stories on the DRM debate, a simple method of contacting legislators (which requires Microsoft Passport), plus T-shirts, coffee mugs, and bumper stickers.

19. In September 2001, Juno Online Services merged with NetZero, Inc. to form United Online, and Juno Advocacy Network ceased operations. United Online website is (http://www.unitedonline.net/about/history.html).

20. The Heritage Forest Campaign was initiated by the Pew Charitable Trusts and funded by several other major foundations. It was hosted by the National Audubon Society, in partnership with American Lands, the Earthjustice Legal Defense Fund, the National Environmental Trust, the National Resources Defense Council, the U.S. Public Interest Research Group, and the Wilderness Society. The online campaign, the OurForests.org, received major support from the W. Alton Jones Foundation, the Turner Foundation, the Brainerd Foundation, and the Bullitt Foundation. Amy Luckey and Rob Stuart, "Our-Forests.org: Online Organizing Comes of Age," TechRocks, Winter 2001, available at (http://techrocks.org/casestudy_ourforests.html).

21. Luckey and Stuart, "OurForests.org."

22. Laura Miller, "One E-mail Message Can Change the World," *The New York Times Magazine,* December 9, 2001, 86.

23. Conservative HQ website (http://www.conservativehq.com) and the Sixty-Second Activist Club is found at (http:www.conservativehq.com/activist/60second/activist-index.htm).

24. Nancy Cleeland, "Goodbye Union Handbills, Hello Net," *Los Angeles Times,* October 11, 1999, C5, and Jim McKay, "AFL-CIO Sees Solidarity Via Online Network," *Pittsburgh Post-Gazette,* October 12, 1999, F1.

25. The Women's Sports Foundation website is available at (http://www.womenssports foundation.org) and Geena Takes Aim is available at (http://www.womenssports foundation.org/cgi-bin/iowa/issues/geena/index.html). Geena Takes Aim won the 2002 Golden Dot award for online civic excellence, given by the Politics Online Conference and the Graduate School of Political Management of the George Washington University.

26. The checklist was adapted from L. Bunker, N. Chaudrey, P. Keller, P. Larkin, and V. Williams, "Check It Out: Is the Playing Field Level for Girls at Your Elementary and Secondary School?"

27. Capitol Advantage website (http://capitoladvantage.com). Brian Krebs, "Congress Diverts Unwanted E-mail," *The Washington Post,* August 8, 2002, available at (http://www.washingtonpost.com/ac2/wp-dyn/A60019-2002Aug8?language=printer). During an interview, Robert Hansan, president of Capitol Advantage, began our conversation by announcing how many total communications there were with elected officials at that moment using Capitol Advantage products, and then gave an update when we had finished. Interview, June 16, 2001, Merrifield, Virginia.

28. Capitol Advantage website (http://capitoladvantage.com/h2/products/capwiz features.html).

29. Several of these companies have working relationships with one another. For example, Democracy Data & Communications (DDC) is affiliated with Direct Impact. Capitol Advantage is affiliated with e-Advocates, and Grassroots Enterprise and Issue Dynamics, Inc. (IDI) have launched a joint software project.

30. Grassroots Enterprise website (http://grassroots.com/products/grassrootsmultiplier/ features.html).

31. Pollard, "Digging Deep: Grass Roots Lobbying."

32. Melanie Fonder, "Despite Anthrax and Disruption, Lobbyists Slow to Use Web Tools," *The Hill*, December 5, 2001, available at (http://www.hill.news.com/120501/elob-bying.htm).

33. The powerhouse law firm of Patton Boggs in Washington, D.C. formed a strategic partnership and invested in Qorvis Communications, a communications firm that specialized in, among other things, grassroots and grasstops management. Patton Boggs news release, August 9, 2000, available at (http://www.pattonboggs.com/news/ pressreleases/2000/08/qorvis.html).

Chapter 3: The Promise of Electronic Government

Epigraph quotes from Robert D. Atkinson, "Digital Government: The Next Step to Re-engi-neering the Federal Government," 2001 Briefing Book, Advisory Committee of the Congressional Internet Caucus, available at (http://www.netcaucus.org/books/egov2001). Atkinson is vice-president of the Progressive Policy Institute and director of its Technology and New Economy Project and author of *e-Government: The Next American Revolution* (Wash-ington, D.C.: The Council for Excellence in Government, 2001).

1. Judi Hasson, "Waitin,' Watching to Make a Move," *Federal Computer Week*, April 17, 2000, available at (http://www.fcw.com/articles/2000/0417/mgt-gop-04-17-00.asp).

2. Citizens, however, have considerable confidence that e-government will help law enforcement at all levels to exchange information and prosecute criminals and terrorists. Hart-Teeter poll for the Council on Excellence in Government cited in William Matthews, "Perception of E-gov Shifting," *Federal Computer Week*, February 27, 2002, available at (http://www.fcw.com/geb/articles/2002/0225/web-egov-02-27-02.asp).

3. See also, Jane E. Fountain, *Building the Virtual State: Information Technology and Insti-tutional Change* (Washington, D. C.: Brookings Institution Press, 2001), chapter 4, "Bureaucracy."

4. Perhaps it is not fair to pick on the government of the District of Columbia. It is just emerging from an agonizingly long period of customer-care and government service that was profoundly third-world in its ineptitude.

5. Darby Patterson, "Winds of Change," *Government Technology*, November 2001, avail-able at (http://www.govtech.net/magazine/sup_story.phtml).

6. Dibya Sarkar, "States Round Up 511 Resources," *Federal Computer Week*, February 28, 2002, available at (http://www.fcw.com/geb/articles/2002/0225/web-drive-02-28-02.asp).

7. Jeffrey W. Seifert and R. Eric Petersen, "The Promise of all Things E? Expectations and Implications of Electronic Government," paper delivered before the 97th annual meeting, American Political Science Association, San Francisco, California, August 30–September 2, 2001, 1. Janine S. Hiller and France Bélanger expand on the basic types of e-government: a) Government delivering services to individuals (G2IS); b) govern-

ment to individuals as part of the political process (G2IP); c) government to business as
a citizen (G2BC); d) government to business in the marketplace (G2BMKT); e) government to employee (G2E); and f) government to government (G2G). Hiller and
Bélanger, "Privacy Strategies for Electronic Government," in Mark A. Abramson and
Grady E. Means, eds., *E-Government 2001* (Lanham, Md.: Roman and Littlefield, 2001),
173–4.

8. Public Technology, Inc., "Is Your Local Government Plugged In?" cited in Dibya Sarkar,
"Most Governments Now Online," *Federal Computer Week*, February 28, 2001, available
at (http://www.fcw.com/print.asp). The survey was based on 1,900 city and county governments with a population of more than 10,000.

9. Seifert and Petersen, "The Promise of all Things E?" The Gartner Group, a leading technology research firm, conceptualized these four stages of website development. See
Christopher Baum and Andrea Di Maio, "Gartner's Four Phases of E-Government
Model," November 21, 2000, available at (http://www.governing.com/gartner/
gartner_intro.html). Hiller and Bélanger add a fifth category, participation: government
websites that provide online voting, registration online, or the posting of comments.
"Privacy Strategies for Electronic Government," 176.

10. David J. Molchany, chief information office for Fairfax County, Virginia, quoted in
C. E. Pelc, "Web Design by the People," *Government Technology*, October 21, 2001,
available at (http://www.govtech.net/magazine/story.phtm).

11. Civic Resource Group, "Cities on the Internet 2001: E-Government Applied," Santa
Monica, California, August 2001, available at (http://www.CivicResource.com). Some
government websites have domain names that are easy to remember and intuitive, for
example, Chicago (cityofchicago.org) and Costa Mesa, California (cityofcostamesa.com).
Many state government sites use this standardized convention: Georgia (state.ga.us) and
Virginia (state.va.us), while other states use a more intuitive domain convention:
Michigan (michigan.gov) or Utah (utah.gov). Many cities and counties use the more difficult "ci" or "co" convention: Durham, North Carolina (ci.durham.nc.us), Bellevue,
Washington (ci.bellevue.wa.us), or the very abbreviated Montgomery County, Maryland
(co.mo.md.us). Some names have a local flavor: Indianapolis, Indiana (indygov.org), or
Louisville, Kentucky (louky.gov), and once in a while domain names are downright zen-
like: City of Richardson, Texas (cor.net) or State of Nebraska (nol.org).

12. Testimony of Costis Toregas before the Committee on Governmental Affairs, U.S.
Senate, July 11, 2001. Public Technology, Inc. (PTI) is a non-profit research and development local government organization and is the technology arm for the National League
of Cities, the National Association of Counties, and the International City/County
Management Association.

13. The Center for Digital Government is a national research and advisory institute and a
division of e.Republic, Inc., the parent company of *Government Technology* magazine.
The Center for Digital Government is based in Folsom, California and its executive
director is Cathilea Robinett.

14. Center for Digital Government website (http://www.centerdigitalgov.com/center/
bow01).

15. Ellen McCarthy, "Government Sites Draw Web Traffic," *The Washington Post*, January
9, 2002, E5.

16. William Matthews, "Setting a Course for E-Government," *Federal Computer Week*,
December 11, 2001, available at (http://fcw.com/fcw/articles/2000/12/11/cov-egov-12-
11-00.asp).

17. "Information Technology Plan, FY 2002," Fairfax County, Virginia, Department of
Information Technology, May 2001.

18. Council for Excellence in Government, poll conducted by Hart-Teeter Research, November 12–19, 2001. "An Appetite for Online Government," *The Washington Post*, April 1, 2002. In other polls and usage surveys, citizens have wanted online access to birth certificates, hunting and fishing licenses, voter registration, and information about state parks and reservations. Meghan E. Cook, "What Citizens Want from E-Government: Current Practice Research." Center for Technology in Government, SUNY at Albany, October 2000. Congressional Internet Caucus, *2001 Briefing Book*, available at (http://www.netcaucus.org/books/egov2001). All responses cited above were between 75 and 50 percent saying they were very likely or fairly likely to conduct those activities over the Web.

19. Congress Online Project, "Constituents and Your Web Site: What Citizens Want to See on Congressional Web Sites," (Washington, D.C., October 2001), written by Dennis W. Johnson, available at (http://www.congressonlineproject.org). The Congress Online Project conducted the first comprehensive focus group research to determine what constituents wanted to see on congressional websites.

20. Steve Towns, "Top of the Heap," *Government Technology*, October 2001.

21. My California is available at (http://my.ca.gov/state/portal/myca).

22. My Virginia is available at (http://www.myvirginia.org).

23. Towns, "Top of the Heap." The Commonwealth of Virginia website address is (http://www.state.va.us); the state of Maine website address is (http://www.state.me.us).

24. Towns, "Top of the Heap." New York City website address is (http://nyc.gov); the Conyers, Georgia web address is (http://www.conyersga.com).

25. Katherine K. Hanley is the chair of the Fairfax County, Virginia, Board of Supervisors.

26. "Information Technology Plan, FY 2002," Fairfax County, Virginia, Department of Information Technology, May 2001, sec. 2, p. 4.

27. Interview, Gregory Scott, acting manager, Public Access Technology Group, and Steve Malo, Department of Information Technology, Fairfax County, Virginia, December 11, 2001.

28. "Fairfax County Web Site Redesign: Summary of Public Questionnaire Responses, February 2001," available at (http://infoweb/redesign/documents/redesignsummary.htm). Also, the Office of Public Affairs held several focus groups with children as part of "Take Your Children to Work Day" activities. A total of twelve focus groups were held throughout the county in March 2001.

29. Pelc, "Web Design by the People."

30. Fairfax County had for years used the older, but more difficult to remember, naming convention: (http://www.co.fairfax.va.us). With its redesign of the website in June 2001, it moved the URL to the more intuitive (http://www.fairfaxcounty.gov).

31. "Texas Launches Web-Based Human Services System," *Government Technology*, October 31, 2001, available at (http://www.govtech.net/news).

32. Your Oklahoma, website is available at (http://www.state.ok.us).

33. Civic Resource Group, "Cities on the Internet 2001: E-Government Applied: Executive Brief," Santa Monica, California, August 2001, available at (http://www.Civic Resource.com).

34. Civic Resource Group, "Cities on the Internet 2001."

35. Elena Larson and Lee Rainie, *Digital Town Hall: How Local Officials Use the Internet and the Civic Benefits They Cite from Dealing with Constituents Online* (Washington, D.C.: Pew Internet and American Life Project, October 2002), available at (http://www.pew internet.org).

36. Bara Vaida, "E-Government Move to Digital Government Sparks State Privacy Concerns," *Tech Daily*, Jan. 4, 2002. In 2002, House Energy and Commerce Committee

Chairman W. J. (Billy) Tauzin (Republican-Louisiana) hoped to have the House approve enactment of a bill to supersede all state laws on privacy. Among other things, the legislation would set guidelines on government use of private information collected electronically.

37. Some have concluded that such talk about privacy on the Internet has already been decided: There is none. As Scott McNealy, chief executive office of Sun Microsystems, infamously noted: "You have zero privacy anyway. Get over it." Quoted in Polly Sprenger, "Sun on Privacy: 'Get Over It,'" *Wired.com*, January 25, 1999, available at (http://www.wired.com/news/politics/0,1283,17538,00.html).

38. Megan's Law was prompted by a New Jersey statute on sex offender registration. As a part of the federal 1994 Violent Crime Control and Enforcement Act, Congress passed the Jacob Wetterling Crimes Against Children and Sexually Violent Offenders Registration Act. In 1996, the Wetterling Law was amended by Megan's Law, which requires states to release relevant information about registered sex offenders to the public. Jacob Wetterling was an eleven-year-old boy who was abducted and never seen again; Megan Kanka was a New Jersey child who was abducted and killed.

39. Department of Corrections, State of Minnesota, website, available at (http://www.doc.state.mn.us/level3/offenders/noncompliant/176250.htm).

40. Klaas Foundation for Children, Sausalito, California, founded by Marc Klaas, father of Polly Klaas, a child who was abducted from her home and murdered in 1993. The Klaas Foundation website is http://www.klaaskids.org. Another private site is Pandora's Box: The Secrecy of Child Sexual Abuse, maintained by Nancy Faulkner, M.D., available at (http://www.prevent-abuse-now.com/register.htm).

41. Charles Lane, "Megan's Laws Affirmed by High Court," *The Washington Post*, March 6, 2003, A1 and Bill Keller, "Government Should Set the Example on Internet Privacy," The Gartner Group, December 14, 2001, Report FT-15-1151, available at (http://www3.gartner.com/DisplayDocument?id=350614&acsFlg+accessBought). The two cases to reach the U.S. Supreme Court were *Connecticut Dept. of Public Safety v. Doe, et al.* (No. 01-1231) and *Godfrey v. Doe* (No. 01-729).

42. Leslie Walker, "Police Records For Anyone's Viewing Pleasure," *The Washington Post*, May 23, E1. ChoicePoint Inc. is a 5,000-employee company that was spun off from Equifax in 1997, and it owns 14 billion records about people and companies. See Richard Hunter, *World Without Secrets: Business, Crime and Privacy in the Age of Ubiquitous Computing*, (New York: Cahners Business Information, Inc., 2002).

43. Sandra G. Boodman, "Accuracy: Please Wait," *The Washington Post*, November 27, 2001, HE1. The months elapsing between the time that the Virginia Board of Medicine was notified of a discrepancy and an action taken by them reflects the due process rights accorded doctors, according to Robert A. Nebiker, deputy director of the Virginia Department of Health Professionals. The website address is (http://www.vahealth-providers.com).

44. Brian Faler, "Nursing Home Web Site is Found Lacking," *The Washington Post*, February 21, 2001, A19. The website is available at (http://www.medicare.gov/NHCompare/home.asp).

45. Steve Towns, "States, Cities Sanitize Web Sites," *Government Technology*, November 2001, available at (http://govtech.net/news/features/news_feature.phtml).

46. Ariana Eunjung Cha, "Risks Prompt U.S. to Limit Access to Data," *The Washington Post*, February 24, 2002, A1 and Renae Merle, "New Job, Newer Realities," *The Washington Post*, June 19, 2002, H1.

47. The St. Paul, Minnesota website (http://stpaul.gov).

48. Legislative Audit Bureau, "A Best Practices Review of Local E-Government Services,"

State of Wisconsin, December 2001, available at (http://www.legis.state.wi.us/lab/Reports/01-0_E-GovFull.pdf).

49. J. H. Snider, "E-Democracy as Deterrence: Public Policy Implications of a Deterrence Model of Democratic Accountability." Paper delivered at the 97th annual meeting of the American Political Science Association, San Francisco, California, August 30–September 2, 2001, at 14.

50. Snider, "E-Democracy as Deterrence," 30–35.

51. Senator Patrick J. Leahy and Representative Robert Goodlatte, "The Internet and the Future of Democratic Governance" (2000), available at (http://www.internetpolicy.org/briefing/leahy_goodlatte.html) and Senator Leahy remarks at panel discussion, "E-Government: Constituent Mail in the Time of Anthrax," The Advisory Committee to the Congressional Internet Caucus, Washington, D.C., March 20, 2002.

52. FirstGov.gov website (http://www.firstgov.gov). The Chief Information Officers (CIO) Council was established by Executive Order 13011, Federal Information Technology, on July 16, 1996. It serves as the principal interagency forum for improving federal government agency information resources. The search engine was a multi-million dollar gift from the Federal Search Foundation, a non-profit charitable organization established by and chiefly funded by Eric Brewer, a University of California-Berkeley professor and co-founder and chief scientist of the Inktomi Corporation. Testimony of Eric Brewer, "FirstGov.gov: Is it a Good Idea?," Subcommittee on Government Management, Information, and Technology, Committee on Government Reform, U.S. House of Representatives, October 2, 2000, available at (http://www.house.gov/reform/gmit/hearings/2000hearings/001002.FirstGov/001002eb.htm). In 2002, AT&T won a contract worth $2 million annually to replace the FirstGov.gov search engine. Gail Repsher Emery, "AT&T Wins GSA Web Hosting Contract," *Washington Technology* (August 21, 2002), available at (http://www.washingtontechnology.com/news/1_1/daily_news/18811-1.html).

53. Available at (http://www.firstgov.gov/Citizens/Services.html).

54. French Caldwell, "FirstGov Will Improve Searches but Needs Content Management," The Gartner Group (FT-15-2847, January 18, 2002), available at (http://www3.gartner.com/DisplayDocument?id=351920&acsFlg=accessBought).

55. "A Blueprint for New Beginnings," White House website, available at (http://whitehouse.gov/news/usbudget/blueprint/budix.html).

56. "OMB Outline New Federal E-Government Strategy," press release, Office of Management and Budget, October 25, 2001.

57. "OMB Outline New Federal E-Government Strategy." Another initiative would be called e-Authentication, headed by the General Services Administration, which would establish a core federal public-key infrastructure which would give the public a secure and consistent way of communicating with the government online. Diane Frank, "E-Gov Initiatives," *Federal Computer Week,* October 29, 2001, updated January 23, 2002, available at (http://www.fcw.com/fcw/articles/2001/1029/web-egovlist-10–29–01.asp).

58. Williams Matthews, "Setting a Course of E-Government," *Federal Computer Week*, December 11, 2000, available at (http://fcw.com/fcw/articles/2000/1211/cov-egov-12–11-00.asp).

59. William Matthews, "Study: E-Gov Prone to Falter," *Federal Computer Week,* May 6, 2002.

60. U.S. Congress, House Committee on Government Reform, Subcommittee on Government Management, Information and Technology, available at (http://house.gov/reform/gmit/ index.htm).

61. Timothy J. Sprehe, "E-Government: Smoke and Mirrors," *Federal Computer Week,* May

6, 2002, available at (http://www.fcw.com/fcw/articles/2002/0506/pol-sprehe-05-06-02.asp). Sprehe is president of Sprehe Information Management Associates, Washington, D.C.

62. Chief Information Officers Council website, available at (http://www.cio.gov/Documents/about_the_cio.html). On the creation of the federal Chief Information Officer, see Jeffrey W. Seifert, *Federal Chief Information Officer (CIO): Opportunities and Challenges* (Congressional Research Service, July 2, 2002) and Jeffrey W. Seifert, *A Primer on E-Government: Sectors, Stages, Opportunities, and Challenges of Online Governance* (Congressional Research Service, January 28, 2003).

63. U.S. Congress. House. Committee on Government Reform, Subcommittee on Technology and Procurement Policy. Testimony of David L. McClure, Director, Information Technology Management Issues, U.S. General Accounting Office, "Enterprise-Wide Strategies for Managing Information Resources and Technology: Learning from State and Local Governments," April 3, 2001, available at (http://www.house.gov/reform).

64. McClure Testimony. H.R. 5024, the Chief Information Officer of the United States Act of 2000, introduced by Rep. Jim Turner (Democrat-Texas) would vest the federal CIO the information resources and technology management responsibilities currently held by OMB together with oversight of the General Services Administration, and promulgation of information system standards developed by the National Institute of Standards and Technology. A second bill, H.R. 4670, introduced by Rep. Thomas Davis (Republican-Virginia) generally did not change the responsibilities of these agencies, but called for a federal CIO to advise the agencies and consult with state and local governments and the private sector; at 22.

65. *e-Government: The Next American Revolution* (Washington, D.C.: The Council for Excellence in Government, 2001); *Mr. President, Appoint a Federal CIO*, (GartnerGroup, TG-12-8984, March 18, 2001) and *Help Wanted: Federal CIO for High-Stress, Rewarding Work* (GartnerGroup, COM-13-0387, March 14, 2001). The Progressive Policy Institute was first to make such a recommendation, and its proposals were contained in federal legislation introduced by Senator Joseph Lieberman (Democrat-Connecticut), S. 803 and Rep. Jim Turner (Democrat-Texas), H.R. 2458, the E-Government Act of 2001. Andrew Leigh and Robert D. Atkinson, *Breaking Down Bureaucratic Barriers: The Next Phase of Digital Government* (Washington, D.C.: Progressive Policy Institute, November 2001), 13.

66. E-Government Act of 2002, H. R. 2458. Judi Hasson, "E-Gov Act Signed into Law," *Federal Computer Week*, December 17, 2002 and Diane Frank and Judi Hasson, "Senate Slashes E-Gov Fund—Again," *Federal Compute*

67. Thomas C. Beierle, "Democracy On-Line: An Evaluation of the National Dialogue on Public Involvement in EPA Decisions," RFF Report: Resources for the Future (January 2002), 8, available at (http://www.rff.org/reports/PDF.files/democracyonline.pdf).

68. Beierle, "Democracy On-Line," 12.

69. Cindy Skrzycki, "U.S. Opens Online Portal to Rulemaking," *The Washington Post,* January 23, 2003, E1.

70. Memorandum from Craig Luigart, Chief Information Officer, Department of Education and James Flyzik, Chief Information Officer, Department of Treasury, to Chief Information Officers, "Publication of Final Regulations Implementing Section 508," December 21, 2000, available at (http://www.cio.gov/Documents/memo_508_final_regs_Dec_2000.html). The relevant federal legislation enacted during the 1990s was the Americans With Disabilities Act (1990); Rehabilitation Act amendments (1998); and Assistive Technology Act (1998).

71. Wendy Lazarus and Francisco Mora, "Online Content for Low-Income and Under-

served Americans: The Digital Divide's New Frontier," The Children's Partnership, March 2000, 9. The Children's Partnership is a non-profit, non-partisan organization based in Santa Monica, California, and Washington, D.C.

72. Health Resources and Services Administration, U.S. Department of Health and Human Services, "Cross-Agency Portal for Low Income Americans," (2001).

73. Benton Foundation, press release, "Bush Abandons National Strategy to Bridge the Digital Divide," February 11, 2002.

74. Center for Democracy and Technology, *CDT Policy Post*, vol. 8, no. 25, November 21, 2002.

Chapter 4: Old Communications and New

Epigraph quote of Carson from Rebecca Fairley Raney, "E-Mail Gets the Cold Shoulder in Congress," *The New York Times*, December 13, 2001, available at (http://www.nytimes.com/2001/12/13/technology/circuits/13CONG.html); quote of Senate press aide from Rebecca Fairley Raney, "Congress Not Yet Plugging in to E-Mail," *The New York Times*, June 15, 1996, available at (http://search1.nytimes.com/library/cyber/week/0615mail.html).

1. Charles O. Jones, *The United States Congress: People, Place, and Policy* (Homewood, Ill.: The Dorsey Press, 1982), 294–295.

2. On congressional procedure, see Walter J. Oleszek, *Congressional Procedures and Policy Processes*, 5th ed. (Washington, D.C.: CQ Books, 2000).

3. Matthew Josephson, *Edison: A Biography* (New York: John Wiley & Sons, 1992), 65–66, in Anthony G. Wilhelm, *Democracy in the Digital Age: Challenges to Political Life in Cyberspace* (New York: Routledge, 2000), 1. See also, Walter J. Oleszek, *The Internet and Congressional Decisionmaking*, at 4–5, a report prepared for the Chairman, House Rules Committee, 107th Cong., 1st sess. (September 2001), available at (http://www.house.gov/rules/internet_congressional_decisionmaking.pdf). Representative Thomas Ferry (Republican-Michigan), a supporter of the Edison invention, observed that during the 40th Congress there were 345 roll call votes, which consumed 115 hours, or a calendar month of time. Oleszek, *The Internet and Congressional Decisionmaking*, at 4.

4. U.S. Congress. Congressional Research Service. Jane Bortnick Griffith and Walter J. Oleszek, *Electronic Devices in the House Chamber*, a Report to the Subcommittee on Rules and Organization, House Rules Committee. 106th Cong., 1st sess., (November 21, 1997), available at (http://www.house.gov/rules/e-devices.htm).

5. Correspondence with R. Eric Petersen, Government and Finance Division, Congressional Research Division, Library of Congress, May 18, 2003.

6. Orrin E. Dunlop, Jr., "Reading Some Radio Mail: Gets Taste of Congress," *The New York Times*, December 11, 1932, 6, retold in Stephen E. Frantzich and John Sullivan, *The C-SPAN Revolution* (Norman: University of Oklahoma Press, 1996), 30. Representative Vincent M. Brennan (Republican-Michigan) introduced the bill to allow radio coverage in 1922.

7. These were the first nationally-televised congressional hearings. See Emile de Antonio and Daniel Talbot, *Point of Order! A Documentary of the Army-McCarthy Hearings*. (New York: Norton, 1964) and Ronald Garay, *Congressional Television: A Legislative History* (Westport, Conn.: Greenwood Press, 1984).

8. Quoted in C. Lawrence Evans and Walter J. Oleszek, "The 'Wired Congress': The Internet, Institutional Change and Legislative Work," in James A. Thurber and Colton C. Campbell, eds., *Congress and the Internet* (Upper Saddle River, N.J.: Prentice Hall, 2003), 104.

9. Griffith and Oleszek, *Electronic Devices in the House Chamber*, 2.

10. U.S. Congress. Library of Congress. Oleszek, *The Internet and Congressional Decision-making*, at 4–5.

11. U.S. Congress. House Committee on House Oversight. *CyberCongress Accomplishments During the 104th Congress*, 105th Cong., 1st sess. (February 11, 1997), available at (http://www.house.gov/cha/publications/cybercongress/body_cybercongress.html). The earliest study of Congress and the use of computer technology was Stephen E. Frantzich, *Computers in Congress: The Politics of Information* (Beverly Hills, Calif.: Sage Publications, 1982). For historical accounts of the growth of computer use in Congress, see Oleszek, *The Internet and Congressional Decisionmaking*. Jane Bortnick Griffith, *Information Technology in the House of Representatives: A Historical Framework of the Trends and Political Impact on Legislative Process for the 104th–106th Congresses*, 106th Cong., 2nd sess. (April 12, 1999), available at (http://www.house.gov/rules/infotech99.htm); and David Dreier, "We've Come a Long Way . . . Maybe," 52–77 in Thurber and Campbell, eds., *Congress and the Internet*; an earlier version is available at (http://www.house.gov/rules/congress_andthe_internet.pdf).

12. *CyberCongress Accomplishments*, 1.

13. *CyberCongress Accomplishments*, 1 and Christopher J. Dorobek, "House Approves Overhaul of E-mail for Cyber-Congress," *Government Computer News* (November 27, 1995), available at (http://www.gcn.com/archives/gcn/1995/November27/comphill.htm).

14. Chris Casey, "Congress and the Internet: Looking Back and Looking Forward," 186–192, in Thurber and Campbell, eds., *Congress and the Internet*. See also Chris Casey, *The Hill on the Net: Congress Enters the Information Age* (Boston: Academic Press, 1996). Casey, one of the first staffers to appreciate the importance of online communications, launched the Kennedy home page.

15. Those first seven House Members were Jay Dickey (Republican-Arkansas), Sam Gejdenson (Democrat-Connecticut), Newt Gingrich (Republican-Georgia), George Miller (Democrat-California), Charlie Rose (Democrat-North Carolina), Fortney (Pete) Stark (Democrat-California), and Mel Watt (Democrat-North Carolina). Howard Rheingold, *The Virtual Community: Homesteading on the Electronic Frontier* (Reading, Mass.: Addison-Wesley Publishing Company, 1993), 93–94.

16. Patrick Jasperse, "'Electronic Democracy' is Under Way as Congress Gets the Word by E-Mail," *The Milwaukee Journal*, November 25, 1994, available at (http://ptg/djnr/ccroot/asp/publib/story_clean_cpy.asp?rndnum=548606).

17. Write Your Representative was run by House Information Resources; another filter software was Citizen Direct, which was run by an independent organization. For a discussion of these filters, see OMB Watch, "Speaking Up in the Internet Age: Congress and Internet Communications," December 1998, available at (http://www.ombwatch.org/npt/resource/reports/congsrvy.html).

18. Rebecca Fairley Raney, "Technology Filters Flow," *The New York Times*, January 15, 1998, available at (http://www.nytimes.com/library/cyber/week/011598congress-tech.html).

19. Eshoo quoted in Wayne Rash, Jr., *Politics on the Nets: Wiring the Political Process* (New York: W. H. Freeman, 1997), 143.

20. Courtney Macavinta, "Congress Has Issues with E-Mail," *News.Com*, February 25, 1998, available at (http://news.com/2100–1023–208492.html).

21. Quoted in Gary Ruskin, "America Off-Line: Gingrich's Unfulfilled Internet Promise," *The Washington Post*, November 16, 1997, C2. Ruskin was the director of the Congressional Accountability Project.

22. Mark Lewyn and John Carey, "Will America Log on to the Intenet," *Business Week*, December 5, 1994, 38.

23. *CyberCongress Accomplishments*, 1.

24. U.S. Congress. Library of Congress. *A Plan for a New Legislative Information System for the United States Congress,* 104th Cong., 2nd sess. (February 16, 1996), submitted to the Committees on House Oversight, Senate Rules and Administration, House Appropriations and Senate Appropriations, pursuant to Public Law 104–53, available at (http://www.house.gov/rules/theplan.txt). Appendix A, submitted by House Information Resources, 36–37. Gingrich was a big fan of futurist Alvin Toffler and his book *The Third Wave* (New York: Bantam Books, 1989).

25. *CyberCongress Accomplishments*, 2.

26. *A Plan for a New Legislative Information System for the United States Congress.*

27. THOMAS is located at (http://thomas.loc.gov).

28. Interview with Jonah Seiger, co-founder, Mindshare Internet Campaigns, Washington, D.C., January 13, 2003.

29. U.S. Congress. Congressional Research Service. Jeffrey W. Seifert and R. Eric Petersen, *House of Representatives Information Technology Management Issues: An Overview of the Effects on Institutional Operations, the Legislative Process, and Future Planning.* Updated April 2, 2003.

30. *CyberCongress Accomplishments*, 6.

31. Barbara J. Saffir, "Bit by Bit, Congress Is Opening Up to the Information Age," *The Washington Post,* June 2, 1997, A17, available at (http://www.washingtonpost.com/wp-srv/politics/govt/fedguide/stories/cong.htm).

32. Graeme Browning, *Electronic Democracy: Using the Internet to Transform American Politics*, 2nd ed. (Medford, New Jersey: Cyber Age Books, 2002), 4, 46–48.

33. Rory J. O'Connor, "Congress: DOS in a Windows World–Members Can't Find On Ramp to the Information Highway," *The Seattle Times*, December 15, 1995, available at (http://ptg/djnr/ccroot/asp/publib/story_clean_cpy.asp?rndnum=548606).

34. Matthew McAllester, "Enlightening Lawmakers: The U.S. Congressional Internet Caucus is Spreading the Word of the World Wide Web Among Colleagues," *Newsday*, October 8, 1997, C3.

35. O'Connor, "Congress: DOS in a Windows World."

36. Marcia Stepanek, "Congressional Caucus Works to Plug Lawmakers into Internet," *The Fort Worth Star-Telegram,* December 22, 1997, 23.

37. Stepanek, "Congressional Caucus Works to Plug Lawmakers into Internet." Chris Casey quipped in 1997 about the future of the Internet Caucus: "Once everybody gets a computer and gets online, the novelty will rub off, and people won't need the caucus anymore. It would be silly to have a caucus, say, on the telephone, wouldn't it?" Rep. White quoted in Saffir, "Bit by Bit, Congress is Opening Up to the Information Age."

38. U.S. Congress. House. Office of the Inspector General. *House Computer Systems Were Vulnerable to Unauthorized Access, Modifications, and Destruction.* 104th Cong., 1st sess., Report No. 95-CAO-18. (July 18, 1995); *Internet Security Weaknesses.* 104th Congress, 1st sess., Report No. 95-CAO-3 (July 18, 1995); and *Information Systems Security Weaknesses,*" Report No. 95-CAO-1 (May 3, 1995).

39. U.S. Congress. House. Office of Inspector General. Letter of Transmittal, John W. Lainhart, IV, Inspector General, to Jeff Trandal, Acting Chief Administrative Officer, May 8, 1997, accompanying, *HIR Management Practices Undermine The House's Ability to Keep Pace with Technological Changes.* 105th Congress, 1st sess. Report No. 97-CAO-09, May 8, 1997, available at (http://house.gov/IG/97cao09.htm).

40. *HIR Management Practices*, at iii.

41. *HIR Management Practices*, at iii. The IG report made 26 specific recommendations and the Acting Chief Administrative Officer, in response to the IG report, fully concurred with its findings and recommendations.

42. U.S. Congress. House. Office of the Inspector General. *Significant Improvements in the Management and Operations of the Office of the Chief Administrative Officer*. 105th Cong., 2nd sess. Report No. 98-CAO-19 (December 16, 1998), i, available at (http://house.gov/IG/98cao19.htm). In other reports, the Office of the Inspector General found that the HIR's Communications Group, which is responsible for data, voice, and video communications, was very successful in accomplishing a number of its initiatives, and that the House telecommunications network reliability was over 99 percent, exceeding industry standards. U.S. Congress. House. Office of the Inspector General. *Proactive Management Approach Can Improve House Telecommunications Services and Operations*. 105th Cong., 1st sess., Report No. 97-CAO-08. (March 24, 1997), available at (http://www.house.gov/IG/97cao08.htm).

43. O'Connor, "Congress: DOS in a Windows World."

44. O'Connor, "Congress: DOS in a Windows World."

45. Diana Owen, Richard Davis, Vincent James Strickler, "Congress and the Internet," *Harvard International Journal of Press/Politics*. Vol. 4, no. 2 (1999), 10–29; see also, Casey, *The Hill on the Net*. Gebe Martinez, "Congress Now Posts Its Politicking on Internet Computers," *Los Angeles Times*, September 4, 1996, A1.

46. OMB Watch survey analyzed in Matt Carter, "Speaking Up in the Internet Age: Use and Value of Constituent E-Mail and Congressional Websites," *Parliamentary Affairs*, July 1999, 464–479. The OMB Watch analysis is available at (http://www.ombwatch.org/npt/resource/reports/congsrvy.html); the Bonner-American University study is available at (http://www.american.edu/academic.depts/spa/ccps/Research.html).

47. Natasha Haubold, "Congress Legislates, Procrastinates on Tech," *Federal Computer Week*, April 17, 2000, available at (http://fcw.com/fcw/articles/2000/0417/mgt-hill-04-17–00.asp).

48. William Matthews, "Web Hasn't Roped in One Congressman," *Federal Computer Week*, February 19, 2001, available at (http://www.fcw.com/fcw/articles/2001/0219/cov-extra-02–19–01.asp).

49. Natasha Haubold, "Hill Shies From Technology," *Federal Computer Week*, April 3, 2000, available at (http://www.fcw.com/fcw/articles/2000/0403/news-hill-04–03–00.asp).

50. Gary Rivlin, "The Things They Carry," *Fortune/CNET Tech Review*, Winter 2002, 70.

51. U.S. Congress. House. Committee on Rules. *Legislating in the Information Age*. 106th Cong., 1st sess. (July 16, 1999) available at (http://www.house.gov/rules/rules_tran05.htm).

52. Saffir, "Bit by Bit."

53. Browning, *Electronic Democracy*, 8.

54. Congressional Management Foundation, *Setting Course: A Congressional Management Guide*, 107th Congress edition (Washington, D.C.: Congressional Management Foundation, 2000), at 262.

55. Browning, *Electronic Democracy*, 56.

56. William Matthews, "Survey Says Congress Should Get Online," *Federal Computer Week*, December 13, 1999, available at (http://fcw.com/fcw/articles/1999/fcw_1213199_survey.asp).

57. Casey, "Congress and the Internet," 190.

58. Brian Krebs, "Senate Getting Badly Needed E-Mail Update," *The Washington Post*, July 19, 2002, available at (http://www.washingtonpost.com/ac2/wp-dyn/A33809-2002Jul19?language=printer).

59. Susan Crabtree, "Changes Are Virtually Certain in Congress' Future," *Roll Call*, 2000, available at (http://www.rollcall.com/election/gtc2.html).

60. Dreier, "We've Come a Long Way . . . Maybe." Representative Dreier is chairman of the House Committee on Rules.

61. U.S. Congress. House. Committee on House Administration. Representative Bob Nye and Representative Steny Hoyer, Dear Colleague letter, "Improving District Office Computer Performance" 107th Cong., 2nd Sess. (February 12, 2002), available at (http://www.house.gov/cha/February_21.htm).

62. Dreier, "We've Come a Long Way . . . Maybe."

63. The Internet Caucus website is available at (http:www.netcaucus.org).

64. Author's assessment and "The Digital Dozen," *Businessweek Online*, April 24, 2000, available at (http://www.businessweek.com:/2000/00_17/63678133.htm).

65. Chris Casey, staffer for the Democratic Technology and Communication Committee, however, was not impressed with Gingrich's pioneering online activities. In an open letter to Gingrich, appearing in *Internet World*, Casey noted: "Speaker Gingrich deserves credit for supporting and promoting the Library of Congress' THOMAS service. However, I think it's worth noting that the Speaker is not among the fifty representatives who as of today [October 1995] maintain Gopher directories, or the thirty-two that maintain home pages on the World Wide Web. As the third-highest elected official in the nation, Gingrich does not post information to the Net as Speaker of the House, nor even as representative of Georgia's sixth district. I'm sure that eventually he will, but for now the fact is that Newt's Net doesn't exist. The emperor has no clothes, and the Speaker has no home page." Correspondence from Casey.

66. Ellen McCarthy, "Guiding the House to the 21st Century," *The Washington Post*, April 11, 2002, E8.

Chapter 5: The E-mail Overload

Epigraph quotes of Rep. Ehlers from Susan Crabtree, "Changes Are Virtually Certain in Congress' Future," *Roll Call*, February 18, 2000, available at (http://www.rollcall.com/election/gtc2.html).

1. William Matthews, "Slow E-Mail Dogs Senate," *Federal Computer Week*, February 19, 2001, available at (http://fcw.com.print.asp).

2. Matthews, "Slow E-Mail Dogs Senate."

3. Mark Preston, "Senate Plagued by E-Mail Snafus," *Roll Call*, February 12, 2001, available at (http://www.rollcall.com/pages/news/00/2001/02/news0212b.html).

4. "Senate Adds Servers to Speed up E-Mail," *Government Computer News*, March 5, 2001, available with I.D. access at (http://www.gcn.com/cgi-bin/udt/im.display.printable?client.id+gcn2&story.id+3769).

5. Patricia Daukantas, "Message Mania," *Government Computer News,* January 8, 2001, available at (http://www.gcn.com/cgi-bin/udt/im.display,printable?client_id+gcn2&story. id=3461).

6. Brian Krebs, "Senate Getting Badly Needed E-Mail Update," *The Washington Post,* July 19, 2002, available at (http://www.washingtonpost.com/ac2/wp-dyn/A33809-2002Jul19?language=printer) and Jason Miller, "With Mail Safety Still Iffy, Hill Upgrades E-mail," *Government Computer News*, January 7, 2002, available at (http://www.gcb.com/cgi-bin/udt/im.display.printable?client.id=gcn2&story.id=17720).

7. *Congress Online Project Newsletter* (August 2002) available at (http://www.congressonlineproject.org/080702volume.html). In addition to outside e-mail, there is extraordinary

traffic within Congress itself. For example, in March 2001 alone, there were nearly 9 million internal e-mails passed between House staffers. House Information Resources data cited by David Dreier, "We've Come a Long Way ... Maybe," in *Congress and the Internet*, eds. James A. Thurber and Colton C. Campbell (Upper Saddle River, N.J.: Prentice-Hall, 2003), 53.

8. Congress Online Project. Kathy Goldschmidt, "E-Mail Overload and the Response of Congress," unpublished presentation, Congress Online Conference, George Washington University, Washington, D.C., December 11, 2002.

9. Goldschmidt, "E-Mail Overload and the Response of Congress."

10. *Computerworld* (April 5, 1999), 70, noted that "spam" originated this way: "It all started in early Internet chat rooms and interactive fantasy games where someone repeating the same sentence or comment was said to be making a 'spam.' The term referred to a Monty Python's Flying Circus scene in which actors keep saying, 'Spam, Spam, Spam and Spam' when reading options from a menu." Noted in footnote 1, in Marcia S. Smith, *'Junk E-Mail': An Overview of Issues and Legislation Concerning Unsolicited Commercial Electronic Mail ('Spam')*, CRS Report to Congress, Congressional Research Service, The Library of Congress, November 6, 2001.

11. Amy Harmon, "'You've Got Mail,' More and More, and Mostly It Is Junk," *The New York Times*, January 24, 2001, available at ⟨http://nytimes.com/2001/12/24/technology/24SPAM.html⟩, and AOL spam e-mail data from *The Washington Post*, February 24, 2003, E2.

12. Smith, *'Junk E-Mail,'* updated March 1, 2002, citing figures from SpamLaws website, ⟨http://www.spamlaws.com⟩.

13. "Overall, the vast majority of e-mail going to members of Congress is outside of their districts, and for the most part, ignored," concluded Jack Bonner, from a joint study by Bonner & Associates and American University Study cited in Courtney Macavinta, "Congress Has Issues with E-Mail," *News.Com*, February 25, 1998, available at ⟨http://news.com.com/2100-1023-208492.html⟩.

14. Cited in OMB Watch, "Speaking Up in the Internet Age: Congress and Internet Communications," (December 1998), available at ⟨http://www.ombwatch.org/npt/resource/reports/ congsrvy.html⟩.

15. Representative Barney Frank ⟨http://www.house.gov/frank⟩.

16. *Setting Course: A Congressional Management Guide*, 285.

17. Rebecca Fairley Raney, "E-Mail Finds the Rare Ear in Congress," *The New York Times*, December 13, 2001, G11.

18. Congress Online Project, *E-Mail Overload in Congress: Managing a Communications Crisis* (Washington, D.C., March 2001), written by Kathy Goldschmidt. This section relies heavily on this study.

19. Matthew McAllester, "Enlightening Lawmakers: The U.S. Congressional Internet Caucus is Spreading the Word of the World Wide Web Among Colleagues," *Newsday*, October 8, 1997, C3.

20. During the late 1980s, Representative Norman Sisisky (Democrat-Virginia) refused to use an auto-pen, the mechanical device that duplicated his signature. Instead, he authorized me, his chief of staff, to check and sign every routine letter. This took about 2–3 hours every week simply to look the letters over and sign them on his behalf. This provided important quality control and it saved the Congressman those hours for more important things.

21. U.S. Congress. House. Committee on House Administration. *Members' Congressional Handbook: Regulations Governing the Members' Representational Allowance of the U.S. House of Representatives*. 107th Cong., 1st sess., at 8, available at ⟨http://www.house.gov/

cha/handbook.handbook.html), and *Setting Course: A Congressional Management Guide*, 76. In addition to the 11,692 personal staff, there are 2,492 employees who work for the majority or minority on congressional committees; the Leadership staff numbers 274, consisting of employees of the Speaker of the House, the Majority Leader, Minority Leader, Majority Whip, and Minority Whip; there are 5,034 in the Institutional staff, among them the Capitol police, legislative clerks, building and maintenance workers; and there are 747 staff in the Congressional Research Service, 232 in the Congressional Budget Office, and 3,500 in the General Accounting Office. Norman Ornstein, Thomas Mann, and Michael Malbin, *Vital Statistics on Congress, 1999–2000* (Washington, D.C.: American Enterprise Institute, 1999).

22. E-mail correspondence from David Pike, Systems Administrator, Office of Senator Jeff Bingaman, April 16, 2002. By contrast, the Washington office of the other New Mexico Senator, Republican Pete Domenici estimated that it received about 500 e-mails per day, with about 70 percent coming from New Mexico residents. Daukantas, "Message Mania."

23. Daukantas, "Message Mania."

24. William M. Bulkeley, "EchoMail Can Sort, Answer Deluge of E-Mails," *The Wall Street Journal*, November 15, 2001.

25. Bulkeley, "EchoMail Can Sort, Answer Deluge of E-Mails." The office of the Senate Sergeant at Arms hosts the EchoMail system in the Senate's main data center, located near Capitol Hill in the Postal Square building. EchoMail runs on two Sun Microsystems Enterprise 450 servers and two additional Enterprise 450 machines host an Oracle8 Release 8.06 database for EchoMail. Daukantas, "Message Mania."

26. Congress Online Project, *E-Mail Overload in Congress*.

27. Daniel Bennett and Pam Fielding, *The Net Effect: How Cyberadvocacy is Changing the Political Landscape* (Merrifield, Virginia: e-Advocates Press, 1999), 134–135.

28. Reps. Robert Ney and Steny Hoyer, Dear Colleague letter, "House Improves Campus Data Network" (August 15, 2001).

29. House of Representatives website (http://www.house.gov) and information about Write Your Representative Service at (http://www/house.gov/writereps/wyrfaqs.htm).

30. Representative Eric Cantor (http://cantor.house.gov), see *Congress Online Project Newsletter* (March 2002), available at (http://www.congressonlineproject.org/march2002.html).

31. *Congress Online Project Newsletter* (August 2002); Congress Online Project, *E-Mail Overload in Congress*, available at (http://www.congressonlineproject.org). An earlier study, conducted in 1998, found that 80 percent of all replies from congressional offices to constituent e-mails are done through regular mail. Study by Bonner and Associates and the American University, cited in Macavinta, "Congress Has Issues with E-Mail."

32. *Congress Online Project Newsletter* (August 2002).

33. David Silverberg, "What Will Become of the Letter to Congress?" *The Hill*, July 10, 2002, available at (http://www.hillnews.com/120501/silverberg.shtm).

34. William Matthews, "Survey Says Congress Should Get Online," *Federal Computer Week*, December 13, 1999, available at (http://fcw.com/print.asp).

35. Dana Milbank, "Errant E-Mails Ruffle House Democrats' Feathers," *The Washington Post*, October 22, 2002, A25.

36. Senator Lieberman website (http://lieberman.senate.gov). The website was accessed on January 31, 2003.

37. Jeri Clausing and Rebecca Fairley Raney, "More Members Are Plugged In, But Few Are Making the Connections," *The New York Times*, January 15, 1998, available at (http://nytimes.copm/library/cyber/week/011598congress.html).

38. Raney, "E-Mail Finds the Rare Ear in Congress."

39. Office of Senator Patrick Leahy, May 17, 2000 news release, available at (http://leahy.senate.gov/text/press/200005/00517.html). Leahy assured his constituents that, as author of the Internet Security Act, which would add a wide range of enforcement tools against computer hacking, that he continued to be a leader in the fight against computer crime.

40. *Congress Online Project Newsletter* (November 2001) available at (http://www.congress onlineproject.org/november.html).

41. William Matthews, "E-mail Keeps Lawmakers in Touch," *Federal Computer Week,* October 29, 2001, available at (http://www.fcw.com).

42. *Congress Online Newsletter* (November 2001).

43. Matthews, "E-mail Keeps Lawmakers in Touch."

44. Johanna Neuman, "Congress Reopening Mail Room," *Los Angeles Times,* December 9, 2001, A46.

45. Senator Bill Frist website (http://senate.gov/~frist).

46. Eliza Newlin Carney, "E-mail Increases on Hill; Lawmakers Not Equipped to Respond," *CongressDailyAM,* November 2, 2001, available at (http://www.cd-alert@ nationaljournal.com).

47. Rebecca Fairly Raney, "Spam Gets the Message Out," *The New York Times,* January 15, 1998, (http://www.nytimes.com/library/cyber/week/011598congress-spam.html). House rules do not permit Members to use e-mail or their websites to solicit petitions from constituents.

48. Raney, "Spam Gets the Message Out."

49. For further details, see Congress Online Project, *E-Mail Overload.*

50. Jeffrey W. Seifert, *Information Technology in the House of Representatives: Trends and Potential Impact on Legislative Process for the 107th Congress,* Congressional Research Service, April 19, 2001, available at the House Rules Committee website (http://house. gov/rules). Among the improvements cited by the House Chief Administrative Office were a doubling of available bandwidth for House Internet access from 10 megabytes (mb) to 21 mb/second; upgrading of software; faster v.90 analog and intergrated services digital network (ISDN) dial access; and better connectivity between Washington and district officers using digital subscriber line (DSL) technology.

Chapter 6: Congressional Websites

Epigraph quote from a focus group participant in Congress Online Project, *Constituents and Your Website: What Citizens Want to See on Congressional Websites* (October 2001), 8. Written by Dennis W. Johnson, available at (http://www.congressonlineproject.org); Congress Online Project, *Congress Online: Assessing and Improving Capitol Hill Websites* (January 2002). Written by Kathy Goldschmidt, Nicole Folk, Mike Callahan, Richard Shapiro, and Brad Fitch of the Congressional Management Foundation, 61, available at (http://www.congressonline project.org).

1. Katherine Bainbridge, *Building Websites Constituents Will Use* (Washington, D.C.: Congressional Management Foundation, 1999). In 1999, three social scientists analyzed congressional websites and found them to be used mainly for advertising the achievements of the Members to constituents back home. D. Owen, R. Davis, and V. J. Strickler, "Congress and the Internet," *Harvard International Journal of Press/Politics,* 4.2 (1999), 10–29. A study in 2001 looked at the hyperlinks made within Member of Congress's websites, principally those of congressional caucuses and state delegation

connections. Dongwook Cha, "Internet Communication Structure in U.S. Congress: A Network Analysis," paper presented at the 2001 Annual Meeting of the American Political Science Association, San Francisco, California, September 2001. See also Jeff Gulati, "Connecting with Constituents: Congress and the Presentation of Self on the WWW," paper presented at the 2002 Annual Meeting of the American Political Science Association, Boston, Massachusetts, September 2002.

2. Congress Online Project. Data compiled by Lisa Wallenda, graduate student, Master of Arts in Legislative Affairs program, the George Washington University, March—June 2001; data assembled by Kathy Goldschmidt, Congressional Management Foundation. See expanded list in Appendix E.

3. Congress Online Project, *Constituents and Your Website.* Focus groups sessions were held in Richmond, Virginia, Washington, D.C., Phoenix, Arizona, and Philadelphia, Pennsylvania, in early 2001, and conducted by Dr. Rosita Thomas of Thomas Opinion Research. Similar focus group sessions were held in Denver, Colorado, for a research project on state legislative websites, under the auspices of the National Council on State Legislatures, also conducted by Thomas Opinion Research. The number one request of the citizens looking at state legislative websites was the same as those viewing congressional websites: voting accountability. Also Dennis W. Johnson, "Communicating with Congress: Citizens, E-Mail, and Websites," in *Congress and the Internet,* eds. James A. Thurber and Colton C. Campbell (Upper Saddle River, N.J.: Prentice Hall, 2003), 123–134.

4. Congress Online Project, *The Public Speaks Out on Congressional-Constituent Communications* (April 2003), prepared by Thomas Opinion Research. Available at (http://www.congressonlineproject.org).

5. The expert panel included Graeme Browning, author of *Electronic Democracy: Using the Internet to Transform American Politics* (2nd ed.); Janet Caldow, Director of the IBM Institute for Electronic Government; Max Fose, partner, Integrated Web Strategy; Kathy McShea, president, Emerald Strategies; and Joiwind Ronen, Director of Intergovernmental Technology Leadership Consortium, the Council for Excellence in Government. For a more complete description of the Best Practices model and website evaluation methodology, see Appendix A.

6. Congress Online Project, *Congress Online.* The evaluations for this January 2002 report were made from August through October 2001; the evaluations for *Congress Online 2003* (March 2003) were made from August through November 2002.

7. Congress Online Project, *Congress Online.* See also, Dennis W. Johnson, "U.S. Congress Responds to Online Communication Needs," *Journal of Political Marketing,* vol. 1, no. 3 (2003).

8. Congress Online Project, *Congress Online,* 55–56.

9. Training was provided primarily by Mike Callahan and Nicole Folk of the Congressional Management Foundation.

10. Congress Online Project, *Congress Online 2003: Turning the Corner on the Information Age* (2003). Written by Nicole Folk and Kathy Goldschmidt, with contributions by Rick Shapiro, Brad Fitch, and Mike Callahan.

11. This includes the congressional offices for the District of Columbia and territories.

12. Senator Harry Reid (http://reid.senate.gov).

13. Senator Patrick Leahy (http://leahy.senate.gov); Representatives John Boozman (http://www.house.gov/boozman), Kay Granger (http://kaygranger.house.gov), Nick Smith (http://www.house.gov/nicksmith), Steve Rothman (http://rothman.house.gov), George Radanovich (http://www.radanovich.house.gov); and Senator Sam Brownback (http://brownback.senate.gov).

14. Congress Online Project, *Congress Online 2003*, 47.
15. Representative Lynn N. Rivers (http://www.house.gov/rivers); no longer available following Rivers' defeat in 2002. Roll call votes taken by Representative Rivers for 1997–1999 were to added to her vote archive, and the site read "under construction," as of June 24, 2002.
16. Representative Jennifer Dunn (http://www.house.gov/dunn). The website was checked on June 24, 2002.
17. Representative Chaka Fattah (http://www.house.gov/fattah); Representative Judy Biggert (http://judybiggert.house.gov); Senator Bill Frist (http://frist.senate.gov).
18. Senator Dianne Feinstein (http://feinstein.senate.gov); Representative Frank Wolf (http://www.house.gov/wolf); Representative Christopher Shays (http://www.house.gov/shays). See *Congress Online Newsletter*, July 8, 2002, available at (http://www.congressonlineproject.org/070802.html).
19. The Office of the Clerk of the House of Representatives website (http://clerkweb.house.gov/evs/index.htm); Congress.org website (www.congress.org); C-SPAN Congressional Votes Library website (http://congress.nw.dc.us/c-span/subjectvote.html); Project Vote Smart website (http://www.vote-smart.org); and the Library of Congress Explanation of Roll Call Votes website (http://thomas.loc. gov/home/votes/votehelp.html).
20. Senator Dianne Feinstein (http://feinstein.senate.gov); Senator Patrick Leahy (http://leahy.senate.gov); Senator Carl Levin (http://levin.senate.gov); Senator Tom Harkin (http://harkin.senate.gov); Senator Kay Bailey Hutchison (http://hutchison.senate.gov).
21. Representatives Chaka Fattah (http://www.house.gov/fattah), Christopher Shays (http://www.house.gov/shays), and Mike Honda (http://www.house.gov/honda). Senator Fred Thompson (http://thompson.senate.gov), but is no longer available after his retirement.
22. Congress Online Project focus group sessions.
23. Representative Lynn Woolsey (http://woolsey.house.gov/schedule.asp); Representatives Melissa Hart (http://www.hart.house.gov/calendar.asp), John Boozman (http://www.house.gov/boozman/calendar), Tom Allen (http://www.tomallen.house. gov) and Senator Larry Craig (www.senate.gov/~craig/portal.htm).
24. While there was a consistent pattern of interest from focus group participants in seeing Member schedule information on websites, there was not a corresponding interest among the respondents to Congress Online Project's March 2003 online poll. Only 9 percent of the 1,085 respondents (the lowest percentage of twelve categories), said they were "extremely likely to look at a Senator's or Representative's daily schedule." Congress Online Project, *The Public Speaks Out on Congressional-Constituent Communications* (April 2003).
25. David Dreier, "We've Come a Long Way ... Maybe," in *Congress and the Internet*, eds. Thurber and Campbell, 52–77.
26. Allen website (http://tomallen.house.gov).
27. Senator Harry Reid (http://reid.senate.gov); Representatives Mike Pence (http://mikepence.house.gov), Kay Granger (http://kaygranger.house.gov), Melissa Hart (http://hart.house.gov), Mike Honda (http://www.house.gov/honda), Richard Pombo (http://www.house.gov/pombo); and Senators Barbara Boxer (http://www.boxer.senate.gov) and Mary Landrieu (http://landrieu.senate.gov).
28. Senator Debbie Stabenow (http://stabenow.senate.gov); *Congress Online Newsletter*, June 24, 2002, available at (http://www.congressonlineproject.org/062402.html).
29. E-Government Project website (http://www.senate.gov/~gov_affairs/egov). When last

checked, March 6, 2003, the website had a dead link to Senator Thompson's official website, which had been taken down upon his retirement from the Senate in January 2003.

30. Mark Leibovich, "Congressional Man of Letters," *The Washington Post,* February 21, 2002, C1.

31. Office of the Clerk, U.S. House of Representatives, website (http://clerkweb.house.gov).

32. Another good example was the website of Rep. Chaka Fattah, which explained, particularly to a young audience, how an actual piece of his legislation passes into law. Available at (http://www.house.gov/fattah).

33. Congress Online Project, *Congress Online* and *Congress Online 2003.* In the 2002 analyses, the Republican Senate committee websites averaged a 0.75 (out of 4.00) rating, while the same websites in 2003 had an average rating of 1.25.

34. Representative W. J. Tauzin (http://house.gov/tauzin).

35. Representative James Langevin (http://www.house.gov/langevin).

36. C. Lawrence Evans and Walter J. Oleszek, "The 'Wired' Congress: The Internet, Institutional Change, and Legislative Work, in *Congress and the Internet,* eds. Thurber and Campbell, 107.

37. *Congress Online Newsletter,* June 10, 2002, available at (http://www.congressonline project.org/061002.html).

38. Congress Online Project, "Accessing Congress Online: Congressional Websites and Accessibility to the Disabled" (2004, forthcoming).

39. House Committee on Energy and Commerce (Minority) website (www.house.gov/commerce_democrats); Representative John D. Dingell (Democrat-Michigan), ranking Member.

40. The House Republican Conference website was first created under the leadership of Representative J.C. Watts (Republican-Oklahoma) and beginning in the 108th Congress was chaired by Representative Deborah Pryce (Republican-Ohio).

41. Congress Online Project, *Congress Online 2003,* 27.

42. U.S. Congress. House. Committee on House Administration. *107th Congress Members' Congressional Handbook: Regulations Governing the Members' Representational Allowance of the U.S. House of Representatives,* 107th Cong., 1st Sess., at 36, available at (http://www.house.gov/cha/handbook/handbook.html).

43. U.S. Senate Internet Services Usage Rules and Policies, adopted by the Committee on Rules and Administration, July 22, 1996, available at (http://www.senate.gov/learning/usage.policies.html).

44. Eve Gerber, "How Congress Resists the Web," *Slate* (December 1, 1999), available at (http://www.slate.com/?id=56807).

45. Statement of Daniel P. Mulhollan before the Subcommittee on Legislative Appropriations, Committee on Appropriations, U.S. Senate, Fiscal 1999 Budget Request, March 12, 1998, 10, quoted in The Project on Government Oversight, "Congressional Research Service Products: Taxpayers Should Have Easy Access," (February 2003), available at (http://www.pogo.org/p/government/go-030201-crs.html).

46. Representative Christopher Shays, press release, "Shays Takes Congressional Research Online," available at (http://www.house.gov/shays).

47. Senator John McCain, press release, "McCain, Leahy Hold Press Conference in Support of Open Access to Government Documents," (February 11, 2003), available at (http://mccain.senate.gov).

48. U.S. Congress. House. Committee on House Administration. Dear Colleague Letter, Bob Ney, Chairman. "Introducing the New and Improved www.House.gov," (January 6, 2003), available at (http://www.house.gov/cha/dearjan6.htm).

49. Senate website virtual tour is available at (http://www.senate.gov/vtour/index.html). Senator Bill Frist also provided a virtual tour of his Senate office, designed for his Ten-

nessee constituents so that they could see where he worked and see the Tennessee artwork and mementos in his office. Senator Bill Frist (http://frist.senate.gov/tour/index.htm). *Congress Online Newsletter*, May 20, 2002, available at (http://congressonline project.org/052002.html).

Chapter 7: Challenges and Opportunities

Epigraph quote from John McCaslin, "Inside the Beltway," *The Washington Times*, March 28, 2002, available at (http://www.washtimes.com/national/20020328-27303984.htm); Jackson quote from Susan Crabtree, "Changes Are Virtually Certain in Congress' Future," *Roll Call*, 2000, available at (http://www.rollcall.com/election/gtc2.html).

1. The pioneering work on Members' work in their districts is Richard F. Fenno, *Home Style: House Members in Their Districts* (Glenview, Ill.: Scott, Foresman, 1978); see also Thomas P. O'Neill, Jr. and Gary Hymel, *All Politics is Local* (New York: Times Books, 1994).

2. U.S. Congress. House. Committee on Rules. Testimony of Stephen E. Frantzich, chair, Department of Political Science, U.S. Naval Academy, on the 21st Century Congress, May 24, 1996, available at (http://www.house.gov./rules/frantzich.html).

3. Congressional Management Foundation, *House Staff Employment Study* (Washington, D.C., 1998), 48–49 and Congressional Management Foundation, *Senate Staff Employment: Salary, Tenure, Demographics, and Benefits* (Washington, D.C., 1998), 89, cited in John S. Pontius, *Casework in a Congressional Office* (Washington, D.C., Congressional Research Service, July 12, 2001), Report 98-878 GOV, 4.

4. Richard H. Shapiro, *Frontline Management: A Guide for Congressional District/State Offices* (Washington, D.C.: Congressional Management Foundation, 1998), 89, cited in Pontius, *Casework in a Congressional Office*, 4.

5. Dwight Thompson, "A Hill Hearing Aid," *The Washington Post*, May 22, 2000, available at (http://www.washingtonpost.com/wp-dyn/articles/A46296-2000May21.html).

6. Timothy Noah, "Privatizing Congressional Hearings," *Slate*, May 24, 2000, available at (http://www.slate.com/?id+1005378).

7. Noah, "Privatizing Congressional Hearings."

8. Website address is (http://www.capitolhearings.org).

9. House Committee on Science website (http://www.house.gov/science/press/107/107-193.htm).

10. J. H. Snider, "E-Democracy as Deterrence: Public Policy Implications of a Deterrence Model of Democratic Accountability." Paper delivered at the 2001 annual meeting of the American Political Science Association, San Francisco, California, August 30–September 2, 2001, at 21.

11. U.S. Congress. Senate. *Senate Ethics Manual*, 499. Available at (http://ethics.senate.gov/downloads/pdffiles/manual.pdf).

12. Michael S. Gerber, "Senate's Website Rules Hurt Lawmakers Seeking Re-election," *The Hill*, April 3, 2002, available at (http://www.hillnews.com/0403/02/website.shtm). Johnson wasn't the only Senator affected: Sens. Mary Landrieu (Democratic-Lousiana), Tom Harkin (Democrat-Iowa), and Max Cleland (Democrat-Georgia) were all challenged by House members who were not under a similar website publication restriction. U.S. Senate Internet Services Usage Rules and Policies found at (http://www.senate.gov/learning/usage.policies.htm).

13. Senate Ethics Rules, XL. See Noah, "Privatizing Congressional Hearings."

14. Senate Allard website (http://allard.senate.gov).

15. *Congress Online Newsletter*, May 20, 2002, available at (http://www.congressonlinepro-ject.org/052002.html); Senator Harkin's website is available at (http://harkin.senate.gov).

16. U.S. Congress. House. Committee on House Administration. Representative Bob Ney and Representative Steny Hoyer. Dear Colleague Letter, "90 Day Election Year Restriction Information," 107th Cong., 2nd Sess. (January 29, 2002), available at (http://www.house.gov/cha/January_29.htm). Unsolicited mass communications include advertisements of town hall meetings; advertisements announcing a personal appearance of a Member at an official event; newspaper inserts, electronic messages and mailings; automated phone calls; facsimiles; purchase of television or radio broadcast time, or production and distribution costs for video and audio services for mass dissemination.

17. Ari Schwartz, "An Unseemly 60-Day Rule," *Federal Computer Week*, December 11, 2000, available at (http://www.fcw.com/print.asp).

18. Jeffrey W. Seifert, *Information Technology in the House of Representatives: Trends and Potential Impact on Legislative Process for the 107th Congress*, Congressional Research Service, April 19, 2001, from the House Committee on Rules website, (http://www.house.gov/rules). Seifert is an analyst in the Information Science and Technology Policy Resources, Science and Industry Division of CRS.

19. National Association of State Chief Information Officers (NASCIO), "The Role of the State Chief Information Officer," March 1, 2001, 1, available at (http://www.nascio.org).

20. David L. McClure, Director, Information Technology Management Issues, U.S. General Accounting Office, testimony before Subcommittee on Technology and Procurement Policy, Committee on Government Reform, U.S. House of Representatives, April 3, 2001.

21. Developed by Research in Motion, Ltd. (RIM), a Canadian firm, the BlackBerry handheld units could store a calendar, list of contacts, browse the Internet, receive PDF files and Word documents; they also could act as mini-laptop computers. For the Senate, LRW Digital, a Baltimore, Maryland, technology firm developed applications so that the Senate could use mailing lists with pin numbers and e-mails together. The pre-programmed e-mail lists were changeable and maintained by the Senate administrative offices. LRW Digital also developed security applications, allowing the BlackBerrys to be shut down remotely from any computer with a simple e-mail. LRW Digital, "Baltimore Technical Company Brings the Wireless World to US Senate," press release, November 5, 2001, available at (http://www.lrwdigital.com/PressSenate.htm).

22. Ephraim Schwartz, "Congress Bets on BlackBerry," *PCWorld.com*, October 12, 2001, available at (http://www.pcworld.com/news/article/0,aid,65803,00.asp). The House Administration Committee chose the BlackBerry 957 model, which has a large screen, could run custom applications, and eventually be equipped with web-browsing capabilities, according to Reynold Schweickhardt. "HandHeld Gadgets Have Become Godsends to Congress," *The New York Times*, November 8, 2001, available at (http://www.newyorktimes.org/learning/students/pop/ articles/08HILL.html). The Hart Senate Office Building was particularly hard hit; 50 Senators and their staffs did not return to Hart until January 22, 2002. Daschle could not return to his office until new furniture and carpets had been installed in March 2002.

23. Jonathan Krim, "House Makes a Plea to Keep BlackBerrys," *The Washington Post*, January 17, 2003, B1. "HandHeld Gadgets Have Become Godsends to Congress" and LRW Digital press release.

24. In January 2003, James M. (Jay) Eagen III, chief administrator of the House of Representatives, pleaded with attorneys to settle their differences in a patent-infringement case involving Research in Motion Ltd. (RIM), makers of the BlackBerry and NTP, Inc., a Virginia firm. A federal court had ruled that RIM had infringed on patents held

by NTP, and the jury had awarded NTP $23 million in damages. NTP also sought an injunction that would shut down the BlackBerry wireless service. Eagen wrote: "The device is used routinely by most members of Congress ... as well as senior staff," and any disruption in service would create "a serious risk to the House's critical communications and could jeopardize the public interest, particularly in the event of an emergency." Krim, "House Makes a Plea to Keep BlackBerrys."

25. Steve Twomey, "A Recipe for Safe Mail," *The Washington Post*, January 30, 2002, A1.
26. Ed Henry, "Next-Day Delivery? Absolutely Not," *Roll Call*, February 4, 2002, available at (http://www.rollcall.com/pages/news/00/2002/02/bews0204c.html).
27. U.S. Congress. House. Committee on House Administration. Testimony of the Honorable James (Jay) M. Eagen III, Chief Administrative Officer, hearing on Mail Delivery Process. 107th Cong., 2nd Sess. (May 7, 2002), available at (www.house.gov/cha/business/050802agenda/eagen_testimony.doc).
28. Eagen testimony.
29. Michael Gerber, "Ney: Burn Bags of House Mail," *The Hill*, November 28, 2001, available at (http://www.hillnews.com/112801/bun.shtm).
30. Eagen testimony.
31. U.S. Congress. House. Office of the Inspector General. *Audit Report–Improvements Are Needed in House Mail Operations*. 105th Cong., 2nd Sess., Report No. 98-CAO-01 (February 27, 1998), available at (http://www.house.gov/IG/98cao01.pdf).
32. David T. Nassef, remarks, Conference on E-Government: Constituent Mail in the Time of Anthrax, the Advisory Committee to the Congressional Internet Caucus, March 20, 2002, Dirksen Senate Office Building, Washington, D.C. "Mail and Document Security," The Pitney Bowes Executive Advisor, n.d., available at (http://www.pb.com/downloads/US/ENG/PitneySecurityBrochure.pdf), 5.
33. David Enrich, "House to Try Scanned-In Letters," *The Washington Post*, July 8, 2002, A15.
34. U.S. Congress. House. Office of the Chief Administrative Officer. Office of Procurement. Request for Proposal, "House Digital Mail Program," RHIR2002079, 107th Cong. 2nd. Sess. [n.d.], available at (http://www.house.gov/cao-opp/PDFSolicitations/RHIR2002079.pdf).
35. Enrich, "House to Try Scanned-In Letters."
36. Henry, "Next-Day Delivery? Absolutely Not."
37. Natasha Haubold, "Congress Legislates, Procrastinates on Tech," *Federal Computer Week*, April 17, 2000, available at (http://fcw.com/print.asp).
38. U.S. Congress. Congressional Research Service. Jane Bortnick Griffith and Walter J. Oleszek, *Electronic Devices in the House Chamber*, a Report to the Subcommittee on Rules and Organizations, House Committee on Rules. 106th Cong., 1st sess. (November 21, 1997), available at (http://www.house.gov/rules/e-devices.htm).
39. Peyman Pejman, "Using Notebooks in Chamber Floors Some Senate Members," *Government Computer News*, October 20, 1997, available at (http://www.gcn.com/archives/gcn/1997/October20/cov4.htm).
40. Courtney Macavinta, "Congress Mulls Laptops in Sessions,"(September 16, 1997) and "Senate Nixes Laptops on Floor," (November 5, 1997), *CNET News.Com*, available at (http://news.com.com/2102-1023-203270.html) and (http://news.com.com/2100-1001-205031.html).
41. Megh Duwadi, "New Request Filed to Bring Laptops to Senate Chamber," *The Atlanta Journal-Constitution*, July 6, 2002, 3F.
42. "Legislators Online," *Federal Computer Week*, May 7, 2001, available at (http://www.fcw.com/print.asp), citing sources from the National Conference of State Legislatures.

43. U.S. Congress. House. Committee on Rules. Hearing on *Legislation in the Information Age*, July 16, 1999. Testimony of Steve Watson, Chief Deputy Director, Nevada Legislature, available at (http://www.house.gov/rules/rules_tran05.htm).

44. Dibya Sarkar, "Politicians Plug In," *Federal Computer Week*, May 27, 2001, available at (http://www.fcw.com/covoc/articles/2001/may/civ-feature-05-01.asp).

45. Sarkar, "Politicians Plug In."

46. Griffith and Oleszek, *Electronic Devices in the House Chamber*, 9.

47. Graeme Browning, *Electronic Democracy: Using the Internet to Transform American Politics*, 2nd ed., (Medford, New Jersey: Cyber Age Books, 2002), 19. Bowen's action was enthusiastically promoted by Jim Warren, one of the early pioneers of cyberspace, and a computer columnist.

48. OMB Watch, "Plugged In, Tuning Up," March 2001, available at (http://www.omb-watch.org/npadv/2001/stlges.html).

49. Dibya Sarkar, "The Web Connection," *Federal Computer Week*, May 7, 2001, available at (http://www.fcw.com/civic/articles/2001/may/civ-feature1b-05-01.asp).

50. Nevada Legislature website (http://www.leg.state.nv.us) and the section asking public opinions is found at (http://www.leg.state.nv.us/71st/opinions).

51. Texas Legislature Online website (http://www.capitol.state.tx.us/tlo).

52. Nebraska Unicameral Information Office website (http://www.unicam.state.ne.us), and the New Jersey Legislature website (http://lis.njleg.state.nj.us).

53. Florida State Senate website (http://www/flsenate.gov).

Chapter Eight: Congress and the Deliberative Process

Epigraph quote from "E-Congress: Prospects, Problems and Alternatives," Statement of Donald R. Wolfensberger before the House Administration Committee, May 1, 2002, and David Fine, "Send the House Home," *Salon*, May 10, 1999, available at (http://www.salon.com/tech/feature/1999/05/10/virtual_congress/print.html). Wolfensberger is Director of the Congress Project at the Woodrow Wilson International Center for Scholars; and David Fine is a writer for *Salon* magazine.

1. Stephen E. Frantzich, "RepresNETation: Congress and the Internet," in *Congress and the Internet,* eds. James A. Thurber and Colton C. Campbell (Upper Saddle River, N.J.: Prentice Hall, 2003), 44.

2. Rep. Jo Ann Emerson website (http://www.house.gov/emerson/r010100.htm).

3. Rep. David Dreier website (http://dreier.gov/cdd_tech.htm).

4. Democratic Leadership Council, "Legislating By Any Means Necessary" (October 23, 2001), available at (http://www.ndol/print.cfm?contentid=3865).

5. Dima Hamdan, "Witness to Testify in U.S. Trial by Satellite," *Jordan Times* (February 19, 2002), noted in (http://www.jordanembassyus.org/02192002005.htm).

6. Bradley Graham, "Bremer: Iraq Focus Shifts to Job Creation," *The Washington Post* (June 13, 2003), A15.

7. Senate Rule XXVI(7). See Congressional Research Service, *Electronic Congress: Proposals and Issues*. Written by Jeffrey W. Seifert and R. Eric Petersen (Updated January 28, 2003) Report RS-21140.

8. U.S. Congress. House. Committee on House Administration. Testimony of the Honorable David Dreier (Republican-California). "E-Congress? Hearing for Conducting Congressional Operations in Emergency Situations." 107th Cong., 2nd Sess. (May 1, 2002).

9. H.J.Res. 67.

10. Out of concern for terrorist attacks came the Continuity of Government Commission. Its first report, *Preserving Our Institutions—The First Report of the Continuity of Government Commission* (June 2003), recommended the creation of a constitutional amendment to ensure that the House of Representatives and the Senate could reconstitute quickly after a terrorist attack. The report is available at ⟨http://continuityof government.org/report/report.html⟩.

11. See, for example, Anthony S. Pitch, *The Burning of Washington: The British Invasion of 1814* (Annapolis, Md.: Naval Institute Press, 1998).

12. The first bill was H.R. 3481, "Ensuring Congressional Security and Continuity Act," introduced in December 13, 2001; the second, H.R. 5007, "To Direct the Comptroller General to Enter Into Arrangements with the National Academy of Sciences and the Library of Congress," was introduced on June 24, 2002, and referred to the Committee on House Administration.

13. Jim H. Snider, address, "Time for an E-Congress?: Helping Bureaucracy," delivered at the U.S. Capitol, November 14, 2001, available at ⟨http://www.votd.com/snider.htm⟩.

14. "Legislating By Any Means Necessary," *New Democrats Online*, October 23, 2001, available at ⟨http://www.ndol.org⟩.

15. Quoted in Susan Crabtree, "Changes Are Virtually Certain in Congress' Future," *Roll Call* (2000) available at ⟨http://rollcall.com/election/gtc2.html⟩.

16. Dreier testimony.

17. U.S. Congress. House. Committee on House Administration. Testimony of Professor Stephen Frantzich. "E-Congress? Hearing for Conducting Congressional Operations in Emergency Situations." 107th Cong., 2nd sess. (May 1, 2002).

18. Frantzich testimony.

19. See John D. Nugent, "If E-Democracy is the Answer, What's the Question? *National Civic Review*, vol. 90, no. 3 (Fall 2001), 221–234.

20. Donald R. Wolfensberger, *Congress and the People: Deliberative Democracy on Trial* (Baltimore: The Johns Hopkins University Press, 2000), 244.

21. Lee Hamilton, "Is Congress Out of Touch?" Center on Congress, Indiana University website, available at ⟨http://www.congress.indiana.edu/outreach/opeds/oped37-2_1.htm⟩.

Index